CW01457188

Real-time Operating Systems

Book 2 - The Practice

Jim Cooling

Published by Lindentree Associates © 2017

From the Lindentree series 'The engineering of real-time embedded systems'

For my granddaughter

Eilish Siobhan Cooling

Labhraíonn na páistí spás i do chroí nach raibh a fhios agat riamh ann
(Grandchildren fill a space in your heart that you never knew was there)

CONTENTS

Chapter 4
Supporting task intercommunication.

PART 3 Visualization of software behaviour using Tracealyzer

Chapter 5
Tracealyzer integration and setup guide.

Chapter 6
Basic features and use of Tracealyzer.

Chapter 7
Introduction to the streaming mode of operation.

Chapter 8
Analyzing resource sharing and task intercommunications.

PART 4 Epilogue - looking to the future

Chapter 9
A self-help improvement guide

PART 5 Useful, helpful and informative online material

Chapter 10
Online material reference guide.

Preface

Why this book?

When you want to become expert in any technical subject you need to understand its theoretical aspects (hardly a ground-breaking piece of advice but true all the same). I call that the 'head's' appreciation. But if you want to become truly proficient this isn't enough - you need to have the 'heart's' understanding as well. By that I mean getting a real feel for the subject. And, in my opinion, the best way to do this is to put your theory into practice: learn-by-doing.

If you look around you'll find many people fall into one or other of the two categories. Leading the field of 'head' experts are University-based computer science theoreticians and the like. In complete contrast the classical 'heart' experts are self-taught programmers with little or no understanding of the subject basics. Rather a large gap here, methinks; and these books set out to help close that gap. Volume 1 of this book deals with the 'head' aspects; volume 2 leads into the 'heart' of the matter. Use this material to help you become expert by turning theory into practice.

Now, while that seems to be a good idea in theory, the practice is a bit more challenging. First, you need a sensible, practical toolset on which to carry out the work. Second, for many self-learners, cost is an issue; the tools mustn't be expensive. Third, they mustn't be difficult to get, use and maintain. So what we have here is *our* approach to providing you with a low cost toolset for RTOS experimentation.

The practical tools.

The toolset used for this work consists of:

- A graphical tool for configuring microcontrollers (specifically STM32F variants) - STM32CubeMX software application.
- An Integrated Development Environment for the production of machine code.
- A very low cost single board computer with inbuilt programmer and debugger

All software, which is free, can be run on Windows, OSX or Linux platforms. The Discovery kit is readily available from many electronic suppliers. The RTOS used for this work is FreeRTOS, which is integrated with the CubeMX tool.

All the exercises given here are designed to execute on the the STM32F4 Discovery kit, http://www.st.com/en/evaluation-tools/stm32f4discovery.html. (confusingly this is also called the STM32F407G-DISC1 board). You can, if you wish, use the cheaper STM32L100C Discovery kit, http://www.st.com/en/evaluation-tools/32l100cdiscovery.html.

The philosophy of this book.

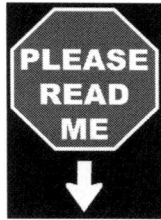

The fundamental philosophy of this book is that 'theory is best understood by putting it into practice'. Great: I think that we can all sign up to that. But then a really important question arises; exactly _how_ should we do it? And underlying that question is an even more basic one; what _precisely_ do we want to achieve? Suppose, for example, you're filled with a burning desire to make your own wooden chair based on the one shown here:

The intended product

Unfortunately you don't have any carpentry knowledge or experience. So you set about learning the theory of carpentry and, armed with this, launch into your project. Well, you may not end up with something as disastrous as that shown in figure below but it's pretty unlikely to be a professional job.

The actual product

What should you have done instead of just jumping into the project, expecting (hoping?) that all will turn out well? It's blindingly clear that before starting any real project you first need to learn _what_ the tools of the trade are and _how_ to use them. Thus, as a novice carpenter, we'll start with the traditional woodworking toolset:

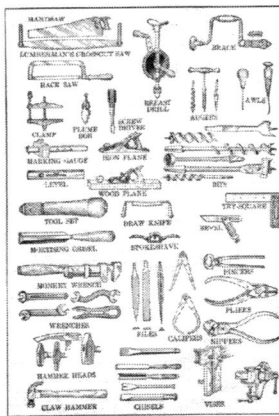

Carpenters traditional woodworking toolset

At this stage you don't really need to know *how* the tools work. What *is* important is what they do and how they're used. Once you've mastered the tools you can then go on to employ them with confidence in real projects And that is the basis of the practical work covered in this book. So don't expect to learn how to design/code operating systems. Nor how to design an embedded system that uses an RTOS. What you *will* learn, however, are:

- What tools are available.
- How each tool works.
- Why and how you should use them.
- What the downsides are in using the various tools.

Put simply, the objective of the exercises is to provide a path for you to truly learn the tools of the trade. The practical work starts with the simplest problem, then gradually builds into more complex aspects. If you are new to all (or most) of the upcoming work please follow this sequence. Don't skip any exercises and do <u>not</u> proceed until you can satisfactorily complete each one in the sequence. If, at the end of the practicals, you feel that you haven't learned the tool fundamentals as outlined, then it's entirely my fault. Mea Culpa!

Acknowledgements.

This updated edition of the book contains material that uses the visualization tool Tracealyzer. I wish to express my great appreciation to the company for all their help in preparing the work, which included free use of the toolset. Also, I am indebted for the amount of technical support provided by the Percepio company, in particular that given by Dr. Johan Kraft, the company CEO. To say it was invaluable is a massive understatement.

Jim Cooling
Markfield November 2017.
(Still a fan of Arthur Guinness)

Book navigation guide

These navigation notes are intended to help you assess the overall structure and intent of the book and its exercises. They are also used as a substitute for a conventional index of entries which, in my view, would be of very limited value in a book like this.

1. Contents guide

PART 1 Developing the practical code

PART 2 The practical exercises

PART 3 Visualization of software behaviour using Tracealyzer

PART 4 Epilogue - looking to the future

PART 5 Useful, helpful and informative online material

2. Navigating the practical exercises.

Chapter 2 - Multitasking design and implementation - the basics.

Prerequisite: Read chapters 1 and 2 of book 1.

Preliminary exercise -Implement simple I/O interfacing.
Fundamental purpose of the exercise: to learn how to drive the LEDs and handle the pushbutton signal of the STM32F407G-DISC board.

Exercise 1 - Create and run a single task that executes repeatedly.
Fundamental purposes of the exercise: learn how to develop one of the simplest, essential functions of a multitasking system: the execution of a single, continuously executing, task.

Exercise 2 - Implement a single periodic task.
Fundamental purpose of the exercise: to create and run a single periodic task having an accurate periodic time.

Exercise 3 - Create and run multiple independent periodic tasks.
Fundamental purpose of the exercise: to create and run multiple independent periodic tasks.

Exercise 4 - Evaluate priority preemptive scheduling policies.
Fundamental purpose of the exercise: to gain a good understanding of task behaviour where a priority preemptive scheduling policy is used.

Chapter 3 - Dealing with shared resources.

Prerequisite: Read chapter 3 of book 1.

Exercise 5. Analyze access contention problems.
Fundamental purpose of the exercise: to demonstrate access contention problems when using shared resources in a multitasking system.

Exercise 6. Eliminate resource contention by suspending the scheduler.
Fundamental purpose of the exercise: to demonstrate a simple way to eliminate resource contention - suspending the scheduler.

Exercise 7. Demonstrate deterioration in system performance.
Fundamental purpose of the exercise: to demonstrate that sharing resources in multitasking designs can lead to deterioration of system performance.

Exercise 8. Use a semaphore to protect critical code sections.
Fundamental purpose of the exercise: to demonstrate how to eliminate resource contention in a selective manner — using a semaphore to protect the critical code section

Exercise 9. Use a mutex to protect the critical code section

Fundamental purpose of the exercise: to demonstrate how to eliminate resource contention in a selective manner — using a mutex to protect the critical code section.

Exercise 10. Use encapsulation techniques to improve system safety and security.

Fundamental purpose of the exercise: to demonstrate that encapsulating an item with its protecting semaphore improves the safety and security of software.

Prerequisite: Read chapter 4 of book 1.

Exercise 11. Demonstrate the effects of priority inversion.

Fundamental purpose of the exercise: to demonstrate the effects of priority inversion in a multitasking design.

Exercise 12. Eliminate priority inversion by using priority inheritance.

Fundamental purpose of the exercise: to demonstrate that priority inversion of tasks can be eliminated by using priority inheritance techniques.

Chapter 4 - Supporting task intercommunication.

Prerequisite: Read chapter 5 of book 1.

Exercise 13. Use flags to coordinate activities.

Fundamental purpose of the exercise: to show how flags can be used to coordinate activities.

Exercise 14. Use event flags to provide unilateral synchronization.

Fundamental purpose of the exercise: to show how event flags can be used to provide unilateral synchronization of tasks.

Exercise 15. Use semaphores to provide unilateral synchronization.

Fundamental purpose of the exercise: to show how semaphores can be used as event flags for unilateral synchronization purposes.

Exercise 16. Use semaphores to provide bilateral synchronization.

Fundamental purpose of the exercise: to show how semaphores can be used to provide bilateral synchronization of tasks.

Exercise 17. Use semaphores to synchronize multiple tasks.

Fundamental purpose of the exercise: to show how semaphores can be used to provide synchronization of multiple tasks - the 'Rendezvous Barrier'.

Exercise 18. Use pools to provide a data sharing mechanism.

Fundamental purpose of the exercise: To show how the pool is used to support data transfer between tasks without any synchronizing actions.

Exercise 19. Use queues for data transfer with task synchronization.

Fundamental purpose of the exercise: To show how the queue is used to support data transfer between tasks without any synchronizing actions.

Exercise 20. Use mailboxes to provide data transfer with task synchronization.

Fundamental purpose of the exercise: To show how the mailbox is used to support data transfer between tasks at designated synchronization points.

Exercise 21. Implement a push-button generated interrupt service routine (ISR).

Fundamental purposes of the exercise: to learn how to implement a push-button generated interrupt service routine (ISR).

Exercise 22. Demonstrate why ISRs should be as fast as possible.

Fundamental purposes of the exercise: to show that using lengthy interrupt-driven aperiodic tasks in multitasking designs can seriously affect system temporal behaviour

Exercise 23. Minimize ISR disruptions by using deferred servers.

Fundamental purposes of the exercise: to show how to minimize the effects of interrupt-driven aperiodic tasks by using the deferred server technique.

3. Navigating the Tracealyzer exercises

Chapter 5 Tracealyzer integration and setup guide.

5.1. Exercise 1 - Introduction to Tracealyzer.

The purpose of this section is act as a guide for the installation, integration and configuration of Tracealyzer on STM32F4 microcontrollers running FreeRTOS. It includes just enough material to get your project working correctly.

Chapter 6 Basic features and use of Tracealyzer.

6.1. Exercise 2 Tracealyzer basics.

The fundamental purpose of this exercise is to help you to gain a basic understanding of the Tracealyzer tool. To do this it is used to record and analyze the simplest of multitasking designs: a single periodic task.

6.2. Exercise 3 Evaluating trace recordings.

The purpose of this exercise is to increase your understanding of the trace recordings. Here we'll perform the recording and analysis of a single task that is slightly more complex than that of exercise 2.

6.3. Exercise 4 Run-time analysis of a two-task design

The purpose of this exercise is to use Tracealyzer to evaluate the run-time behaviour of a simple two-task design (similar to that specified in the original practical exercise 3).

6.4. Exercise 5 Investigating priority preemptive scheduling.

The aim of this exercise is to use Tracealyzer to observe the run-time behaviour of a two-task design that uses a priority preemptive scheduling policy.

6.5. Exercise 6 Evaluating the FreeRTOS delay functions.

The purposes of this exercise are to:

- Investigate task behaviour when the *osDelayUntil* function is used.
- Investigate task behaviour when the *osDelay* function is used.
- Compare the two behaviours.

Chapter 7 Introduction to the streaming mode of operation.

7.1 Exercise 7. Using the streaming mode for trace recording.

The objective of this work is to introduce you to the streaming mode of operation. This mode must be used if you wish to make significantly longer trace recordings than those gathered by the snapshot operation.

Chapter 8 Analyzing resource sharing and task intercommunications.

8.1. Exercise 8. Evaluating the use of protected shared resources.

The purpose of this exercise is to use Tracealyzer to observe task executions that involve accesses to a protected shared resource.

8.2. Exercise 9. Investigating non-synchronized data transfer between tasks.

The objective of this exercise is to investigate the use of a queue to support data transfer between tasks without any synchronizing actions.

8.3. Exercise 10. Investigating synchronized data transfer between tasks.
The aim of this exercise is to demonstrate task synchronization with data transfer.

8.4. Exercise 11. Evaluating the use of deferred server techniques.
This exercise demonstrates the use of Tracealyzer to observe the activation of a deferred server task using interrupt-driven operations.

Part 1

Developing the practical code

Until you turn theory into practice you'll never truly, fully and deeply understand a subject. And we assume, because you've parted with your hard earned money to buy this book, _that_ is your key aim. Put concisely; your objective is to turn your designs into practical software that actually runs on real hardware. Moreover, in our view, the actual process should be as straightforward, simple and cheap as possible; masochism is not the _ordre du jour (_as the French would say). Furthermore, it should be based on professional-level tools so that you can, if you wish, employ them later in your own work.

   To that end we've put together a toolset that consists of:

- A graphical tool for configuring microcontrollers - the STM32CubeMX software application.
- An RTOS (specifically FreeRTOS), which is integrated with the CubeMX tool.
- A very low cost single board computer with inbuilt programmer and debugger, the STM32F4 Discovery kit.
- An Integrated Development Environment for the production of machine code.

All software, which is free, can be run on Windows, OSX or Linux platforms. The Discovery kit is readily available from many electronic suppliers.

   Now, it's one thing to have the tools; it's another to know how to use them. _This_ is the essence of part 1 of the book.

Chapter 1

Processes, tools, toolchains and hardware.

1.1 Design to code - a practical approach

1.1.1 Overview.

What is described here is a particular way of turning a software design into machine code. This consists of two major steps, figure 1.1:

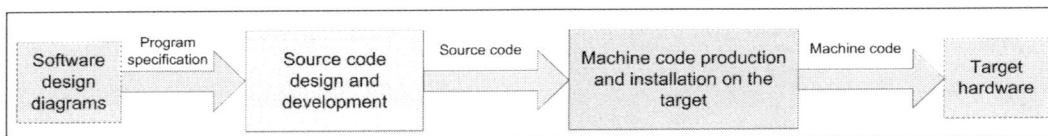

Figure 1.1 Design to machine code - the major steps

- Step 1 is the process used to produce the source code of the design. For convenience we'll call this the *source code production phase.*
- Step 2 involves turning this source code into machine code and installing this on the target processor. We'll call this step the t*arget code production phase.* This process relies on the use of an Integrated Development Environment (IDE), to be described later.

1.1.2 Source code production.

Let's first have a brief look at the source code production phase. The complete source code can be split into three major parts: application-level code, initialization code and platform-specific code, figure 1.2.

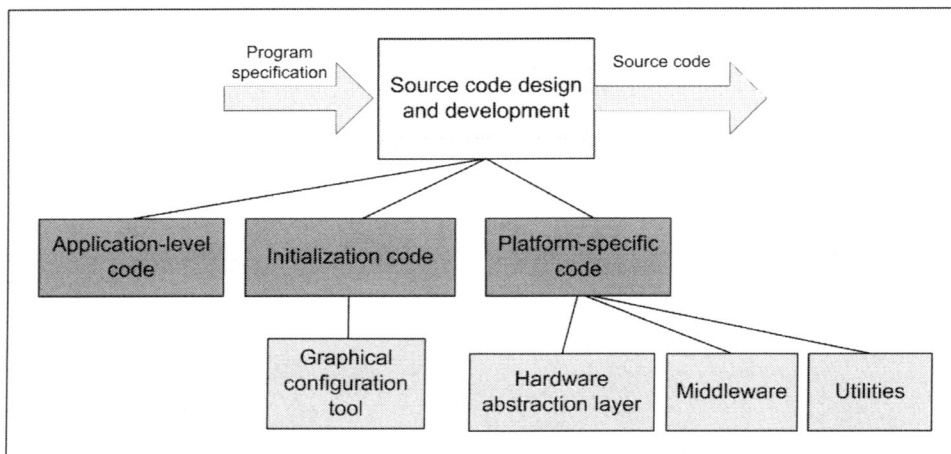

Figure 1.2 Source code components

It may surprise some readers that initialization code is treated as being a distinct, visible, explicit separate unit.   But there are goods reason for this.   Any of you familiar with modern microcontrollers will know that they are generally very complex devices. The range of functions available is extensive; moreover many functions often (usually) require detailed programming to set them up. And it gets worse. There is an extra layer of complexity when handling functions that deal with the external world. In many cases there aren't sufficient pins on the IC package to simultaneously interface to all the internal functions.   Thus you have to configure the microcontroller to define exactly which function is provided on a specific pin.

Device manufacturers often provide tools to simplify the configuration process, the best of these being graphics-based. More of this in a moment.

Platform-specific code can generally be grouped into three categories: the hardware abstraction layer (HAL), middleware and lastly, utilities. What you get here depends on individual vendors.

1.1.3 Target code production.

Let us now consider the target code production phase and the software tools needed for this work.   Now, there isn't a single tool that provides everything needed to develop software (machine code) for a target system; it takes many tools working together to perform all the required functions.   This group of tools is collectively called a software toolset or *toolchain* (because the tools are chained together to produce the final executable application for the microcontroller).   In its basic form a toolchain consists of a compiler, assembler, linker and locator, figure 1.3.

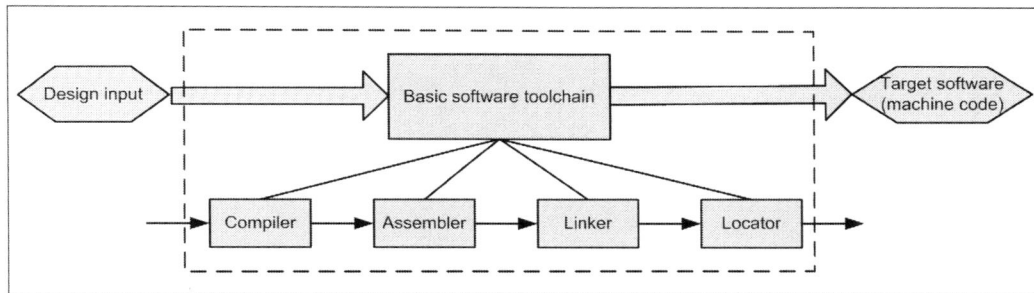

Figure 1.3 Software toolchain - overview

We'll now show how to implement the more general development process described in figure 1 as a project-specific one, figure 1.4.   Here, for general applications, the toolchain consists of two major software items: the STM32Cube tool and an Integrated Development Environment tool (which includes or is augmented by JTAG software).

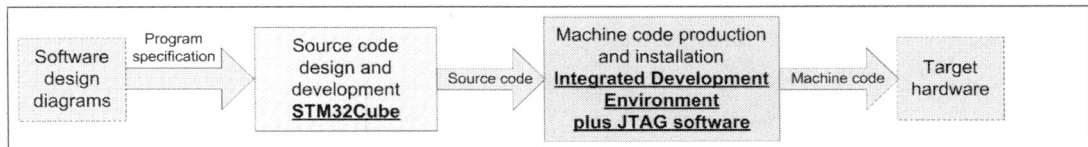

Figure 1.4 Design to code - project specific

The purpose of the STMicroelectronics software tool (STM32Cube) is to generate source code based on the program specification.   From user-provided input it automatically outputs all initialization and hardware-specific code. However it does *not* produce application code: this has to be implemented by the programmer (but see later notes relating to the use of an RTOS).

The second tool implements all the functions of the basic software toolchain of figure 3 (and more).   Its output, the run-time machine code, is downloaded into the target system using (in this case) a JTAG device.   Note that some IDE'S can import the STM32Cube tool to form an extended toolset.

These tools will now be described in more detail, sufficient for you to appreciate what they do and how they do it.   However, to actually use the tools you'll need to consult their detailed manuals and application notes. First for consideration is the STM32Cube tool.

1.2 The STM32Cube software tool - an introduction.

1.2.1 Tool overview.

The structure of the STM32Cube tool is shown in figure 1.5.

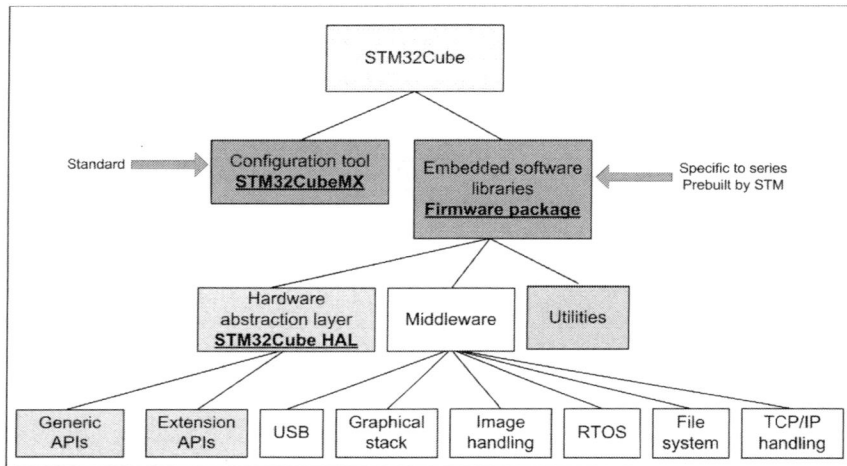

Figure 1.5 Structure of the STM32Cube tool

This consists of the:

- STM32CubeMX graphical configuration tool and the
- STM32Cube embedded software libraries - the firmware package.

These can be used either together or independently. They can be downloaded from:

http://www.st.com/web/catalog/tools/FM147/CL1794/SC961/SS1533/PF259242?sc=stm32cube#

1.2.2 STM32CubeMX features.

- Configuration C code generation for pin multiplexing, clock tree, peripherals and middleware setup with graphical wizards.
- Generation of full project source code for input to an integrated development environment tool chain.
- Power consumption calculation for a user-defined application sequence.
- Direct import of STM32 Cube embedded software libraries from st.com.
- Integrated updater to keep STM32CubeMX up-to-date.

Relevant manuals:

- STM UM1718 STM32CubeMX for STM32 configuration and initialization C code generation.

1.2.3 STM32Cube embedded software libraries and documentation.

- The HAL hardware abstraction layer, enabling portability between different STM32 devices via standardized API calls
- A collection of Middleware components, like RTOS, USB library, file system, TCP/IP stack, Touch sensing library or Graphic Library (depending on the MCU series).
- All embedded software utilities.

All packages come with a large number of examples and demonstration code, ready to be used with a wide range of development environments including IAR EWARM, Keil MDK or GCC-based IDEs.

Important user manuals:

- STM UM1779 Firmware package getting started for STM32F0 series.
- STM UM1847 Firmware package getting started for STM32F1 series.
- STM UM1739 Firmware package getting started for STM32F2 series.
- STM UM1766 Firmware package getting started for STM32F3 series.
- STM UM1730 Firmware package getting started for STM32F4 series.

- STM UM1785 Description of STM32F0xx HAL drivers.
- STM UM1850 Description of STM32F1xx HAL drivers.
- STM UM1940 Description of STM32F2xx HAL drivers.
- STM UM1786 Description of STM32F3xx HAL drivers.
- STM UM1725 Description of STM32F4xx HAL drivers.

For an excellent overview of Cube go to:

www.st.com/stm32cube-pr11

Run the featured video 'STM32Cube Basics'.

   At this stage the most relevant document is:

- DB2164 STM32Cube for STM32F4 - a simple overview.

Overview information is also provided there for other STM32F devices but really it just repeats the F4 material.

1.3 The practical toolset.

1.3.1 Hosting the software tools - Integrated Development Environments.

The basic software toolchain, essentially a collection of individual tools, must run within some sort of software development environment. In order to produce machine code for a target system we need, at the very minimum, those shown in figure 1.3. However, adding tools to extend its functionality results is a much more powerful, useful and adaptable product. Typically such extras include:

- Code-aware text editors for source code production.
- GUI builders.
- Board and device emulators.
- Profilers (e.g. runtime behaviour, memory usage, cpu usage etc.).
- Analysis tools (static and dynamic).

All these tools need to act in an integrated fashion, leading to the term Integrated Development Environment (IDE). An IDE is built as an application that runs on some specified operating system; thus it is a complete software package.

Well known IDEs include Microsoft Visual Studio, Apple Xcode and Java NetBeans. In general IDEs are proprietary items, including those designed for embedded applications (e.g. IAR EWARM and Keil (ARM) µVision). Free versions of these are available; they are usually subsets of the full tool which (unfortunately) limit the extent of the software development (e.g. Keil µVision limits code size to 32 kB). At the moment the Cube tool generates source code that can be processed by the following IDEs:

- IAR EWARM.
- KEIL mdk-arm.
- ATOLLIC TrueSTUDIO
- System Workbench for STM32 — SW4STM32.
- Other Toolchains (GPDSC).

One 'Other Toolchain' that is well worth looking at is the free open-source IDE **Eclipse**. This has many interesting and useful features, in particular it can be hosted on Mac (OSX) and Linux devices. More details are given later. An aside: both TrueSTUDIO and SW4STM32 are based on the Eclipse IDE.

1.3.2 The hardware - STM32F4 Discovery kit.

This kit — strictly speaking *the STM32F4 Discovery kit for STM32F407* — will allow you to run all the practical exercises without the need to use any other hardware. The reason for using this board is that:

- There is extensive support for it from STM.
- The code generated by the Cube tool (and then processed using one of the designated IDEs) is guaranteed to run on the board.
- It is the cheapest Discovery board that contains all items essential to the exercises.
- There isn't a need to perform any software porting or configuration operations (to use a cliche 'it runs out of the box').
- If any of your practical code exercises fails to run correctly you can almost always guarantee that *you* have got it wrong — it's not down to a hardware fault!
- It is also an excellent platform for further experimentation of your own choosing.

The following is a summary of its features (an STM blurb):

The STM32F4DISCOVERY Discovery kit allows users to easily develop applications with the STM32F407 high performance microcontroller with ARM® Cortex®-M4 32-bit core. It includes everything required either for beginners or for experienced users to get quickly started.
Based on the STM32F407VGT6, it includes an ST-LINK/V2 or ST-LINK/V2-A embedded debug tool, two ST MEMS digital accelerometers, a digital microphone, one audio DAC with integrated class D speaker driver, LEDs and push buttons and an USB OTG micro-AB connector. To expand the functionality of the STM32F4DISCOVERY Discovery kit with the Ethernet connectivity, LCD display and more, visit the www.st.com/stm32f4dis-expansion webpage. The STM32F4DISCOVERY Discovery kit comes with the STM32 comprehensive software HAL library, together with various packaged software examples,

A photo of the board itself is shown in figure 1.6.

Figure 1.6 The STM32F4-discovery board

Two important documents that you should get are:
1. ST User Manual UM1467
Getting started with software and firmware environments for the STM32F4DISCOVERY Kit
2. ST User Manual UM1472
Discovery kit with STM32F407VG MCU

There is a some information overlap between the two user manuals. However, UM1467 is basically tool/software oriented whilst UM1472 concentrates on the hardware.

NOW FOR GOOD ADVICE:
1. Download the user manuals and, at the very least, have a good browse of their contents.
2. If you haven't used any of the IDEs listed above then go and evaluate them. Select the one that suits you best, then make sure you become totally familiar with its features.
3. Now, at the very least, produce a short test program, download it into a target board and make sure it runs. Once you've done that you can go ahead and include the Cube tool in the overall process.

1.4 The STM32Cube graphical tool - STM32CubeMX details.

1.4.1 Overview.

To produce initialization code the following process must be carried out:

I.   Start the STMCube32CubeMX application and create a new project.
II. Select the microcontroller (or board) to be used (selection tool or 'wizard).
III. Set the pin functions as required in your design (pinout wizard).
IV. Set the parameters of the peripherals and middleware (peripherals and middleware configuration wizard).
V.   If required, set the clock system (clock tree wizard - clock configuration).
VI. If required, check the estimated power consumption (power consumption wizard).
VII. Generate the initialization code.

Steps III and IV can be carried out in an iterative fashion until the design is complete.
   What follows here is a broad outline of the process in action. It is meant to give you a good understanding of the overall process, not detailed activities (more of this later).

1.4.2 Selecting the microcontroller.
When *New Project* is selected in the app the following screen, the selection wizard, appears, figure 1.7. You can see that its lists a whole range of STM32 devices together with memory and peripheral information

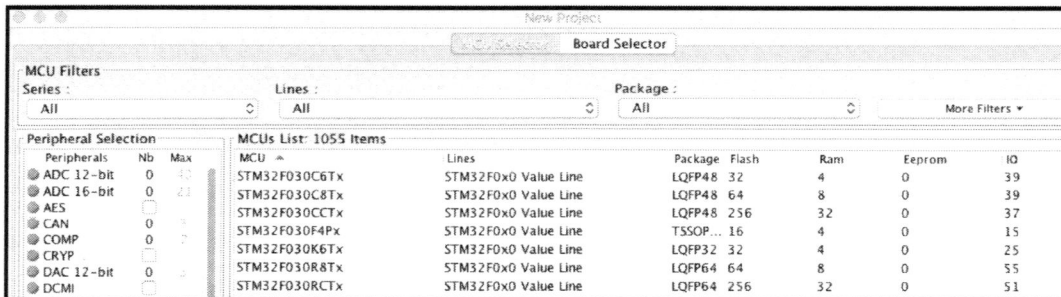

Figure 1.7 The selection wizard

Use "MCU filters" (series, lines, packages) to quickly define the required device.

Once a device is chosen the display changes to show the outline of the device together with all pins, figure 1.8.

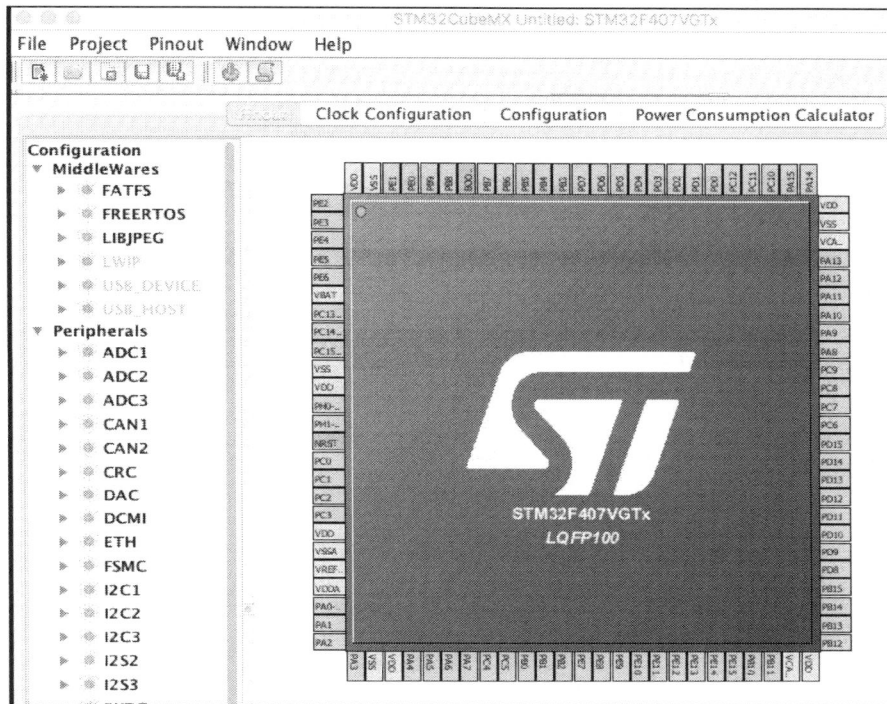

Figure 1.8 The pinout view after the microcontroller is selected

The functions of several pins are predefined (e.g. power connections); the rest may be configurable. Note that there are four selectable tabs: Pinout, Clock Configuration, Configuration and Power Consumption Calculator. Observe that here the Pinout tab is selected; hence the pinout wizard is active.

If the configuration tab is selected the following display appears (figure 1.9). This shows the default configuration of the peripherals and middleware.

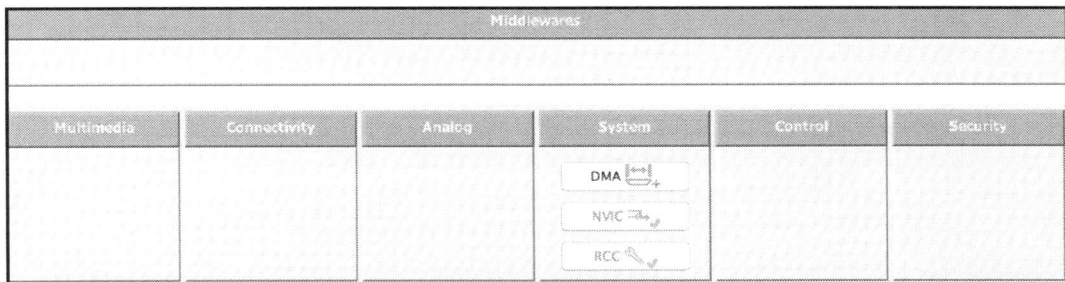

Figure 1.9 The peripherals and middleware configure view (initial).

You can see that, by default, we can configure the DMA controller, the nested vectored interrupt function (NVIC) and the reset and clock controller (RCC).

1.4.3 Using the pinout wizard to set pin functions.

To set a pin function, you merely have to select that pin, figure 1.10.

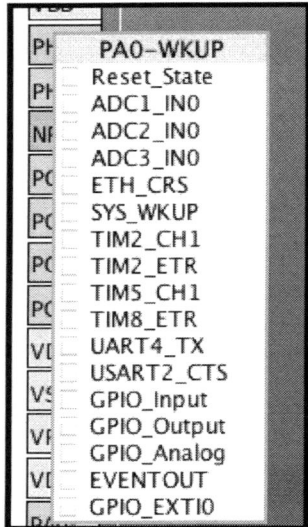

Figure 1.10 Functions available on pin PA0.

Choose, from this list , the required function.
  So, let us set PA0 to GPIO_Output. As a result the pin changes colour and its function is shown on the pinout view, figure 1.11.

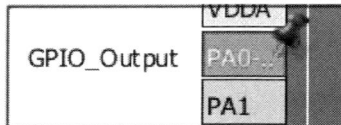

Figure 1.11 Pinout view after a pin function selected

If the configuration view is opened you'll see that GPIO functions have been added to the available configurable System functions, figure 1.12.

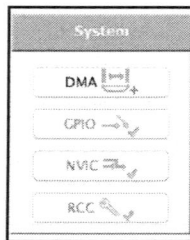

Figure 1.12 Configuration view - configurable system functions after pin selection

When GPIO is selected the following window opens (figure 1.13):

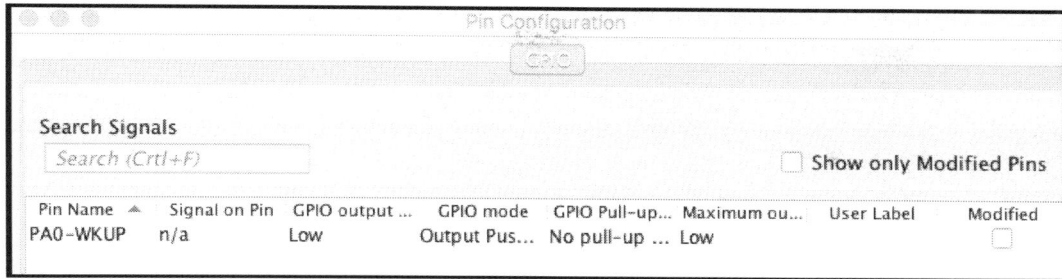

Figure 1.13 Pin configuration information

We can name this pin by right clicking (just a detailed point) on the pin. This produces a pop-up form that we can fill in with the signal details, figure 1.14.

Figure 1.14 Naming pins

The result of typing in 'LED1 drive' is then shown on the pinout view, figure 1.15.

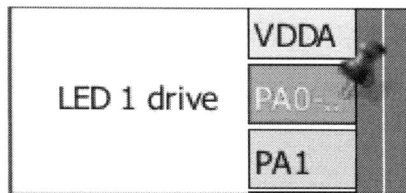

Figure 1.15 Pinout view - named pin

A return to the system configuration view for GPIO now shows the pin User Label, figure 1.16.

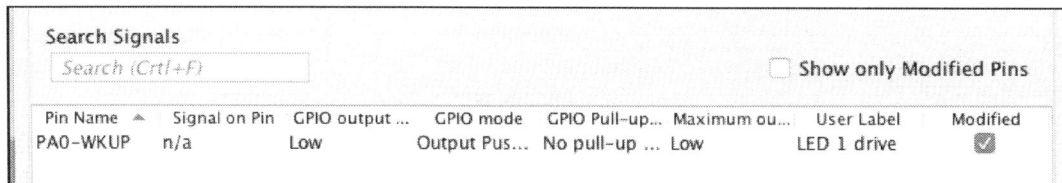

Figure 1.16 Updated pin configuration information

We're now ready to generate code.

1.4.4 Generating the code.

First, set up the project; select 'Project', then 'Settings'. In the Project Settings window (figure 1.17) enter a name for your project, define the folder that is to hold it and then specify your IDE (e.g.EWARM, Keil MDK, etc.).

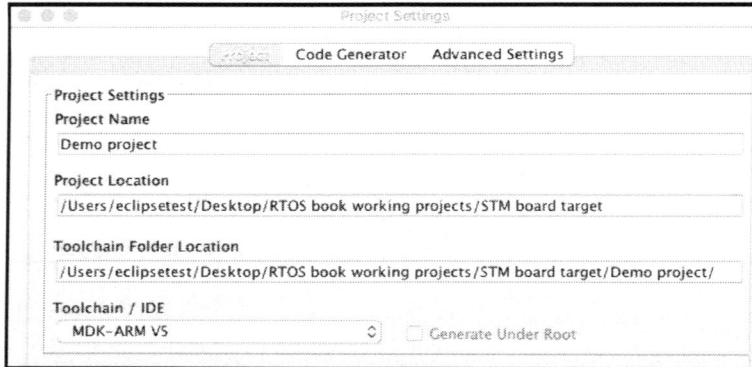

Figure 1.17 Project Settings window

After selecting 'Ok' go to the project folder and check that the project has been created, figure 18.

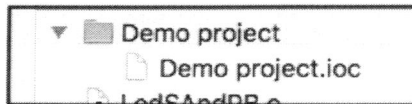

Figure 1.18 Project folder and its contents (initial)

Observe that one file only is present, a .ioc one. Code generation can now be initiated by using the code generation wizard icon or the drop-down *Project* menu (just more detail). After you've performed the required steps you'll find that the project folder is populated with the required set of folders/files, figure 1.19.

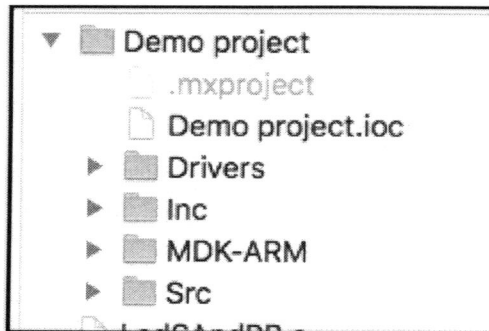

Figure 1.19 STM32 Cube generated project info.

In this example the generated code was intended to be compiled by the IAR IDE, EWARM. Note that all the driver software has automatically been added. However our interest, at this point, lies with the code of main.c, shown below. For the moment scan this to gain an appreciation of its content and structure.   After that read the information that follows in section 4.4. (*Automatically generated code*); then return and work your way carefully through this code.

```
/*******************************************************************************
  * File Name          : main.c
  * Description        : Main program body
  *******************************************************************************
  *
  * COPYRIGHT(c) 2016 STMicroelectronics
  *
  * Redistribution and use in source and binary forms, with or without modification,
  * are permitted provided that the following conditions are met:
  *   1. Redistributions of source code must retain the above copyright notice,
  *      this list of conditions and the following disclaimer.
  *   2. Redistributions in binary form must reproduce the above copyright notice,
  *      this list of conditions and the following disclaimer in the documentation
  *      and/or other materials provided with the distribution.
  *   3. Neither the name of STMicroelectronics nor the names of its contributors
  *      may be used to endorse or promote products derived from this software
  *      without specific prior written permission.
  *
  * THIS SOFTWARE IS PROVIDED BY THE COPYRIGHT HOLDERS AND CONTRIBUTORS "AS IS"
  * AND ANY EXPRESS OR IMPLIED WARRANTIES, INCLUDING, BUT NOT LIMITED TO, THE
  * IMPLIED WARRANTIES OF MERCHANTABILITY AND FITNESS FOR A PARTICULAR PURPOSE ARE
  * DISCLAIMED. IN NO EVENT SHALL THE COPYRIGHT HOLDER OR CONTRIBUTORS BE LIABLE
  * FOR ANY DIRECT, INDIRECT, INCIDENTAL, SPECIAL, EXEMPLARY, OR CONSEQUENTIAL
  * DAMAGES (INCLUDING, BUT NOT LIMITED TO, PROCUREMENT OF SUBSTITUTE GOODS OR
  * SERVICES; LOSS OF USE, DATA, OR PROFITS; OR BUSINESS INTERRUPTION) HOWEVER
  * CAUSED AND ON ANY THEORY OF LIABILITY, WHETHER IN CONTRACT, STRICT LIABILITY,
  * OR TORT (INCLUDING NEGLIGENCE OR OTHERWISE) ARISING IN ANY WAY OUT OF THE USE
  * OF THIS SOFTWARE, EVEN IF ADVISED OF THE POSSIBILITY OF SUCH DAMAGE.*
  *******************************************************************************
  */
/* Includes ------------------------------------------------------------------*/
#include "stm32f0xx_hal.h"

/* USER CODE BEGIN Includes */

/* USER CODE END Includes */

/* Private variables ---------------------------------------------------------*/

/* USER CODE BEGIN PV */
/* Private variables ---------------------------------------------------------*/

/* USER CODE END PV */

/* Private function prototypes -----------------------------------------------*/
void SystemClock_Config(void);
static void MX_GPIO_Init(void);

/* USER CODE BEGIN PFP */
/* Private function prototypes -----------------------------------------------*/

/* USER CODE END PFP */

/* USER CODE BEGIN 0 */

/* USER CODE END 0 */

int main(void)
```

```
{

  /* USER CODE BEGIN 1 */

  /* USER CODE END 1 */

  /* MCU Configuration---------------------------------------------------------*/

  /* Reset of all peripherals, Initializes the Flash interface and the Systick. */
  HAL_Init();

  /* Configure the system clock */
  SystemClock_Config();

  /* Initialize all configured peripherals */
  MX_GPIO_Init();

  /* USER CODE BEGIN 2 */

  /* USER CODE END 2 */

  /* Infinite loop */
  /* USER CODE BEGIN WHILE */
  while (1)
  {
  /* USER CODE END WHILE */

  /* USER CODE BEGIN 3 */

  }
  /* USER CODE END 3 */

}

/** System Clock Configuration
*/
void SystemClock_Config(void)
{

  RCC_OscInitTypeDef RCC_OscInitStruct;
  RCC_ClkInitTypeDef RCC_ClkInitStruct;

  RCC_OscInitStruct.OscillatorType = RCC_OSCILLATORTYPE_HSI;
  RCC_OscInitStruct.HSIState = RCC_HSI_ON;
  RCC_OscInitStruct.HSICalibrationValue = 16;
  RCC_OscInitStruct.PLL.PLLState = RCC_PLL_NONE;
  HAL_RCC_OscConfig(&RCC_OscInitStruct);

  RCC_ClkInitStruct.ClockType = RCC_CLOCKTYPE_HCLK|RCC_CLOCKTYPE_SYSCLK
                  |RCC_CLOCKTYPE_PCLK1;
  RCC_ClkInitStruct.SYSCLKSource = RCC_SYSCLKSOURCE_HSI;
  RCC_ClkInitStruct.AHBCLKDivider = RCC_SYSCLK_DIV1;
  RCC_ClkInitStruct.APB1CLKDivider = RCC_HCLK_DIV1;
  HAL_RCC_ClockConfig(&RCC_ClkInitStruct, FLASH_LATENCY_0);

  HAL_SYSTICK_Config(HAL_RCC_GetHCLKFreq()/1000);

  HAL_SYSTICK_CLKSourceConfig(SYSTICK_CLKSOURCE_HCLK);

  /* SysTick_IRQn interrupt configuration */
```

```
  HAL_NVIC_SetPriority(SysTick_IRQn, 0, 0);
}

/** Configure pins as
      * Analog
      * Input
      * Output
      * EVENT_OUT
      * EXTI
*/
void MX_GPIO_Init(void)
{

  GPIO_InitTypeDef GPIO_InitStruct;

  /* GPIO Ports Clock Enable */
  __GPIOA_CLK_ENABLE();

  /*Configure GPIO pin Output Level */
  HAL_GPIO_WritePin(LED_1_drive_GPIO_Port, LED_1_drive_Pin, GPIO_PIN_RESET);

  /*Configure GPIO pin : LED_1_drive_Pin */
  GPIO_InitStruct.Pin = LED_1_drive_Pin;
  GPIO_InitStruct.Mode = GPIO_MODE_OUTPUT_PP;
  GPIO_InitStruct.Pull = GPIO_NOPULL;
  GPIO_InitStruct.Speed = GPIO_SPEED_LOW;
  HAL_GPIO_Init(LED_1_drive_GPIO_Port, &GPIO_InitStruct);

}

/* USER CODE BEGIN 4 */

/* USER CODE END 4 */

#ifdef USE_FULL_ASSERT

/**
   * @brief Reports the name of the source file and the source line number
   * where the assert_param error has occurred.
   * @param file: pointer to the source file name
   * @param line: assert_param error line source number
   * @retval None
   */
void assert_failed(uint8_t* file, uint32_t line)
{
  /* USER CODE BEGIN 6 */
  /* User can add his own implementation to report the file name and line number,
    ex: printf("Wrong parameters value: file %s on line %d\r\n", file, line) */
  /* USER CODE END 6 */

}

#endif


/********************* (C) COPYRIGHT STMicroelectronics *****END OF FILE****/
```

1.4.5 Automatically-generated code: the really important points.

Listed below are the salient points of the automatically-generated code (minus that of the initialization functions).

(a) Automatic include files
```
/* Includes -------------------------------------------------------------*/
#include "stm32f0xx_hal.h"
```

(b) Prototypes of functions used to initialize the micro.
```
/* Private function prototypes ---------------------------------------------*/
void SystemClock_Config(void);
static void MX_GPIO_Init(void);
```

(c) Actual initialization code function calls (in main).
```
  /* MCU Configuration-------------------------------------------------------*/

  /* Reset of all peripherals, Initializes the Flash interface and the Systick. */
  HAL_Init();

  /* Configure the system clock */
  SystemClock_Config();

  /* Initialize all configured peripherals */
  MX_GPIO_Init();
```

Note that the functions HAL_Init() and SystemClock_Config() will always be generated; other functions produced depend on the pin configuration settings.

(d) User includes sections
You can see that there are a number of sections in the code that are similar to the following;

```
  /* USER CODE BEGIN 1 */

  /* USER CODE END 1 */
```

THE key point is that anything inserted between the begin and end points is always preserved when (if) you regenerate the code.

Now go back and read study the code of main.c in detail. Make sure, in the end, that you fully understand all aspects of the file contents.

1.4.6 The next step.

Download the user manual *STM UM1718 STM32CubeMX for STM32 configuration and initialization C code generation*. Follow the instructions for installing and running STM32CubeMX. Study and experiment with the tutorials until you are comfortable with the tool.

1.5. The STM32Cube HAL.

The HAL drivers consist of a set of driver modules, each module being linked to a standalone peripheral. Each driver consists of a set of functions covering the most common peripherals. Some important features:

• Three API programming models are supported: polling, interrupt and DMA.
• All APIs are RTOS compliant:

- - Fully reentrant APIs
  - - Systematic usage of timeouts in polling mode.
- • Callback functions are provided for:
  - - Peripherals interrupt events
  - - Error events.
- • Timeouts are used for all blocking processes.
- • Objects can be locked (an access control mechanism).

An example of a set of automatically-generated HAL include files is shown in figure 1.20.

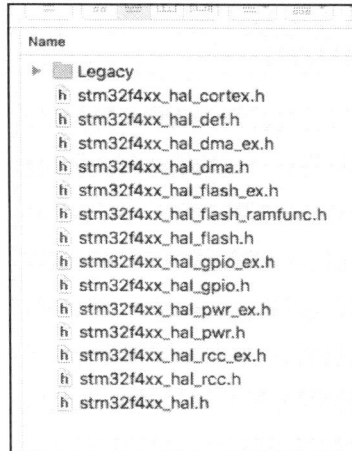

Figure 1.20 Example of HAL include files.

These were produced (for a specific project) when the project code was generated in CubeMX. Note that, in practice, the *actual* HAL file set produced depends on the microcontroller being used in the project. These files are defined in the user manuals of the various STM32F families (listed earlier, repeated here for convenience):

- • STM UM1785 Description of STM32F0xx HAL drivers.
- • STM UM1850 Description of STM32F1xx HAL drivers.
- • STM UM1940 Description of STM32F2xx HAL drivers.
- • STM UM1786 Description of STM32F3xx HAL drivers.
- • STM UM1725 Description of STM32F4xx HAL drivers.

A full list of HAL driver acronyms and definitions is given in these user manuals.
There's little point is saying much more about the HAL as it's quite an extensive subject. Consult the user manual as and when you need information. A good idea (at this point) is to download the relevant manual and assess its overall content.

1.6. Example - FreeRTOS configuration in a Cube project.

The real-time operating system FreeRTOS is included in the middleware package of the STM32Cube tool. This is a good, well proven and relatively simple RTOS; its use is highly recommended. The process to incorporate FreeRTOS in a Cube-generated multitasking design is relatively straightforward; however it must be carried out in a very specific, prescriptive manner. This is described in more detail in the following section.
An example of a Cube project pinout is shown in figure 1.21 where the FreeRTOS is enabled (observe that in the configuration information FREERTOS is highlighted). Observe also that SYS

timebase source has been set to TIM1 (any timer would do but it must be changed from the default setting of SysTick).

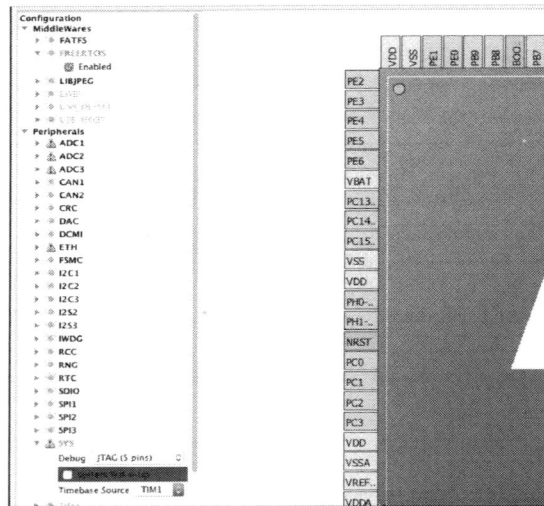

Figure 1.21 Example Cube project - screenshot of the pinout view

When this is compiled the resulting Cube-generated project folders/files are (figure 1.22):

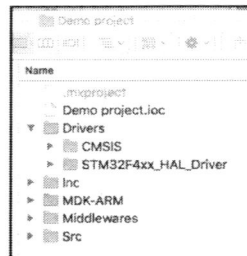

Figure 1.22 Cube-generated project folders and files

The Cube project RTOS configuration details are given below. First, in figure 1.23, is the list of tasks in the project. The default one is created automatically by Cube; any others are added by the designer.

Tasks							
Name	Priority	Stack Size (Words)	Entry Function	Code Generation Option	Allocation	Buffer	Control Block
defaultTask	osPriorityNormal	128	StartDefaultTask	Default	Dynamic	NULL	NULL

Figure 1.23 List of FreeRTOS tasks in the project

Next is shown the Config parameters of the project, figure 1.24. This is where we configure the system as specifically required by the project.

The third item is that of the Include parameters, figure 1.25, where we can enable or disable the FreeRTOS (native) functions. It is very important to check this to see which items are disabled (note especially vTaskDelayUntil).

The final Cube screenshot displays the heap usage information, figure 1.26.

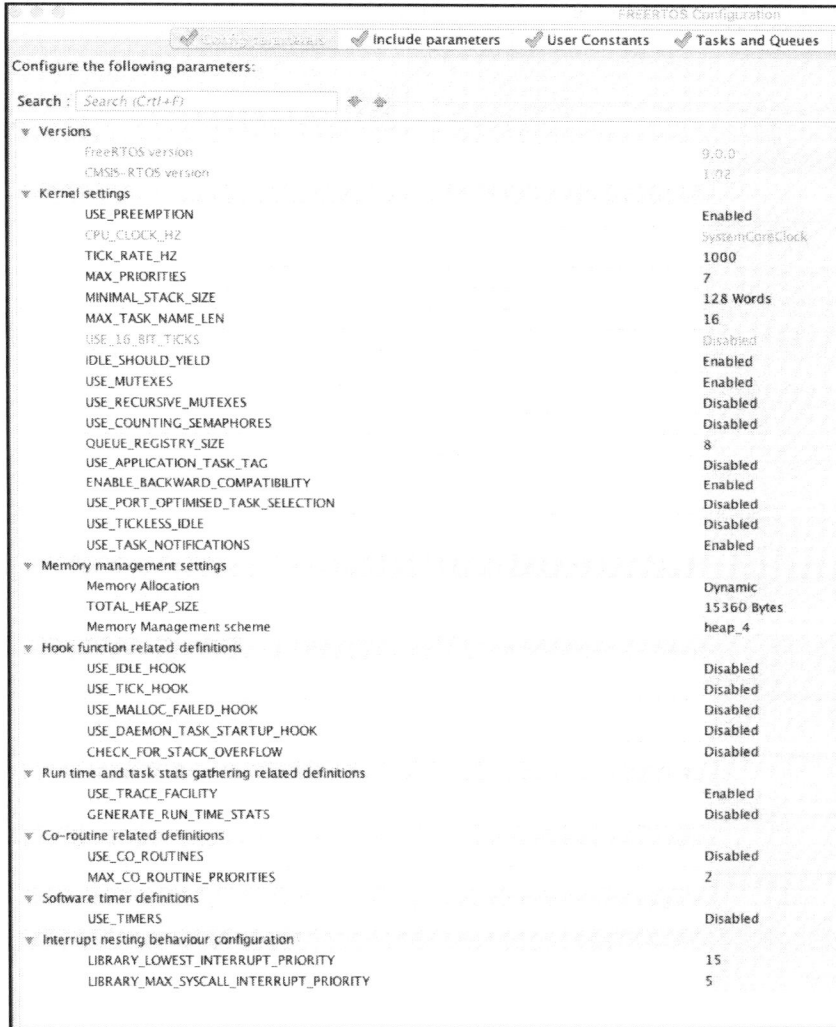

FREERTOS Configuration

	Include parameters	User Constants	Tasks and Queues

Configure the following parameters:

Search : Search (Crtl+F)

Versions		
FreeRTOS version		9.0.0
CMSIS-RTOS version		1.02
Kernel settings		
USE_PREEMPTION		Enabled
CPU_CLOCK_HZ		SystemCoreClock
TICK_RATE_HZ		1000
MAX_PRIORITIES		7
MINIMAL_STACK_SIZE		128 Words
MAX_TASK_NAME_LEN		16
USE_16_BIT_TICKS		Disabled
IDLE_SHOULD_YIELD		Enabled
USE_MUTEXES		Enabled
USE_RECURSIVE_MUTEXES		Disabled
USE_COUNTING_SEMAPHORES		Disabled
QUEUE_REGISTRY_SIZE		8
USE_APPLICATION_TASK_TAG		Disabled
ENABLE_BACKWARD_COMPATIBILITY		Enabled
USE_PORT_OPTIMISED_TASK_SELECTION		Disabled
USE_TICKLESS_IDLE		Disabled
USE_TASK_NOTIFICATIONS		Enabled
Memory management settings		
Memory Allocation		Dynamic
TOTAL_HEAP_SIZE		15360 Bytes
Memory Management scheme		heap_4
Hook function related definitions		
USE_IDLE_HOOK		Disabled
USE_TICK_HOOK		Disabled
USE_MALLOC_FAILED_HOOK		Disabled
USE_DAEMON_TASK_STARTUP_HOOK		Disabled
CHECK_FOR_STACK_OVERFLOW		Disabled
Run time and task stats gathering related definitions		
USE_TRACE_FACILITY		Enabled
GENERATE_RUN_TIME_STATS		Disabled
Co-routine related definitions		
USE_CO_ROUTINES		Disabled
MAX_CO_ROUTINE_PRIORITIES		2
Software timer definitions		
USE_TIMERS		Disabled
Interrupt nesting behaviour configuration		
LIBRARY_LOWEST_INTERRUPT_PRIORITY		15
LIBRARY_MAX_SYSCALL_INTERRUPT_PRIORITY		5

Figure 1.24 Project configuration parameters

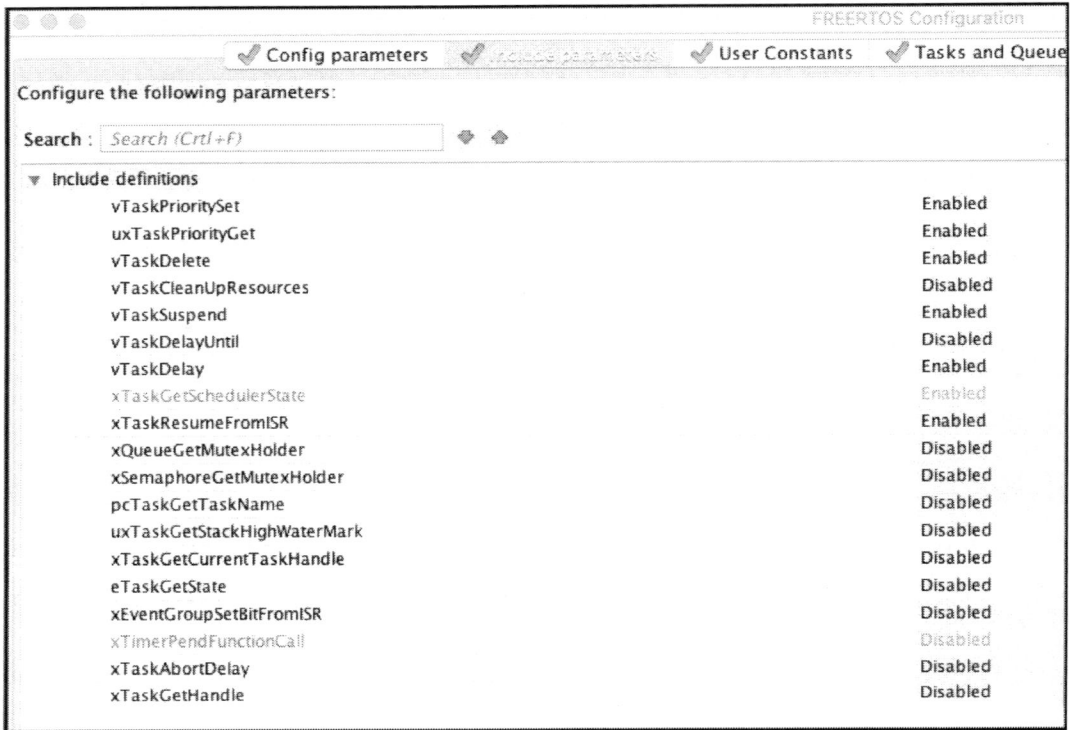

Figure 1.25 Config parameters settings

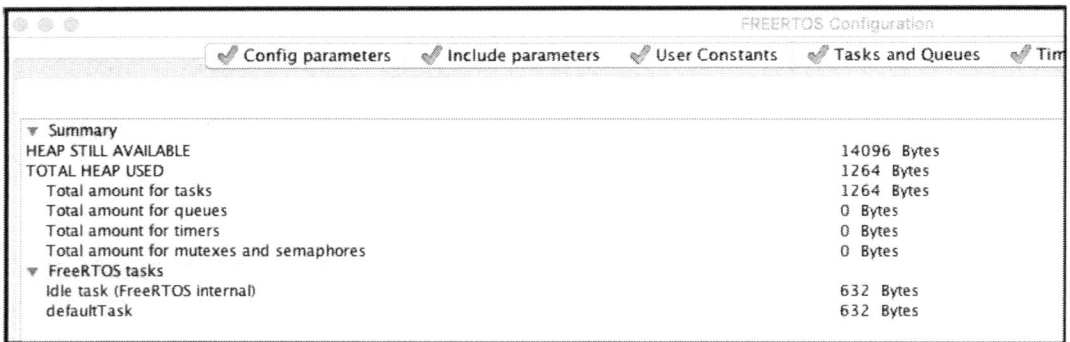

Figure 1.26 Cube-generated heap usage data

Part 2

The practical exercises.

These exercises are a vehicle to help you learn how to turn RTOS theory into practice. Specifically they relate to the material contained in chapters 1 to 5 of book 1, this being the bedrock of all modern general purpose real-time operating systems.
   The RTOS used here is FreeRTOS, chosen for the following reasons:

- It is integrated as middleware with the Cube tool.
- It is very easy and straightforward to configure it.
- The API set is comprehensive without being complex.
- Most of the APIs are similar to those found in other mainstream RTOSs.

Pretty-well all RTOSs have 'quirky' features; FreeRTOS is no exception. However these are few and far between, and shouldn't be a barrier to your learning how to use other RTOSs
   The key tenet of the exercises is that the work should be as simple and straightforward as possible. Also they — the exercises — must be self-contained and not rely on the use of external devices or other software tools.   In fact all that is needed are the on-board LEDs and the pushbutton of the STM32F4Discovery board. Thus it is essential that you totally understand how to use these items before embarking on the exercises. If you haven't already experimented with the target board, do so now. You can, if you wish, limit yourself to producing small test programs concerned only with LED and pushbutton operations. If you are embarking on target board work for the first time you'll find that the following documentation is helpful:

STM UM1725 Description of STM32F4xx HAL drivers.
Tutorial CubeMx - 1 - GPIO Out STM32F4Discovery STM32CubeMX
https://www.youtube.com/watch?v=TcCNdkxXnJY
Tutorial STMCubeMX - 3 - GPIO In Out on STM32F4 Discovery
https://www.youtube.com/watch?v=p_WyLNI40uU

   Just a memory jog: the practical work starts with the simplest problem, then gradually builds into more complex aspects. If you are new to all (or most) of the upcoming work please follow this sequence. Don't skip any exercises and do not proceed until you satisfactorily complete each one in the sequence. And please: always try to predict the expected visual information produced by the exercises before actually checking them out!

Chapter 2

Multitasking design and implementation - the basics.

2.1 Preliminary exercise - implement simple I/O interfacing.

Fundamental purpose of the exercise: to learn how to drive the LEDs and handle the pushbutton signal of the STM32F407G-DISC board.

2.1.1 Introduction.

Before getting into detail we need to answer four important questions:

- What is the point in doing this exercise?
- What will you learn from carrying it out?
- What should you know (or have done) before starting this exercise?
- How, in general, are you going to perform the work?

(a) What is the point in doing this exercise?
You will learn how to use the software development toolset for code development. This includes downloading code to the target board and then executing it.

(b) What will you learn from carrying it out?
By carrying out this exercise you will learn:
- The basic steps needed to turn a source code design into machine code that runs on a real target board.
- Precisely what source code 'elements' are produced by the graphical design tool.
- The difference between what the *tools* do and what *you* need to do.

At the end of the work you'll have acquired enough knowledge to take on more complex tasks.

(c) What should you have done before starting this exercise?
Before you do this exercise you must:
- Install the CubeMX graphical tool and exercise it.
- Install the IDE of your choice and learn how to use its essential features.
- Obtain an STM32F407G-DISC board, get to know its features and check that it is operational.

(d) How are you going to perform the work?
The work is carried out in a clearly defined manner, as follows:
- Start the CubeMX graphical tool, choose the 'new project' option and then select the board type (this will automatically set the microcontroller pins to the correct conditions for that board).
- Create a project and set it to generate code for your IDE.
- Generate the source code.
- Open the IDE; build the project using this source code.
- Download machine code to the target board and set it running.

For the exercises in the main section of the book we'll assume that the Keil µVision IDE is used. If you are embarking on target board work for the first time you'll find that the following documentation may be helpful:

STM UM1725 *Description of STM32F4xx HAL drivers.*
Tutorial CubeMx - 1 - GPIO Out STM32F4Discovery STM32CubeMX
https://www.youtube.com/watch?v=TcCNdkxXnJY
Tutorial STMCubeMX - 3 - GPIO In Out on STM32F4 Discovery
https://www.youtube.com/watch?v=p_WyLNI40uU

2.1.2 The problem.

For this problem the overall system structure is shown in figure 2.1 below.

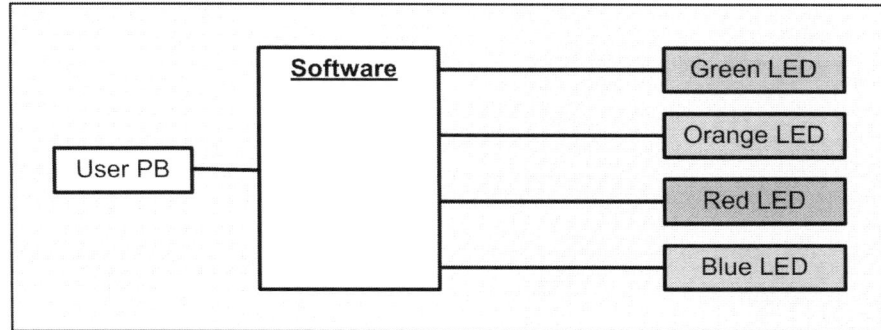

Figure 2.1 System diagram

The aim here is to learn how to develop software for handling the push button signal and for driving the four LEDs.

2.1.3 Implementing the design.

As this is likely to be your first exercise for real, we'll go through it in some detail.   This is essentially a 'hand-holding' approach, to make it easy for you to reach your final goal.   But be warned; after this you'll be very much on your own, so learn the lessons well.

(a) Start the CubeMX graphical tool, choose the 'new project' option. You will now be presented with the following screen display, figure 2.2:

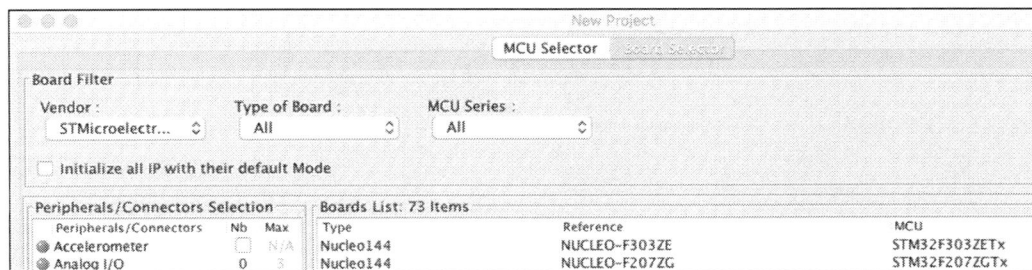

Figure 2.2 Initial screen - creation of a new project

Click on 'board selector' (if it isn't already active). Now choose the Vendor, board type and MCU series, as shown in figure 2.3.

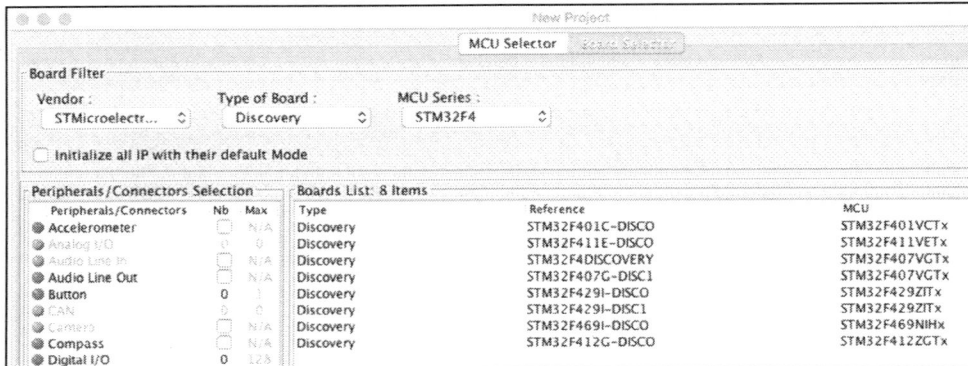

Figure 2.3 Detailed selection features - board and MCU type

Choose the STM32F407G-DISC1 board and tick the box 'Initialize all IP with their default Mode'. The result is that the CubeMX tool displays the pinout view of the microcontroller on this board, figure 2.4.

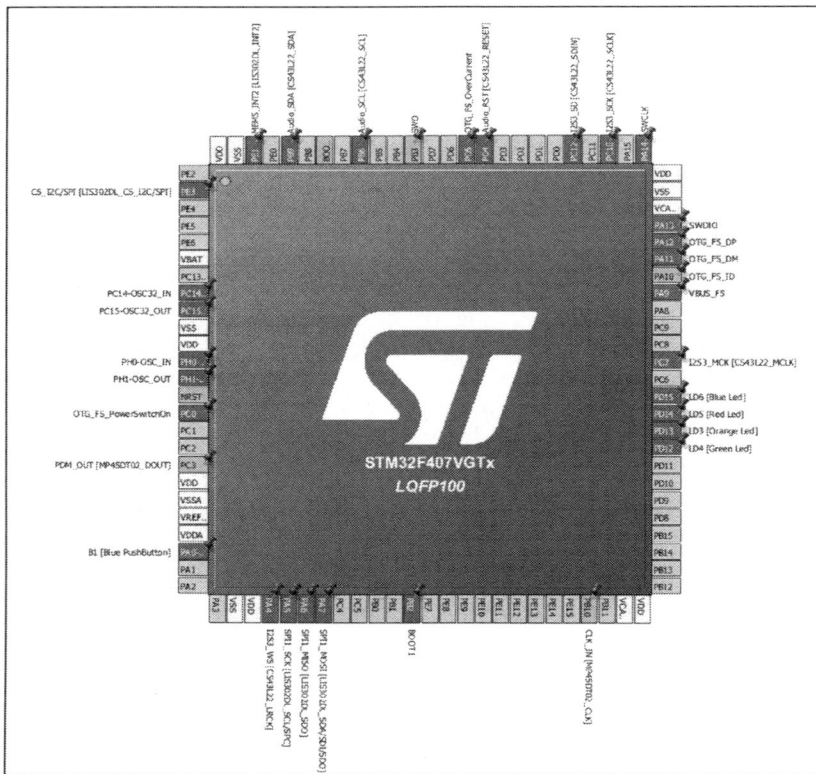

Figure 2.4 Pinout view of the microcontroller

(b) Create a project and set it to generate code for your IDE (here it's the Keil IDE).
Select 'Project' on the toolbar, then select 'Settings'. You will be presented with the 'Project Settings' window, figure 2.5. Set the project name and its location as you wish, then set the Toolchain/IDE selection to MDK-ARM V5 (or whatever version you have).

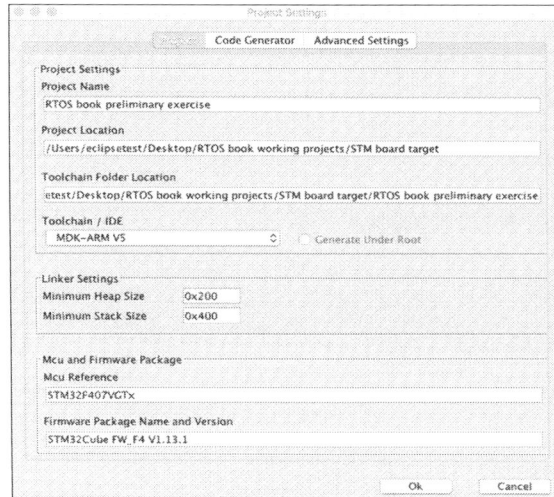

Figure 2.5 The CubeMX project settings window

When you first create a CubeMX project a project folder is created, figure 2.6.

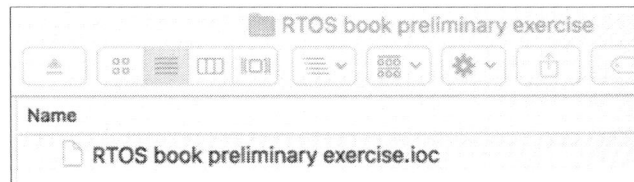

Fig 2.6 CubeMX project folder (initial)

At this stage it contains one file only: *RTOS book preliminary exercise.ioc*.

(c) Produce a simple test program.
At the stage the automatically-generated code doesn't do anything apart from initializing the micro; you have to provide the 'application' code. And note well: this is a sequential, not a concurrent, code unit. I suggest that you start with a very simple test program which toggles the Green LED.
   Insert the following code into the infinite loop of main:

```
// Green LED 4 — Pin PD12
HAL_GPIO_TogglePin(GPIOD, GPIO_PIN_12);
```
A one second software delay here (your own code, timing isn't critical)

(d) The final stages: building the project and downloading the code.
Now generate the project source code. You will now find that additional folders/files are automatically generated, figure 2.7.

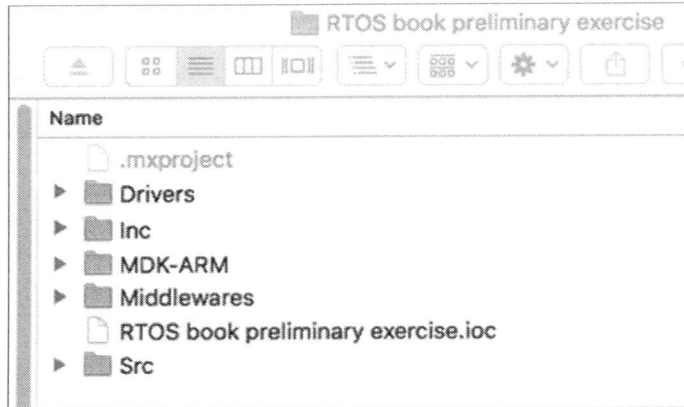

Figure 2.7 CubeMX project folder (final)

The MDK-ARM folder contains all files need by the Keil µVision IDE, which can be launched from this folder. So start the Keil IDE and proceed in the usual way to build, download and run the project. Observe and measure the flashing times of the LED. Check that these correspond to the program code (itself a design specification for executable code).
   Now modify your code to exercise all four Leds, Led 3 (Orange), 4 (Green), 5 (Red) and 6 (Blue). Once this has been completed successfully produce a test program to check out the operation of the 'User' pushbutton.

2.1.4 Preliminary exercise — API quick reference guide.

(i) Set/reset a pin output signal.

General format:
WritePin(PortID, PortPinID, SignalSetting);

Function prototype:
void HAL_GPIO_WritePin(GPIO_TypeDef* GPIOx, uint16_t GPIO_Pin, GPIO_PinState PinState);

Example function calls to control the signal on pin 14 of port D.
HAL_GPIO_WritePin(GPIOD, GPIO_PIN_14, GPIO_PIN_SET);
HAL_GPIO_WritePin(GPIOD, GPIO_PIN_14, GPIO_PIN_RESET);

(ii) Toggle a pin output signal.

General format:
TogglePin(PortID, PortPinID);

Function prototype:
void HAL_GPIO_TogglePin(GPIO_TypeDef* GPIOx, uint16_t GPIO_Pin);

Example function call to toggle pin 14 of port D.
HAL_GPIO_TogglePin(GPIOD, GPIO_PIN_14);

(iii) Get the status of the User pushbutton signal.

General format:
HAL_GPIO_ReadPin(PortID, PortPinID);

Function prototype:
GPIO_PinState   HAL_GPIO_ReadPin(GPIO_TypeDef* GPIOx, uint16_t GPIO_Pin);

(iii) Example function: read the User Pushbutton status (pin 0 of port A).

GPIO_PinState UserPushButtonState;
UserPushButtonState = HAL_GPIO_ReadPin(GPIOA, GPIO_PIN_0);

Note: return value is GPIO_PIN_SET or GPIO_PIN_RESET;

2.1.5 Preliminary exercise review.

If you've completed all parts of this exercise you will:

- Know how to create a CubeMX project for the STM32F discovery board.
- Know what default folders/files are generated by the CubeMX tool.
- Understand the structure and content of the source code *main.c* file.
- Understand clearly what code is automatically generated and what *you* have to provide.
- Have successfully compiled, downloaded and executed code on the target board that exercises Leds 3 (Orange), 4 (Green), 5 (Red) and 6 (Blue) and also deals with the User pushbutton signal.

2.2 Exercise 1 - Create and run a single task that executes repeatedly.

In this exercise you will learn how to develop one of the simplest, essential functions of a multitasking system: the execution of a single, continuously executing, task. By carrying out this exercise you will see how simple it is to produce a periodic task structure. At the end of the work you'll have acquired enough knowledge to take on more complex work.

2.2.1 The problem.

The tasking model of a very simple system is shown in figure 2.8, consisting of a single task which drives a Led. Implement this so that the the Red Led on the Discovery board is flashed. This is to have an on time of approximately 2000 milliseconds and an off time of approximately 500 milliseconds.

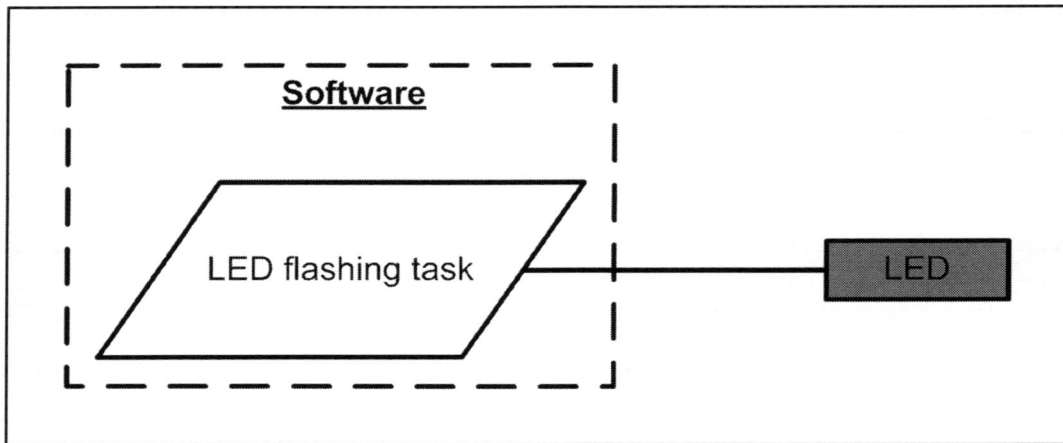

Figure 2.8 Task diagram

2.2.2 Implementing the design - exercise 1(a).

(b) Set up the CubeMX environment.
Start the CubeMX graphical tool, choose the 'new project' option. Click on 'board selector' (if it isn't already active). Now choose the Vendor, board type and MCU series and, as before, select STM32F407G-DISC1 from the boards list.

(b) Create a project and set it to generate code for the IDE.
Select 'Project' on the toolbar, then select 'Settings'. Set the project name and its location as you wish, then set the Toolchain/IDE selection to MDK-ARM V5 (or whatever tool you have).

(c) Configure it to include the FreeRTOS software; select a timer to be used for basic timing functions.
The FreeRTOS software is automatically included when you enable it in the Configuration Middlewares list, figure 2.9

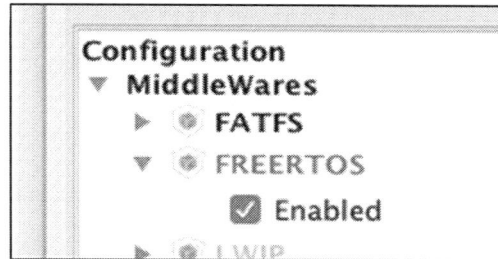

Figure 2.9 Enabling FreeRTOS

Next, the HAL timebase source needs to be set, figure 2.10.

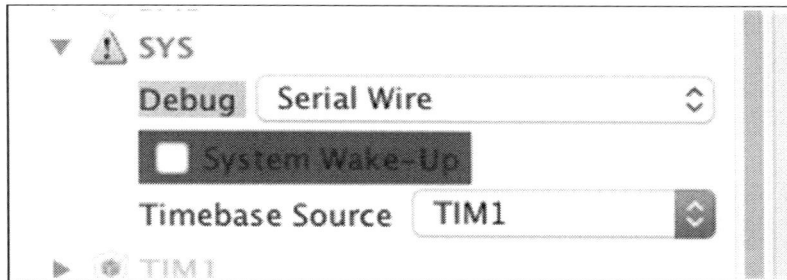

Figure 2.10 Setting the timebase source

Note that any available timer can be used.   Please ensure that the 'System Wake-Up' box is
unticked.

(d) Generate the source code.
Generate the source code as you've done in previous work. Most of what you'll find in main.c will
be familiar.   However, it now also includes RTOS-specific code, the key aspects being shown in
figure 2.11. This illustrates three important points:

- First, this is the way that FreeRTOS does things when part of the CubeMX environment.
- Second, this is what is generated when you use the default settings.
- Third, you don't have to know a great deal about the FreeRTOS APIs to understand how the
code works.

Let us walk our way through this.

1. A thread (task) identifier is created:
        osThreadId defaultTaskHandle;
2. A default thread is defined and created:
        osThreadDef(defaultTask, StartDefaultTask, osPriorityNormal, 0, 128);
        defaultTaskHandle = osThreadCreate(osThread(defaultTask), NULL);
3. The scheduler is started:
        osKernelStart();

4. A function is created to hold the code of the task:
        void StartDefaultTask(void const * argument)

```
/* Private variables ------------------------------------------------------*/
osThreadId defaultTaskHandle;

int main(void)
{
/* Create the thread(s) */  /* definition and creation of defaultTask */
    osThreadDef(defaultTask, StartDefaultTask, osPriorityNormal, 0, 128);
    defaultTaskHandle = osThreadCreate(osThread(defaultTask), NULL);

/* Start scheduler */
    osKernelStart();

    /* We should never get here as control is now taken by the scheduler */

} /* end main

*//* StartDefaultTask function */
void StartDefaultTask(void const * argument)
{

    /* USER CODE BEGIN 5 */
    /* Infinite loop */
    for(;;)
    {
       FOR INFO: NOT TOOL-GENERATED.
       THIS IS WHERE YOUR CODE IS INSERTED
    /* USER CODE END 5 */
}
```

Figure 2.11 Generated code - key RTOS features

The structure of FreeRTOS is such that there isn't a conventional background task; all code is executed by FreeRTOS tasks. Hence, after the scheduler is started, all subsequent operations are controlled by the RTOS.
    At the stage the default task doesn't do anything; you have program it. And note well: this is a sequential code unit. Now insert the following code into the body of the task function:

```
    HAL_GPIO_WritePin(GPIOD, GPIO_PIN_14, GPIO_PIN_SET);
    Your 2 second software delay here
    HAL_GPIO_WritePin(GPIOD, GPIO_PIN_14, GPIO_PIN_RESET);
    Your 0.5 second software delay here
```

(e) The final stages: building the project and downloading the code.
Start your IDE and proceed in the usual way to build, download and run the project. Observe and measure the flashing times (both on and off) of the Led. Check that these correspond to the program code.

2.2.3 Modifying the code - using the osDelay function (exercise 1b).

If you need precise timing in your design a software-based timer isn't good enough. Instead use the RTOS-provided delay function osDelay, as follows:

```
    HAL_GPIO_WritePin(GPIOD, GPIO_PIN_14, GPIO_PIN_SET);
    osDelay(2000);
    HAL_GPIO_WritePin(GPIOD, GPIO_PIN_14, GPIO_PIN_RESET);
    osDelay(500);
```

Replace your existing task code with this and then execute the software (experiment with different time values if you so wish).

2.2.4 Modifying the code - using native FreeRTOS constructs.

This is provided for those who are especially interested in working with the FreeRTOS product. Replace the osDelay function with the FreeRTOS native function, vTaskDelay, and verify that the task behaviour is unchanged.

```
HAL_GPIO_WritePin(GPIOD, GPIO_PIN_14, GPIO_PIN_SET);
vTaskDelay(2000);
HAL_GPIO_WritePin(GPIOD, GPIO_PIN_14, GPIO_PIN_RESET);
vTaskDelay(500);
```

Important note: From the details of the osDelay function—given at the end of this document—you can see that it actually invokes the vTaskDelay function. Note also that the actual timing produced depends on the tick period (the FreeRTOS default setting is 1 millisecond).
 Read the document at http://www.freertos.org/a00127.html for further details of the vTaskDelay function.

2.2.5 A further design exercise.- exercise 1c.

It is important that you carry out this exercise as it provides a good lead-in to exercise 3.
   Amend the task code by inserting a software-generated delay (your own code) of approximately one second after the pin is set (i.e.Led On), viz.:

```
HAL_GPIO_WritePin(GPIOD, GPIO_PIN_14, GPIO_PIN_SET);
Your 1 second software delay here
vTaskDelay(2000);
```

This is the only change; leave the rest as-is. Now rebuild the project, run it, and observe its behaviour. Having done this work out why it's changed and exactly what's taking place.
   Now modify your code to exercise all four Leds.

2.2.6 Exercise 1 review.

If you've completed all parts of this exercise you will:

• Know how to create a CubeMX project for the STM32F discovery board and configure this to use the FreeRTOS.
• Know what default folders/files are generated by the CubeMX tool.
• Understand the structure and content of the source code main.c file, in particular the RTOS constructs.
• Understand clearly what code is automatically generated and what you have to provide.
• Have successfully compiled, downloaded and executed code on the target board for a single FreeRTOS task that exercises Leds 3, 4, 5 and 6.
• Appreciate precisely how the vTaskDelay (aka osDelay) function behaves.

Now is the time to further explore the workings of FreeRTOS. Open your CubeMX project and change from the Pinout view to the Configuration view, figure 2.12.

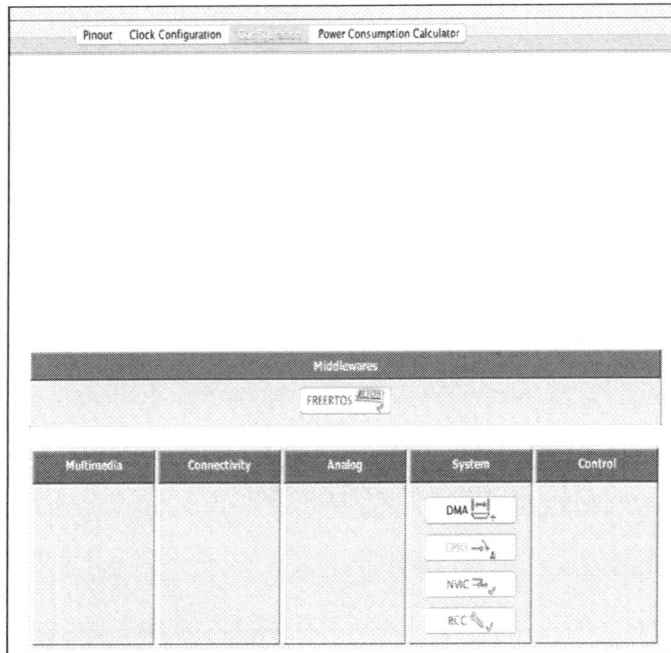

Figure 2.12 Configuration view of the CubeMX project

Click on FREERTOS and select the 'Config parameters' tab. You'll now be presented with the project configuration parameters window (figure 2.13):

For the moment just familiarise yourself with the information contained here.

For detailed information on the FreeRTOS see the following:

http://www.freertos.org/implementation/a00008.html

http://www.freertos.org/Documentation/RTOS_book.html

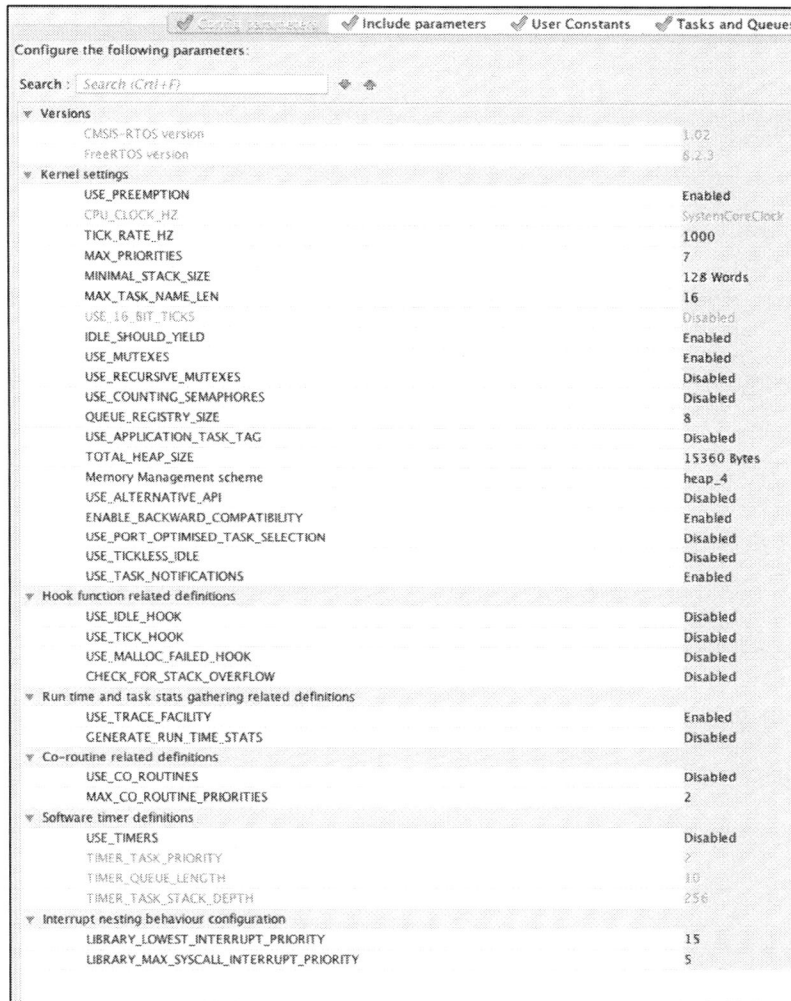

Figure 2.13. FreeRTOS configuration parameters (default shown)

2.2.7 Exercise 1 addendum

(a) Generic Wait Function

```
/********************* Generic Wait Function *******************************/
/**
* @brief   Wait for Timeout (Time Delay)
* @param    millisec     time delay value
* @retval  status code that indicates the execution status of the function.
*/
osStatus osDelay (uint32_t millisec)

#if INCLUDE_vTaskDelay
```

```
    TickType_t ticks = millisec / portTICK_PERIOD_MS;

    vTaskDelay(ticks ? ticks : 1);        /* Minimum delay = 1 tick */

    return osOK;
#else
  (void) millisec;

    return osErrorResource;
#endif
}
/
**************************************************************************/
```

(b) RTOS types and APIs to be used.

You can find relevant information in: /Drivers/CMSIS/RTOS/Template/cmsis_os.h

(i) Types
• osThreadId

(ii) APIs
• osThreadDef
• osThreadCreate
• osKernelStart
• StartDefaultTask
• osDelay

2.3 Exercise 2 - Implement a single periodic task.

Fundamental purpose of the exercise: to create and run a single periodic task having an accurate periodic time.

2.3.1 Introduction to the problem.

What you should have deduced from exercise 1 is that the delay function puts the task into a timed suspension state. The transition from *running* to *suspended* takes place immediately the function is entered; the transition from *suspended* to *ready* occurs when the designated delay time elapses. And, as this is the only task in the system, it is immediately set running.

Well, that's fine as it stands: using it to provide defined delay operations in the run-time code (an essential construct in many embedded applications). Now let's look at a different aspect of the last exercise; the inclusion of a software delay in the source code. You'll have found (if you performed the exercise) that the Led is on for __approximately__ three seconds and off for two. This is, of course, exactly what you'd expect to happen. But what if I asked that the on/off timing should be precise? From the previous work you'll appreciate that this requirement cannot be met by using the delay function (the total time for each execution is slightly longer than the delay time). The solution to this need leads neatly into the next RTOS construct : the os*DelayUntil* (aka the FreeRTOS *vTaskDelayUntil)* function.

First, though, you need to return to the CubeMX project and change from the Pinout view to the Configuration view. When you click on the FREERTOS symbol here it opens up the FreeRTOS configuration window; now select the *Include parameters* tab, figure 2.14.

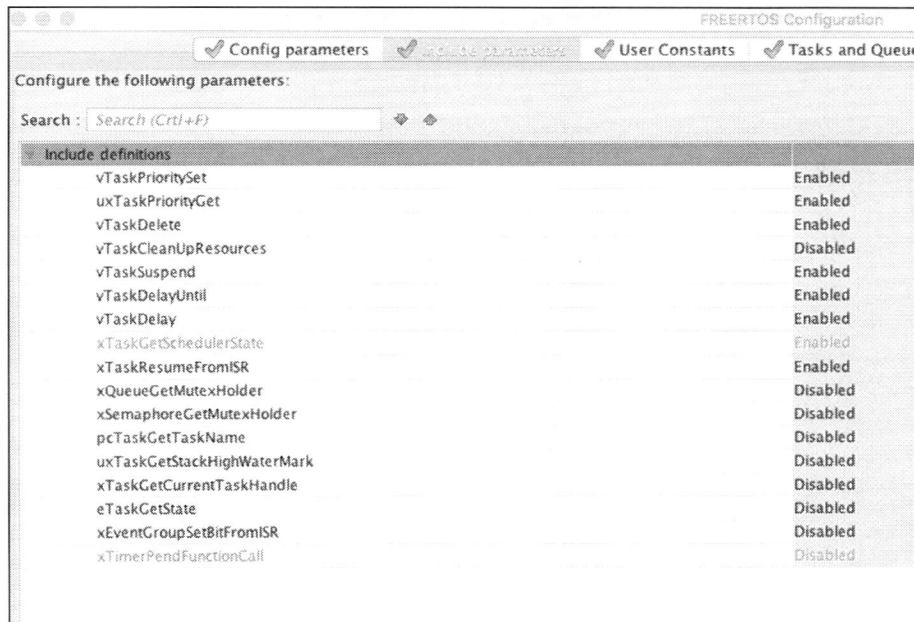

Include definitions	
vTaskPrioritySet	Enabled
uxTaskPriorityGet	Enabled
vTaskDelete	Enabled
vTaskCleanUpResources	Disabled
vTaskSuspend	Enabled
vTaskDelayUntil	Enabled
vTaskDelay	Enabled
xTaskGetSchedulerState	Enabled
xTaskResumeFromISR	Enabled
xQueueGetMutexHolder	Disabled
xSemaphoreGetMutexHolder	Disabled
pcTaskGetTaskName	Disabled
uxTaskGetStackHighWaterMark	Disabled
xTaskGetCurrentTaskHandle	Disabled
eTaskGetState	Disabled
xEventGroupSetBitFromISR	Disabled
xTimerPendFunctionCall	Disabled

Figure 2.14 FreeRTOS configuration window (*Include parameters* selected)

You will find that the include definition *vTaskDelayUntil* is, by default, *Disabled*. Set it to *Enabled*, as shown above.

2.3.2 The problem.

The purpose of this exercise is to create and run a single task that has an accurate periodic time. This structure will form the basis of all later exercises that use periodic tasking.
   The specific problem: Create a periodic task to flash the Green Led (two seconds on followed by two seconds off), repeating this with a periodic time of four seconds.

Memory jog: for details of the toggle function see
       Drivers/STM32F4xxHAL_Driver/inc/stm32f4xx_hal_gpio.h

Now regenerate the CubeMX project source code in the usual way, then open the file main.c. Copy and paste the following code into the task code section :
```
========================================================
/* USER CODE BEGIN 5 */
      TickType_t    TaskTimeStamp;
      TickType_t    DelayTimeMsec = 2000;

      TaskTimeStamp = xTaskGetTickCount();
/* Infinite loop */
for(;;)
{
     HAL_GPIO_WritePin(GPIOD, GPIO_PIN_14, GPIO_PIN_SET);
     YOUR SOFTWARE DELAY - approximately 1 second
     osDelayUntil(&TaskTimeStamp,DelayTimeMsec);
     HAL_GPIO_WritePin(GPIOD, GPIO_PIN_14, GPIO_PIN_RESET);
     osDelayUntil(&TaskTimeStamp,2000); // just a style variation
}
 /* USER CODE END 5 */
========================================================
```

Compile this, download the machine code to the target board, then set it executing. What you'll find is that the Led on and off times are now the same: two seconds each.
   As an exercise: change the delay time of 2000 to 500, rebuild/download/run the project and check the Led flashing times.

2.3.3 Evaluation of the exercises.

What exercise 1 showed was that the *Delay* function sets a fixed delay, which begins at the moment it is called. What *this* example shows is that the *DelayUntil* function creates a delay relative to a specific point in time, defined in terms of tick counts. This value is held in a variable called *TaskTimeStamp*.
   What follows now is a simplified explanation of the *DelayUntil* operation:

1. Load the *TaskTimeStamp* with the current (starting) tick value:
       (TaskTimeStamp = xTaskGetTickCount()
2. Execute the application code.
3. Call the DelayUntil function:
       (osDelayUntil(&TaskTimeStamp, 2000);

From the moment the application code is started value of *TaskTimeStamp* is constantly updated by the tick counter. So when the DelayUntil function is called it:

• Suspends the task and notes the current value of *TaskTimeStamp*.
• Computes how long the suspension time should be.
• Sets this value as the time (in tick counts) when the task is to be re-readied.

Example 1:
Starting tick value = 0
Now execute the application code for 1000 ticks.

Thus the current tick value = 1000.
Computed re-readying tick count for a 2000 tick delay = (StartTickValue + DelayTime):
(0 + 2000) = 2000 ticks.
Computed suspension time = (DelayTime - ApplicationCodeExecutionTime):
(2000 - 1000) = 1000 ticks.

Example 2:
Starting tick value = 2000
Now execute the application code for 500 ticks.
Current tick value = 2500.
Computed re-readying tick count for a 2000 tick delay = (2000 + 2000) = 4000.
Computed suspension time = (4000 - 2500) = 1500 ticks.

To recap: in general, when *vTaskDelayUntil(&TaskTimeStamp, SpecifiedDelayTime);* is called, a calculation is made to define how long the task should *actually* spend in suspension. It uses the *TaskTimeStamp* value together with the number of ticks corresponding to the specified delay.
   In our example the code is housed in an infinite loop. Hence the next piece of code to be executed after

        osDelayUntil(&TaskTimeStamp, 2000);

is

        HAL_GPIO_WritePin(GPIOD, GPIO_PIN_14, GPIO_PIN_SET);

After this, when the code reaches

        osDelayUntil(&TaskTimeStamp, DelayTimeMsec);

the required suspension time is now re-calculated, and the process continues as described above.
   A very important part of the operations is to set the initial value of *TaskTimeStamp,* otherwise behaviour is unpredictable. We do that by setting it to the current value of the tick count just before entering the infinite loop:

        TaskTimeStamp = xTaskGetTickCount();

Before going further check out the following documents:

vTaskDelayUntil function:
http://www.freertos.org/vtaskdelayuntil.html

xTaskGetTickCount function:
http://www.freertos.org/a00021.html#xTaskGetTickCount

TickType_t:
http://www.freertos.org/FreeRTOS-Coding-Standard-and-Style-Guide.html#DataTypes

2.3.4 Additional exercise.

Insert a software delay of about five seconds into the code, then redo the project. Run the target and observe the result. Deduce what has led to the change in behaviour and what lesson(s) can be learned from this.

2.3.5 Exercise 2 review.

You will now:

- One - be able to implement FreeRTOS-based periodic tasks using using the CubeMX/Keil-MDK toolset.
- Two - know that it is essential to execute all the code of a task *within* its periodic time if correct timing is to be maintained.

This last point should be self-evident!   If you checked the weblink for the *vTaskDelayUntil* function you should be aware that:
   vTaskDelayUntil() will return immediately (without blocking) if it is used to specify a wake time that is already in the past.
   A brief digression, just for your broader education: the <u>only</u> way to implement periodic tasking in FreeRTOS is by using the *DelayUntil* function.   However, many RTOSs use a very different approach, as follows:

- First, define the periodic time as part of the task creation/configuration stage.
- Second, allow the scheduler to control the (re)starting of tasks.
- Third, return control from the task to the scheduler by using some variant of a 'TaskSleep' function.

In my view this is a better approach. However, it does bring home an important point; once you choose an RTOS for your project, you have to live with its features.

2.3.6 Exercise 2 addendum - description of the DelayUntil function.

```
/**
* @brief  Delay a task until a specified time
* @param   PreviousWakeTime   Pointer to a variable that holds the time at which the
*    task was last unblocked. PreviousWakeTime must be initialised with the current *time *   *
prior to its first use (PreviousWakeTime = osKernelSysTick() )
* @param   millisec   time delay value
* @retval  status code that indicates the execution status of the function.
*/
osStatus osDelayUntil (uint32_t *PreviousWakeTime, uint32_t millisec)
{
#if INCLUDE_vTaskDelayUntil
  TickType_t ticks = (millisec / portTICK_PERIOD_MS);
  vTaskDelayUntil((TickType_t *) PreviousWakeTime, ticks ? ticks : 1);

  return osOK;
#else
  (void) millisec;
  (void) PreviousWakeTime;

  return osErrorResource;
#endif
}
```

2.4 Exercise 3 - Create and run multiple independent periodic tasks.

Fundamental purpose of the exercise: to create and run multiple independent periodic tasks.

2.4.1. Introduction to the problem.

At this point you should have no difficulty in implementing a single-task design, in particular a periodic one. This knowledge, however, should be seen as a stepping stone to being able to build real systems, those based on multiple tasks. This exercise here is going to take you up to the first level of difficulty: producing software that runs two independent tasks. This particular problem is especially simple in that the tasks are independent of each other — both in software and hardware terms.

2.4.2 The problem.

Produce a design that implements the tasking model of figure 2.15, one which flashes the Green and Red Leds on the board. Led on and off times are to be one second each for the Red Led and two seconds for the Green one. For simplicity use the *TogglePin* function. Set both tasks to have equal priorities.

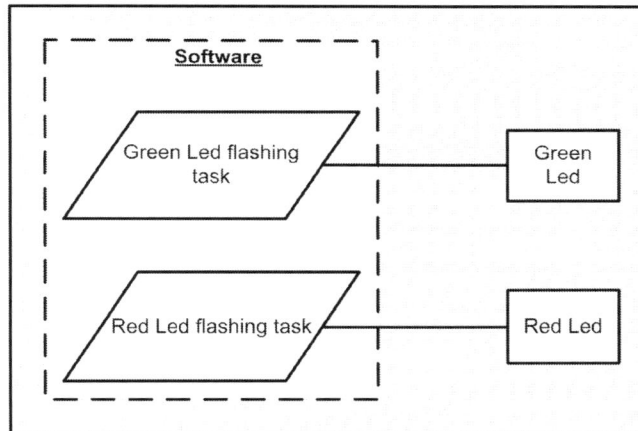

Figure 2.15 System task diagram

Green Led: identified as Led 4, driven by pin PD12 of the microcontroller.
HAL_GPIO_TogglePin(GPIOD, GPIO_PIN_12);

Red Led: identified as Led 5, driven by pin PD14 of the microcontroller.
HAL_GPIO_TogglePin(GPIOD, GPIO_PIN_14);

2.4.3 Implementing the design.

Create a CubeMX project (as covered previously), with FreeRTOS enabled. Name this project 'RTOS book Ex.3' (or any name of your choice).
    Now open the Configuration tab, figure 2.16, select *System*, then *GPIO*. When the GPIO configuration window opens modify the user labels of pins PD12 (GreenLed) and PD14 (RedLed). To do this merely click on the entry for the each pin individually in the *User Label* field of the Pin configuration window, figure 2.17. A drop-down window appears; now modify the name (as you wish) in the appropriate field.

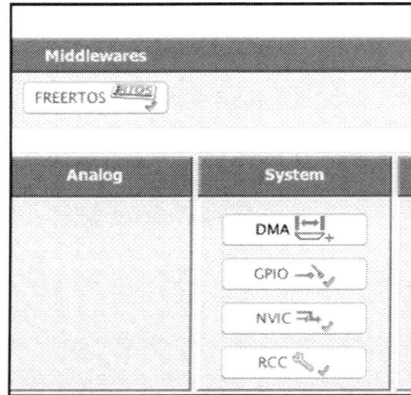

Figure 2.16 Cube configuration window

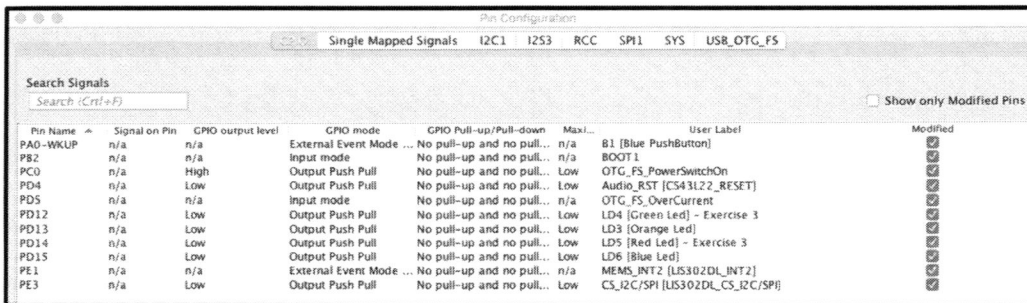

Figure 2.17 Pin configuration window

(i) Open *Pinout* view and check that these names show on the diagram.
(ii) Now open *Configuration* —> *FreeRTOS*, select *include parameters*, and enable *vTaskDelayUntil*.
(iii) Next step: select the *Task and Queues* tab, figure 2.18: Change the name of *defaultTask* to *FlashGreenLedTask* and change its entry function name to *StartFlashGreenLedTask*.
(iv) Add a new task, name it *FlashRedLedTask*, name its entry function *StartFlashRedLedTask* and set its priority to *osPriorityNormal*.

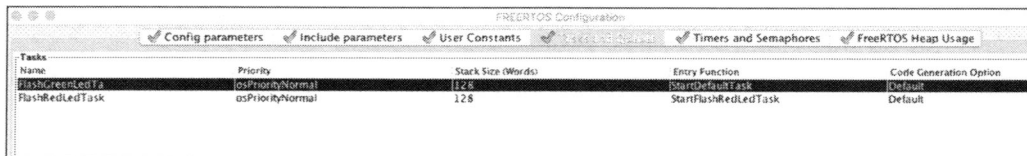

Figure 2.18 Task settings
Regenerate the project, open the main.c file and check that it now includes the code relevant to the two tasks, figure 2.19.

```
/* Private variables -------------------------------------------------------*/
osThreadId FlashGreenLedTaskHandle;
osThreadId FlashRedLedTaskHandle;
////////////////////////////////////////////////////////////////////////////////////////
/* Private function prototypes -------------------------------------------*/
void StartGreenLedTask(void const * argument);
void StartFlashRedLedTask(void const * argument);
////////////////////////////////////////////////////////////////////////////////////////
 /* Create the thread(s) */

  /* definition and creation of FlashGreenLedTa */
  osThreadDef(FlashGreenLedTask, StartGreenLedTask, osPriorityNormal, 0, 128);
  FlashGreenLedTaskHandle = osThreadCreate(osThread(FlashGreenLedTask), NULL);

  /* definition and creation of FlashRedLedTask */
  osThreadDef(FlashRedLedTask, StartFlashRedLedTask, osPriorityNormal, 0, 128);
  FlashRedLedTaskHandle = osThreadCreate(osThread(FlashRedLedTask), NULL);
////////////////////////////////////////////////////////////////////////////////////////////////////

/* StartGreenLedTask function */
void StartGreenLedTask(void const * argument)
{
  /* USER CODE BEGIN 5 */
  /* Infinite loop */
  for(;;)
  {
    osDelay(1);
  }
  /* USER CODE END 5 */
}

/* StartFlashRedLedTask function */
void StartFlashRedLedTask(void const * argument)
{
  /* USER CODE BEGIN StartFlashRedLedTask */
  /* Infinite loop */
  for(;;)
  {
    osDelay(1);
  }
  /* USER CODE END StartFlashRedLedTask */
}
```

Figure 2.19 Automatically-generated source code - task related

Update the source code of the task functions to perform the specified flashing operations (you should be able to work that out for yourself, based on the previous exercise). Now compile the source code to machine code, download it to the target and start executing it.

Figure 2.20 shows the time-based behaviour of the two tasks, on a relative time scale (i.e. time 0 in absolute time for the Red Led is not necessarily the same as time 0 for the Green Led.

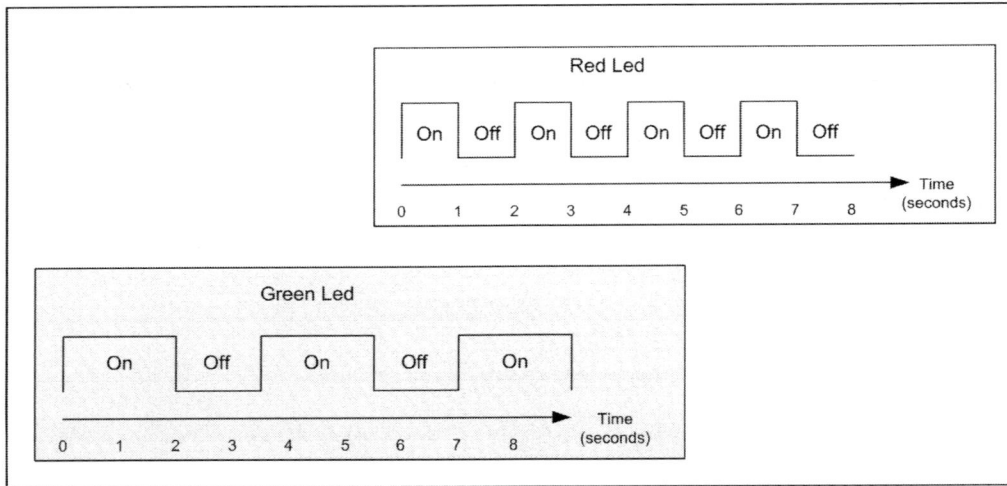

Figure 2.20 Timing diagram of Led flashing operations

Check that the flashing times of the individual leds correspond with this diagram.   Now sketch both timing diagrams on the one time scale, taking into account that the time taken to toggle the leds is insignificant. Check that the actual flashing behaviour corresponds with your predictions.

2.4.4 Review of exercise 3.

You will now:

- Know how to implement a design that consists of a number of independent tasks.
- Have observed the behaviour of periodic non-interacting tasks where these have equal priorities.
- Been able to predict the expected behaviour of the run-time system and then confirm this by observation.

2.5 Exercise 4 - Evaluate priority preemptive scheduling policies.

Fundamental purpose of the exercise: to gain a good understanding of task behaviour where a priority preemptive scheduling policy is used.

2.5.1 Introduction to the problem.

An essential factor in the design of embedded multitasking systems: a very good understanding of task run-time behaviour. In particular you must appreciate how and why priority preemptive scheduling can significantly affect performance. Because, if you don't, you may end up with unpredicted, unpredictable and undesirable run-time behaviour in your designs.

The purpose of this exercise is to take you through a number of scenarios, each intended to demonstrate various effects produced by interference between tasks. An important point: the exercise is *not* intended to be a quantitative demonstration of these effects (you need proper run-time analysis tools for that). Instead it is qualitative in nature, to give you a 'feel' for task behaviour where priority preemptive scheduling is used. The work here is based on a two-task design where each task controls two Leds; the overall behaviour is assessed by observing the run-time light patterns.

2.5.2 Problem overview.

Figure 2.21 shows the system task diagram for this problem.

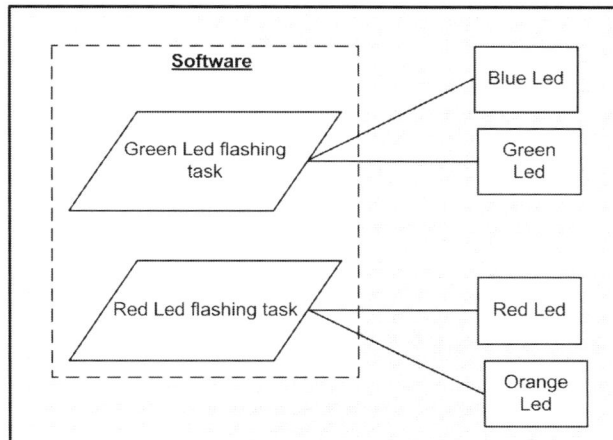

Figure 2.21 System task diagram

The normal mode of operation for each pair of Leds, i.e. Blue/Green and Orange/Red, is exactly the same (as defined in figure 2.22, for the Blue/Green pair). The following description applies to the Green Led flashing task; the other task is to behave in a identical fashion (though timings are different).

The Green Led is used to show when task execution is *actually* taking place; the Blue Led shows the period during which the task is *not suspended* (i.e. is in the active or ready state). For 'normal' operation — one in which task preemption doesn't occur — your system should behave as follows:

- When the *Green Led flashing task* starts, the Green Led is to start flashing (F) and the the Blue Led is to be put on.
- The Green Led is to flash *only* while the task code is actually executing.

- When the *Green Led flashing task* completes both Leds are to be turned off.

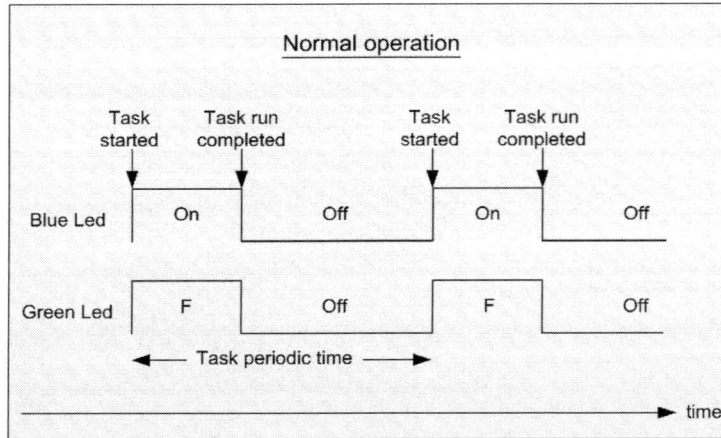

Figure 2.22 Timing diagram — normal operation (no task preemption)

However, if task preemption *does* occur (figure 2.23), the Green Led will go steady (either on or off) during the preemption time. This particular Led light pattern will happen only during a task preemption period, thus allowing you to observe such preemptions.

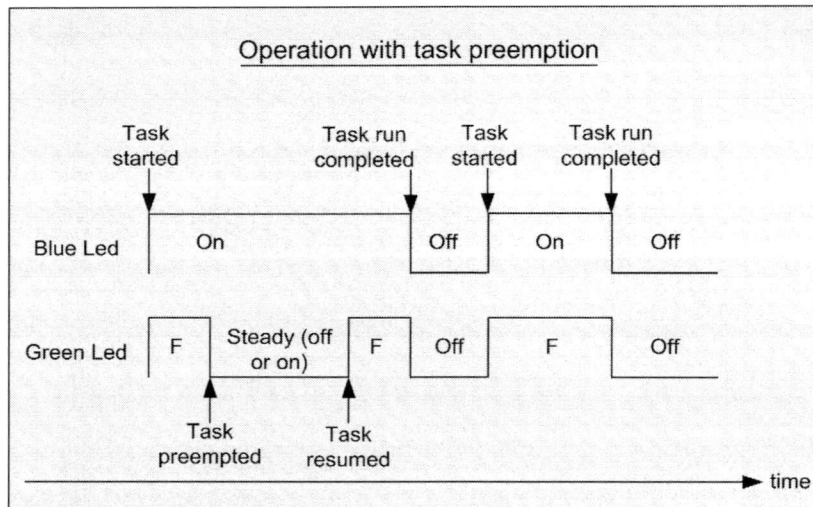

Figure 2.23 Timing diagram — task preemption occurs

2.5.3 The problem details.

Four different scenarios are covered in this exercise, based on a two-task design: *FlashGreenLedTask* and *FlashRedLedTask*. Reuse your code from the previous exercise, adapting it where necessary.

The basic (and constant) attributes of the tasks are as follows:

FlashGreenLedTask
> Periodic time: 10 seconds.
> Task execution time: four seconds.

FlashRedLedTask
> Periodic time: two seconds.
> Task execution time: 0.5 second.

Task structure — FlashGreenLedTask.
Start infinite loop
> 1. Turn the Blue Led on.
> 2. Simulate task execution — toggle the Green Led for four seconds.
>   (Suggested toggling rate — 20 Hz.).
> 3. Turn the Green Led off.
> 4. Turn the Blue Led off.
> 3. Suspend for six seconds(use the osDelay function).
End infinite loop.

Task structure — FlashRedLedTask.
Start infinite loop
> 1. Turn the Orange Led on.
> 2. Simulate task execution — toggle the Red Led for 0.5 seconds.
>   (Suggested toggling rate — 20 Hz.).
> 3. Turn the Red Led off.
> 4. Turn the Orange Led off.
> 3. Suspend for 1.5 seconds(use the osDelay function).
End infinite loop.

2.5.4 Exercise details.

(a) Exercise 4.1 Check that your code implementation of the individual tasks is correct.
Before generating the source code set the *FlashRedLedTask* to have the higher priority.
Download your code to the target system. Run each task individually and verify that the actual timings comply with the problem specification.
Note — Just comment out the following to prevent the creation of a task:
> *osThreadDef*
> *FlashRedLedTaskHandle*

(b) Exercise 4.2 Execute your code with both tasks active.
Before you do this predict the expected behaviour: then check the *actual* behaviour. Explain the results obtained. If your prediction is correct, excellent. If your prediction is wrong work out why you didn't get it right.   You can learn a great deal by doing this and it will improve your understanding of multitasking operations.

(c) Exercise 4.3.
Reverse the priority ordering of the tasks (i.e. *FlashGreenLedTask* to have the higher priority).
Once again predict the expected behaviour; then check the *actual* behaviour.

(d) Exercise 4.4.
Calculate the approximate processor utilization figure.

2.4.5 Exercise 4 review.

You should now realize how important it is to define the timing (temporal) aspects of multitasking software. Some important outcomes from these set of exercises:

- The only task guaranteed to satisfy its timing specification is the one having the highest priority.
- *Actual* run-times (i.e. start to completion) of lower-priority tasks will be longer than the specified ones if they are preempted. Moreover these times are likely to vary, depending on exactly *when* preemption occurs.
- It is much easier to observe preemption in action in exercise 4.2 than that in exercise 4.3. This is a consequence of the relatively short execution time of the FlashRedLedTask.
- Exercise 4.3 shows how disruptive it can be if a task having a long execution time is given highest priority.
- The message from this exercise is that if you are designing critical embedded software you need to:
    - Specify your timing requirements fully.
    - Plan your schedules carefully and, where possible, predict performance.
    - Use task analyser tools to measure exactly what takes place in your run-time code.
    - THINK before DO.
- The processor utilization, approximately 65%, would be considered to be very low in many software system (e.g. desktop applications, mobile devices, supercomputers, etc.). And yet you'll have seen here just often the actual run-times of tasks exceed their specified values. Is this important? Well, it all depends how important it is to you that a task *must* complete in a specified period of time (i.e. has a critical deadline). As a general rule systems that must be highly reactive must also have low processor utilization (research work carried out in the 1990s suggested that, where there is a mix of periodic and non-periodic tasks, utilization should be less than 20%).

Chapter 3

Dealing with shared resources.

3.1 Exercise 5 - Analyze access contention problems.

Fundamental purpose of the exercise: to demonstrate access contention problems when using shared resources in a multitasking system.

3.1.1 Introduction to the problem.

If you've diligently worked through the most recent exercises you'll be in a good position to implement multitasking designs. However, these exercises, important as they are, are quite limited; they've dealt only with sets of independent, non-interacting tasks. And that, in the real world, is a rarity. In most practical designs task usually interact with each other via shared software and/or hardware items. As a result, unfortunately, tasks may unwittingly interfere with each other by making 'simultaneous' accesses to the shared items.

The purpose of this exercise is to demonstrate that this is a real issue and not merely an abstract academic problem. It is designed to show that interference *will* occur unless protection measures are used.

3.1.2 The problem — overview.

Figure 3.1 shows the task diagram for this problem, where the software consists of two tasks and a shared data item. The purpose of the shared item is to hold data that is used

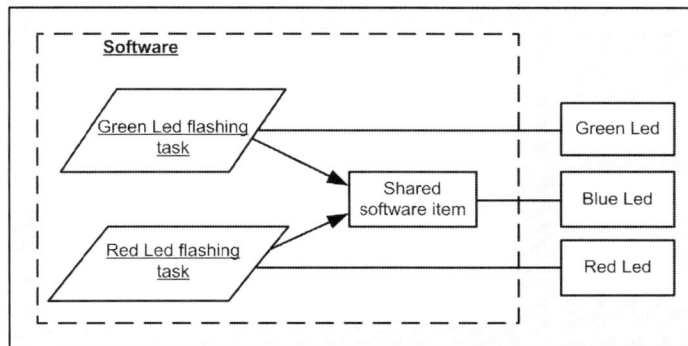

Figure 3.1 System task diagram

by both tasks (a data store); it also enables them to exchange information in a simple, straightforward manner. In general, data can be written to and read from the store. This store:

- Is a well-defined software component.
- Is visible in the overall tasking design.
- Eliminates the use global variables for information interchange.

However, it's important to understand that the 'whens' of read and write operations are dictated by the individual tasks; there is no overall control. Thus there is always a possibility that individual tasks may simultaneously write to the store, for example; or one may be writing while the other is reading. This contention for resources can result in data being corrupted, leading (possibly) to task misbehaviour.

True simultaneous access can take place only in multicomputer/multicore systems; it cannot occur in single processor designs. With these it is a form of 'apparent' simultaneous access; unfortunately this can still lead to corrupted data being used by the tasks.

3.1.3 The problem — exercise details.

(a) General aspects.

In this exercise the shared data item is intended to mimic the action of a read-write data store that:

- Holds a number of data items.
- Can be accessed by all tasks for both reading and writing operations.
- Has an access time that is significant (in processor time, that is), something which must be taken into account in the system time budget.

One effective way to mimic such operations is to use the data item to send messages to a terminal device. This will give you a visual display of any task interactions in the message sending process. Unfortunately this has a down side; providing terminal access from your STM board is not trivial. In general to implement this you can:

- Use the simple serial comms facilities of the microcontroller (but this needs extra hardware for line interfacing) or
- Use the OTG USB facilities of the micro (but this is quite a challenging software task).

So for this example a very simple method is used; the read/write processes are simulated using a straightforward software delay. Of course this leaves us with the need to detect if any 'simultaneous access' has occurred. One easy way to do this is to employ an access indicator — the 'Start flag' — within the access function. This is a binary flag having two values, *Up* and *Down* (initialized to *Up*). *Up* indicates that the resource is *not* in use; conversely *Down* shows that a task is executing the code of the shared item.

So, when a task makes an access to the critical area, it may find:

1. Start flag is *Up*: all is well or
2. Start flag is *Down*: the *other* task had been executing the shared code but has now been preempted.

In this exercise we'll detect resource contention by illuminating the Blue Led. Thus a suitable program design for the complete access function (pseudo-code) is as follows:

> **(Note: Start flag initialized to Up)**
>
> **1. Check Start flag is Up.**
> **2. If Start flag is Up set it to Down**
>   **else show an alert - turn on the Blue Led.**
> **3. Simulate read/write operations - run software delay.**
> **4. Set Start flag to Up.**

This, if you wish, can easily be modified so that a count can be made of task 'collisions'. The focus here is just to detect that a collision has happened.

(b) Specific aspects.

Task 1: Flash the Green Led.
Suggested code:
Loop:
    1. Turn the Green Led on.
    2. Access the shared data.
    3.Turn the Green Led off.
    4. Delay for 0.5 seconds.
End loop.

Task 2: Flash the Red Led.
Suggested code:
Loop:
    1. Turn the Red Led on.
    2. Access the shared data.
    3. Turn the Red Led off.
    4. Delay for 0.1 seconds.
End loop.

Important: set the priority of the *RedLedFlashingTask* to be the greater one.

Access shared data function.
Suggested code:
    1. Check if the Start flag is Up.
      If Up then set the Start flag to Down
      else turn the Blue Led on.
    2. Simulate read/write operations for 500 milliseconds.
    3. Set Start flag to Up.

First compile, download and run each task individually to check your timings. Once you're satisfied run with both tasks active. If you've used the recommended timings then it won't be very long before the Blue Led will turn on, showing that task interference has taken place.

(c) Additional check (optional).

If you've understood the exercise you'll appreciate that the Blue Led is turned on when contention is first detected: and is never subsequently turned off. Now, you can get a 'rough and ready' feel for the frequency of contention by flashing the Led instead of leaving it on. Clearly the 'on' time must be long enough for you to be able to actually see when the Led is lit. So, modify the access function so that Blue Led stays on for approximately 0.1 seconds.

As has already been said, this exercise is somewhat rough and ready, and isn't meant to provide accurate numbers. But it's instructive and well worth doing.

3.1.4 Exercise 5 review.

You should now:

- Realise that when tasks share items there is always a likelihood that 'simultaneous accesses' will occur.
- Understand that this can produce problems, their extent depending entirely on what the shared items are and how they are used.
- Recognize that such unwanted contentions may go entirely undetected unless special measures are taken.
- Appreciate that we can have similar issues when using global items in programs.

- Have deduced that the only sane, safe and robust way of handling contention issues is to design the code so that simultaneous accesses <u>cannot</u> occur.
- See that a typical multitasking model consists of concurrent units (tasks or active objects) and non-current items (passive objects - in this case the data store).
- Realize that non-concurrent items are sequential code units which run only when called on by tasks. They then run *within* the context of the calling task.

3.2 Exercise 6 - Eliminate resource contention by suspending the scheduler.

Fundamental purpose of the exercise: to demonstrate a simple way to eliminate resource contention - suspending the scheduler.

3.2.1 Introduction.

If we ensure that one, and only one, task can ever use the shared item at any one time then it is impossible for interference to occur. And the simplest way to do this is to suspend the scheduler for the duration of the access. In practice this can be done by disabling interrupts during the access process (using RTOS-provided facilities).

3.2.2 Exercise details.

We'll use two FreeRTOS functions to disable and enable interrupts, as follows:

Disable interrupts: taskENTER_CRITICAL();
Enable interrupts: taskEXIT_CRITICAL();

(http://www.freertos.org/taskENTER_CRITICAL_taskEXIT_CRITICAL.html)

Modify the code of **each** task of the previous exercise (Exercise 5) as follows:

1. Disable interrupts.
2. Access the shared resource.
3. Enable interrupts.

The task details are unchanged.

As before, compile, download and run your code. You should now find that the Blue Led never comes on.

3.2.3 Exercise 6 review.

You should now:

- Understand why stopping the scheduler while accessing critical code sections prevents unwanted effects.
- See that the technique is very simple to implement.

Now, think more deeply about this technique. The upside is that it's very simple to use and absolutely guaranteed to work. The downside is that stopping the scheduler effectively stops the execution of concurrent units; all multitasking ceases. And the longer the time spent with interrupts disabled, the greater the impact will be. So the golden rule is: if you're going to use this technique then get in and out of suspension as quickly as possible.

3.3 Exercise 7 - Demonstrate deterioration in system performance.

Fundamental purpose of the exercise: to demonstrate that sharing resources in multitasking designs can lead to deterioration of system performance.

3.3.1 Introduction.

When designing multitasking systems it is essential to develop a good model of its run-time behaviour. A first step in this is to establish the execution times of the individual tasks: then model their collective behaviour. This is reasonably straightforward when tasks are independent; unfortunately when they interact things can become complex. If such interactions aren't taken into account then at best they reduce system responsiveness (compared with predicted values, that is): at worst they can cause catastrophic system failures.

   The aim of this exercise is to demonstrate the impact of resource sharing on the performance of a three task design. Here the purpose of each task is to flash a Led (as specified below); any changes to system performance will lead to changes in the flashing pattern of the Leds. Just a small proviso: we'll make the access time somewhat long so that we can actually see the changes (unrealistic in practice but necessary for this exercise).

   Important note: this is a very instructive exercise, so please complete all of it. Use the recommended timings as these *will* produce observable effects.

3.3.2 Exercise details

(a) Problem overview and key code aspects.

Figure 3.2 shows the task diagram for this exercise where the software consists of three tasks and a single shared software item. The objective here is to demonstrate that using shared resources in a multitasking design degrades overall system performance.

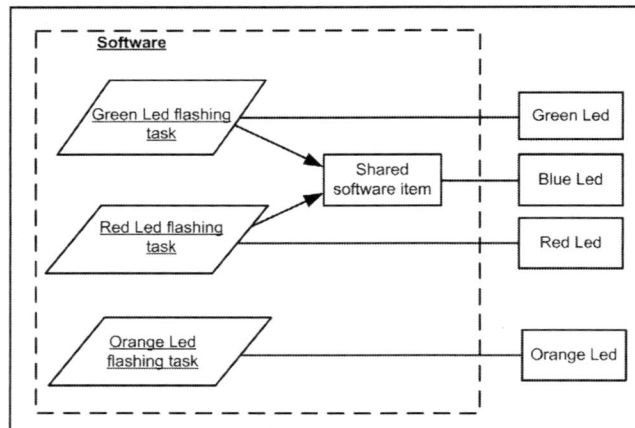

Figure 3.2 System task diagram

Set the priorities of the Green and Red led flashing tasks to 'normal' and the Orange led flashing task to 'above normal' (i.e. highest priority of the task set).

For the Green and Red led flashing tasks use the following task code (or something similar):

///

```
for(;;)
    {
      HAL_GPIO_WritePin(GPIOD, GPIO_PIN_xx, GPIO_PIN_SET);
      AccessSharedData();
      osDelay(DelayTimeMsec);
      HAL_GPIO_WritePin(GPIOD, GPIO_PIN_xx, GPIO_PIN_RESET);
      osDelay(DelayTimeMsec);
    } // end for
```

Flash green Led: DelayTimeMsec   = 200 milliseconds
Flash Red Led: DelayTimeMsec   = 550 milliseconds
(Important note: use osDelay, not osDelayUntil).

///

For the Orange led flashing task use the following code (or something similar):

```
 for(;;)
   {
     HAL_GPIO_TogglePin(GPIOD, GPIO_PIN_13);
     osDelay(50);
   } // end for
```

This will produce a 10 Hz. flashing rate.

///

Access shared data function — suggested code:

  1. Check if the Start flag is Up.
     If Up then set the Start flag to Down
     else turn the Blue Led on.
  2. Simulate read/write operations for one second.
  3. Turn the Blue Led off**.
  4. Set Start flag to Up.
** Insert this if you wish the Blue Led to turn off after a contention is detected.

///

Part of the exercise calls for a resource access control mechanism to be provided. Implement this, when required, by inhibiting interrupts. Simply modify the code of the Green and Red tasks as follows:

  1. Disable interrupts — taskENTER_CRITICAL();
  2. Access the shared resource.
  3. Enable interrupts — taskEXIT_CRITICAL();

The rest of the task details are unchanged

///

The basic (approximate) run-time timing data for each task is given in figure 3.3.

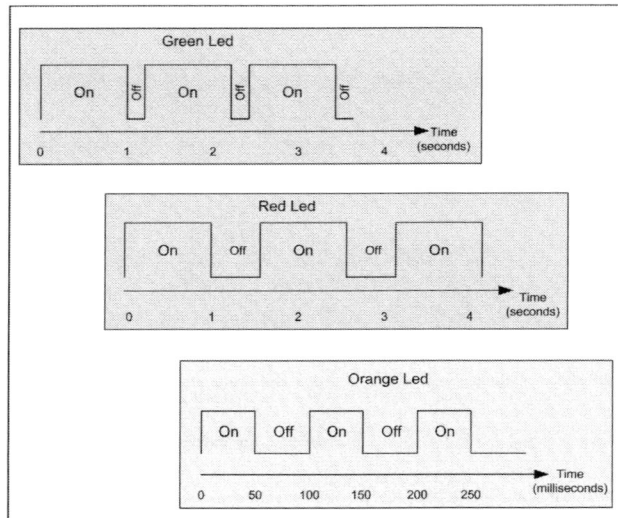

Fig 3.3 Timing diagram of Led flashing operations

(b) Exercise details.

This is a three-step exercise:

(i) Confirmation of individual task run-time timing values by running one task at a time.
(ii) Demonstration of system behaviour (all tasks active) when access to the shared resource is *uncontrolled* (i.e. no mutual exclusion in use).
(iii) Demonstration of system behaviour when access to the shared resource is *controlled*.

Exercise 7.1: Execute the system with one, and only one, task active at a time. Check that the actual run-time behaviour corresponds with predicted values.

Exercise 7.2: Execute the system with all tasks active. Compare the run-time behaviour with that of exercise 7.1. Ensure that your code doe not invoke mutual exclusion for the shared resource.

Exercise 7.3: Repeat 7.2, but now use mutual exclusion (implemented by using the *taskENTER_CRITICAL();* and *taskEXIT_CRITICAL();* functions). Compare the run-time behaviour with that of 7.2.

3.3.3 Exercise 7 review.

It was earlier pointed out that the usage time of the shared resource is unrealistically long. However, it really does exaggerate the effects of task interactions on system performance, demonstrating them visually.   Note that we could minimise these effects by reducing the processor utilization to sensible levels: but they would still occur. Moreover, it would be much more difficult to observe such interactions — we'd certainly have to use a run-time analysis tool.
   So, having done this exercise you should now:

• Realize that executing tasks in a multitasking implementation may produce quite different results to running them in isolation.

- Recognize that when tasks share resources then, in general, it's almost certain that contention will occur.
- Appreciate that it may be extremely difficult (or even impossible) to predict *exactly when* an access contention will occur.
- Understand that it may also be quite difficult to predict precisely *what* effects may be produced by resource contention
- Have seen that contention can be eliminated by inhibiting task switching (by disabling interrupts) *during* access to a critical resource.
- Have also seen that disabling interrupts has a major impact on run-time behaviour.
- Have deduced that great care should be taken with the use of the interrupt disabling mechanisms in multitasking programs.
- Understand why interrupts should never be disabled for very long periods of time.
- Finally, see that the task that disables interrupts effectively becomes the highest priority one in the system.

This simple exercise should bring home to you some really important points when designing time-critical real-time multitasking systems:

- First, the temporal performance of your design needs to be thoroughly evaluated.
- Second, timing uncertainties must be minimized. This can be done by keeping the number of shared resources to a minimum. An important contributing factor here is the number of tasks in your design. As a generalization: more tasks means more shared resources. You will now appreciate why this will definitely produce greater variations in task run-times. So the golden rule is: minimize the task count in your designs.
- Third, keep the times during which shared resources are used to an absolute minimum; *never* have them perform lengthy processing.

3.4 Exercise 8 - Use a semaphore to protect critical code sections.

Fundamental purpose of the exercise: to demonstrate how to eliminate resource contention in a selective manner — using a semaphore to protect the critical code section

3.4.1 Introduction

Exercise 7 has demonstrated that using interrupt disabling as an access control mechanism:

- Is very simple to implement but
- Can produce severe disruptions in the run-time behaviour of multitasking systems and
- Definitely isn't something to be used as a general-purpose scheme.

The basic problem here is that when interrupts are disabled the *whole* system is affected. Clearly this, in general, is undesirable; what we need is a much more focussed mechanism that generates minimal disturbance. Fortunately three such access control (mutual-exclusion) mechanisms are available (discussed in book 1): the semaphore, mutex and mini-monitor ('protected object').
    The aim of this exercise is to introduce and show the use of the first one, the semaphore.

3.4.2 Exercise details.

(a) Introduction and semaphore creation.

This exercise involves a very simple change to the code of exercise 7.3: just replace the interrupt disabling calls with semaphore calls. Now, a semaphore can be considered to be an RTOS-defined program variable. And, like all variables, it must be created before it can be used. The creation process, in overall terms, involves the following steps:

1. Define a reference to the semaphore (the 'handle').
2. Define the semaphore.
3. Create the semaphore.

All the code needed to do this can be generated automatically by CubeMX. Just load the Cube project, go to the FreeRTOS Configuration section, and select 'Timers and Semaphores', figure 3.4.

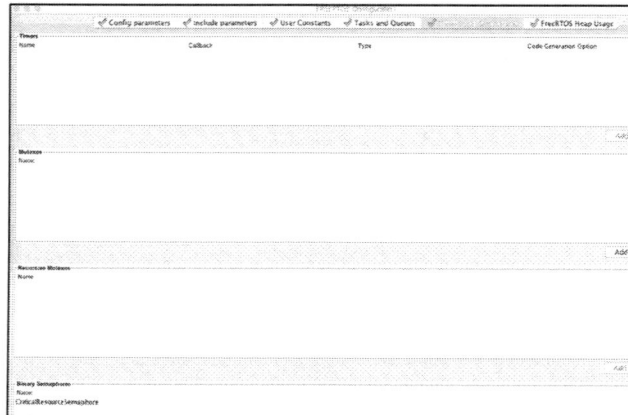

Figure 3.4 CubeMX semaphore configuration

Add a binary semaphore and give it a name (in this case 'CriticalResourceSemaphore'). Now generate and examine the project source code. You'll find that additional code has been produced (compared with that of exercise 7), the salient points being:

//

```
/* Private variables ---------------------------------------------------*/
        osSemaphoreId CriticalResourceSemaphoreHandle;


  /* Create the semaphores(s) */
   /* definition and creation of CriticalResourceSemaphore */
        osSemaphoreDef(CriticalResourceSemaphore);

        CriticalResourceSemaphoreHandle =
                osSemaphoreCreate(osSemaphore(CriticalResourceSemaphore), 1);
```

//

Note that the second parameter of the function *osSemaphoreCreate* is a timeout value for the semaphore. Its units are milliseconds, and 1 (one) is the automatically-generated default value.

(b) Using the semaphore.

First, a recap. The semaphore:

- Is a task flow control mechanism.
- Has two states.
    - State 1 - Released (synonyms include free, available, unlocked).
    - State 2 - Locked (synonyms include taken, unavailable, acquired).
- Either stops tasks (when Locked) or permits them to continue (when Released).

When a task wants to know whether it should stop or continue executing it queries the semaphore state, as follows:

```
        osSemaphoreWait (CriticalResourceSemaphoreHandle, WaitTimeMilliseconds);
```

The parameter *WaitTimeMilliseconds* allows us to decide how long a task should wait before it proceeds with code execution. The value of this, defined by the programmer, depends on the design objectives. For example, when a task merely wishes to check the status of a semaphore, it makes the wait call with the wait time set to zero.
    If a task wishes to free up a semaphore it sends the following message to the semaphore:

```
        osSemaphoreRelease (CriticalResourceSemaphoreHandle);
```

These APIs are used as follows:
//

```
        /* JUST A SIMPLE REPRESENTATION OF THE PROTECTED ACCESS CODE */
        //Acquire the semaphore: semaphore Wait.
        osSemaphoreWait (CriticalResourceSemaphoreHandle, WaitTimeMilliseconds);
                Use the shared (critical) resource.
        //Signal the semaphore: semaphore Release.
        osSemaphoreRelease (CriticalResourceSemaphoreHandle);
```

Important note: when semaphores are created they should *normally* be set to Free (Released). This is the default setting for FreeRTOS.

//

(c) Exercise content.

This is a two-step exercise.

Exercise 8.1: Modify the code of exercise 7.3 as follows;
1. Replace   taskENTER_CRITICAL();   with
        osSemaphoreWait (CriticalResourceSemaphoreHandle, WaitTimeMilliseconds);
2. Replace   taskEXIT_CRITICAL();   with
        osSemaphoreRelease (CriticalResourceSemaphoreHandle);

Build, download and run the software. Observe the Led behaviour; compare this with your findings in exercise 7.3.

Exercise 8.2: Set the *WaitTimeMilliseconds* value to zero and execute the resulting software. Once again observe the behaviour of the Leds.

3.4.3 Exercise 8 review.

Exercise 8.1, done correctly, will have produced one very noticeable change in Led flashing behaviour: that of the Orange Led flashing task. It now executes exactly as specified (precisely what you'd expect as it's the highest-priority task). The reason for this is that the scope of the mutual exclusion mechanism has been limited; now it applies only to tasks that share the critical resource.
    You should also have seen that there isn't any resource contention; the Blue Led never turns on.
When running the code of exercise 8.2 you should have found that the Blue Led *does* come on; contention is taking place. This is to be expected as a semaphore with zero wait time does *not* block the progression of the task.

3.5 Exercise 9 - Use a mutex to protect the critical code section.

Fundamental purpose of the exercise: to demonstrate how to eliminate resource contention in a selective manner — using a mutex to protect the critical code section.

3.5.1 Introduction and exercise details.

This exercise involves a very simple change to the code of exercise 8: just replace the semaphore with a mutex.

(a) Creating a mutex.

All the code needed to create a mutex can be generated automatically by CubeMX. Just load the Cube project, go to the FreeRTOS Configuration section, and select 'Timers and Semaphores', figure 3.5.

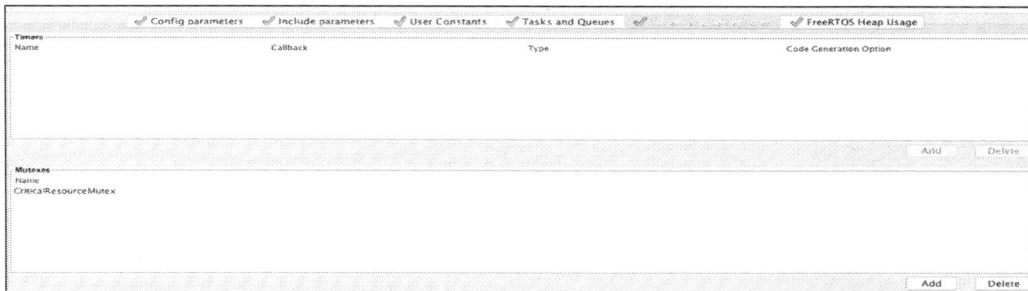

Figure 3.5 CubeMX mutex configuration

Add a mutex and give it a name (in this case 'CriticalResourceMutex'). Now generate and examine the project source code. You'll find code has been produced similar to that of exercise 8, but with the semaphore replaced by a mutex:

```
/////////////////////////////////////////////////////////////////////////////////////////

/* Private variables -------------------------------------------------*/
       osMutexId CriticalResourceMutexHandle;


 /* Create the mutex(es) */
  /* definition and creation of CriticalResourceMutex */
       osMutexDef(CriticalResourceMutex);

       CriticalResourceMutexHandle = osMutexCreate(osMutex(CriticalResourceMutex));

/////////////////////////////////////////////////////////////////////////////////////////
```

(b) Using the mutex.

When a task wants to know if it should stop or continue executing it queries the mutex state, as follows:

```
       osMutexWait (CriticalResourceMutexHandle, WaitTimeMilliseconds);
```

The parameter *WaitTimeMilliseconds* allows us to decide how long a task should wait before it proceeds with code execution (exactly the same with the semaphore).

If a task wishes to free up a semaphore it sends the following message to the mutex:

        osMutexRelease (CriticalResourceMutexHandle);

These APIs are used as follows in the code of **each** task that intends to use the shared resource:

///

```
        /* JUST A SIMPLE REPRESENTATION OF THE PROTECTED ACCESS CODE */
        //Acquire the mutex: mutex Wait.
        osMutexWait (CriticalResourceMutexHandle, WaitTimeMilliseconds)
                Use the shared (critical) resource.
        //Signal the mutex: mutex Release.
        osMutexRelease (CriticalResourceMutexHandle);
```

///

Important note: when FreeRTOS creates a mutex it sets to Free (Released).

Now build and run your software; observe the results.

3.5.2 Exercise 9 review.

You should have found that the run-time behaviour is exactly the same as that of exercise 8.1. Thus we can deduce that the mutex performs exactly the same function as a semaphore. And that's true in this particular case. However, there's more to the mutex than this, because:

- Only the task that locks the mutex can release it (the 'ownership' property).
- The FreeRTOS mutex incorporates a priority inheritance scheme (and *that* is a really important feature).

This particular exercise doesn't show these two mutex-specific properties; however we will demonstrate those in later work.

3.6 Exercise 10 - Use encapsulation to improve system safety and security.

Fundamental purpose of the exercise: to demonstrate that encapsulating an item with its protecting semaphore improves the safety and security of software.

3.6.1 Introduction to the problem.

By now you should fully understand how to eliminate resource contention in multitasking systems. But these exercises also have a second (really important) message; critical resources should *always* be protected if you wish to produce robust software. And that, for quality work, should be your default position as a designer.

You have seen that both the semaphore and the mutex can be used as protection mechanisms. Unfortunately, unless they are used with great care, they can cause more problems that they solve. Take the semaphore, for example, and consider the following issues (as already pointed out in Book 1):

- A semaphore isn't automatically associated with a specific protected item. Yet it is essential in practice to correctly link these up.
- Wait and Signal operations form a pair. Regrettably the basic mechanism *does not* enforce this pairing. As a result a task could call either one in isolation, which would be accepted as valid source code. This may lead to very unusual run time behaviour.
- Nothing prevents Signal being called before Wait, again possibly a source of odd behaviour.
- A semaphore must be visible and in scope to all tasks that share the protected resource. This means that *any* task can 'release' the semaphore (by calling Signal), even if this is a programming error.
- Just because a resource has a semaphore associated with it does *not* guarantee protection. Safeguards can be bypassed if there is a 'back-door' route into the protected area (using a resource which is declared to be global to the program, for example).

The mutex is a little bit more robust, but still suffers from most of these drawbacks.

So, the key question is 'how we can improve things'? Two things are clear; we need to:

- Link the protected item — the critical item — with its protecting mechanism (semaphore or mutex) and
- Ensure that tasks cannot directly access the protected item.

A simple way to satisfy *most* of our needs is to house the protected item and its protection mechanism in a single program unit (as described below). Such a structure we'll call a 'simple monitor'.

3.6.2 Problem overview.

Fundamentally the simple monitor prevents tasks directly accessing a shared resource by:

- Encapsulating the resource (the critical code section) with its protecting semaphore within a program unit.
- Keeping all semaphore/mutex operations local to the encapsulating unit.
- Hiding these from the 'outside' world, i.e. making them private to the program unit.

- Preventing *direct* access to the semaphore/mutex operations and the critical code section.
- Providing means to *indirectly* use the shared resource.

From a conceptual aspect the simple monitor can modelled as shown in figure 3.6.

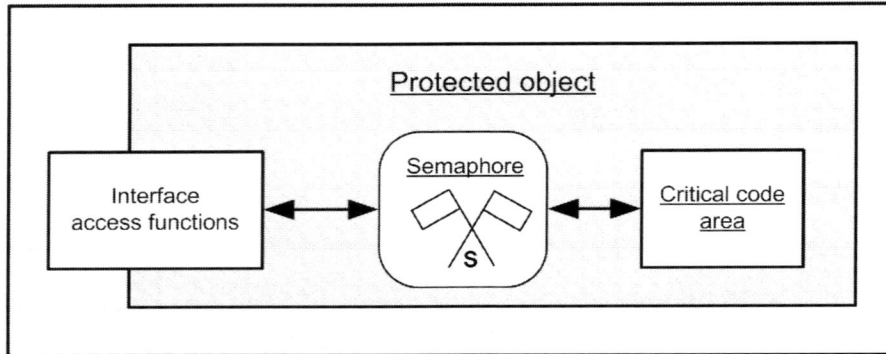

Figure 3.6 The simple monitor (protected object)

This denotes that the semaphore and the critical code area are encapsulated within a program unit. As before, access to the critical code area is controlled by a semaphore. Encapsulated items are not visible to external software; all accesses to them has to go via an interface function.

A basic form of encapsulation in C programming is the function; this we'll now use to build an elementary form of the simple monitor.

Please note: although a semaphore is used in this exercise we could equally well have employed a mutex. Later we'll explain why, when using FreeRTOS to implement mutual exclusion, the mutex is the preferred method. But, for the moment, it doesn't really matter which one you use. If you can solve the problem with a semaphore you'll have no difficulty in applying the mutex.

3.6.3 The problem details.

Figure 3.7 shows the task diagram for this problem, this being based on that of exercise 8. Use the timings as specified for that exercise. In your user code implement a function 'AccessSharedData', having a form similar to:

///
Outline pseudo-code of the simple monitor function 'AccessSharedData();'.

Lock the semaphore (osSemaphoreWait)
//Start of the critical code section
        Check and act on the status of the Start flag
        Simulate read/write operations
        Set the start flag up.
//End of the critical code section
Unlock (release) the semaphore (osSemaphoreRelease)

///

When either the Green or Red task wishes to access the critical code it should simply make a call on this function.

Build, download and run the software. Observe the Led behaviour; compare this with your findings in exercise 8.1. What you should end up with is code that behaves identically, as far as the user is concerned, to that of exercise 8 (where the semaphore was first used). Yet this implementation is a much more secure, robust one.

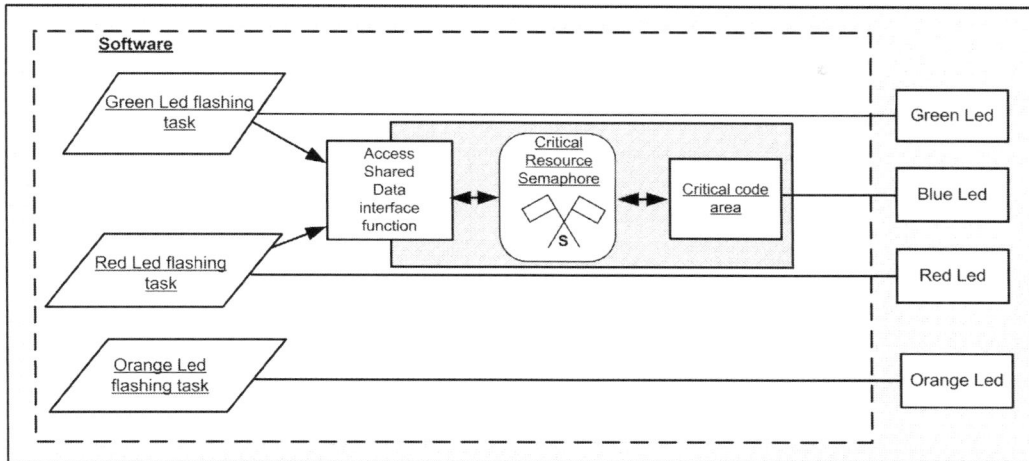

Figure 3.7 System task diagram

3.6.4 Exercise 10 review.

If you've successfully completed this exercise: excellent. What you've done here has shown how to deal with resource contention in a very controlled way. You will have seen that:

- There are *no* semaphore calls in the code of the tasks.
- The protected code is private.
- Application code cannot directly use the protected code.
- The only way for application code to manipulate the protected code is to call the monitor function. This call, a public item, acts as the public interface function for the monitor.
- The approach used here provides safer, more secure and more robust program operations then those of exercise 8.

There's no doubt that the monitor (as described here) has significantly improved the code quality, robustness, etc., of the earlier work. Unfortunately it still has one major weakness; the semaphore itself, as generated by CubeMX, is a global item. As such it isn't protected; thus it is open to abuse or misuse by *any* of the tasks. In a later exercise we'll look at how we can overcome this problem, to produce a truly robust and portable simple monitor.

3.7 Exercise 11 - Demonstrate the effects of priority inversion.

Fundamental purpose of the exercise: to demonstrate the effects of priority inversion in a multitasking design.

3.7.1 Introduction.

By now you should have worked out that it may not be easy to predict the temporal behaviour of multitasking systems. Our predictions are likely to be correct only in simpler cases (e.g. those involving sets of independent periodic tasks requiring low processor utilization). Unfortunately, the moment tasks share software items, it becomes much more difficult to produce deterministic timings. And this problem may be further complicated when priority-preemptive scheduling is used. Such aspects have been discussed in Book 1, showing how extra delays can be produced by the priority inversion problem.

This exercise is designed to produce a practical running example of the effects of priority inversion.

3.7.2 Problem overview and key code aspects.

Figure 3.8 shows the system task diagram for this problem. It consists of three tasks and a single non-concurrent protected object (exactly the same as that of exercise 10). However, there are important differences in the code, so be careful when reusing any software.

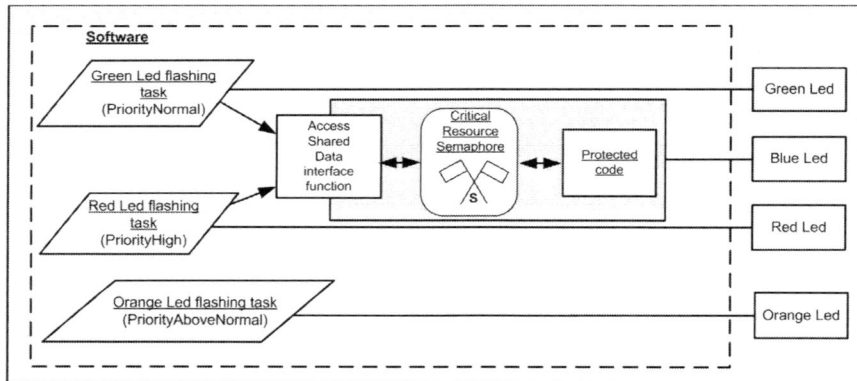

Figure 3.8 System task diagram

This is a four-step exercise:

(a) Exercise 11.1 — Demonstration of the run-time behaviour when all tasks execute in an unimpeded fashion: no resource contention and no delays introduced by task interactions.
(b) Exercise 11.2 — Demonstration of mutual exclusion to prevent resource contention (essentially a recap operation but provides reference timing data for the later priority inversion demo).
(c) Exercise 11.3 — Demonstration of the classical priority inversion problem.
(d) Exercise 11.4 — Repeat of (c), but now providing extra visual information relating to task execution.

As before, the run-time behaviour of the code can be deduced by observing the Led flashing patterns. Now, for this exercise, it's important to use the recommended timings; this will allow you to compare your results with the ones given here (although always feel free to experiment).

The reasons for using this particular set of exercises are explained as we go through the work.

3.7.3 Exercise details.

The most important aspect of this exercise is that tasks are *not* to be run as periodic ones. Instead they are executed in 'single-shot' run-to-completion mode. This is done to make the run time behaviour easy to observe, record and then compared with your theoretical predictions. To do this each task must have a 'suspend this task' statement as the final code item. In FreeRTOS this is done using the following API:

vTaskSuspend(NULL);

See http://www.freertos.org/a00130.html

The task functional behaviours are very similar but not *exactly* the same.   First, the program structure for the Orange Led flashing task is:

Start of code:
   1. Flash Orange Led for four seconds at a 10 Hz. rate.
   2. Suspend this task.
End of code

The *basic* structure of the other two tasks is:

Start of code:
   1. Access shared data (Note: MUST be the first operation).
   2. Flash Led for four seconds at a 10 Hz. rate.
   3. Suspend this task.
End of code

The program structure of the protected object is:

Start of code:
   1. Take semaphore.
   2. Simulate r/w operations; flash the Blue Led for two seconds at a 10 Hz. rate.
   3. Release the semaphore.
End of code

Don't worry about producing precise timings and *don't* use the osDelay/osDelayUntil APIs unless specified; all timing *must* be done in software. The reason is that these APIs invoke rescheduling, which would completely change the run-time behaviour.
   Note that the relative priority of the tasks is shown in figure 3.8: highest is the Red Led flashing task 'Red task'), next is Orange, the lowest being the Green one. Set these using the CubeMX configuration feature.

(a) Exercise 11.1.

One of the major points of this exercise is to get you to think about how sharing resources affects system responsiveness.
   Execute the code with all tasks started simultaneously (normal default FreeRTOS operation). Re-run the code by resetting the processor until you have correctly noted the actual Led flashing sequence. You should find this to be the same as that of figure 3.9 (actual results may vary slightly, depending on the values of your software delays).
   Bear in mind that the code of the protected object executes in the context of either the Green or Red tasks. Hence the total run time is:
   (3 x 4) + (2 x 2) = 16 seconds.

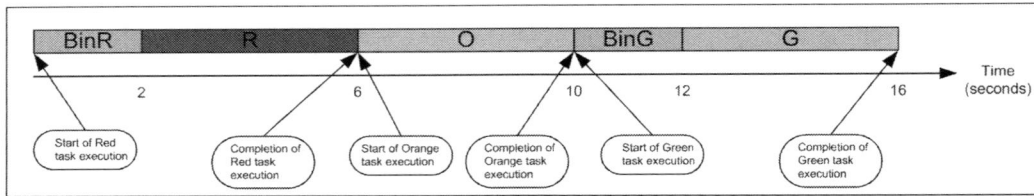

Figure 3.9 Led flashing sequence and timing for exercise 11.1

It is really very important that you fully understand how this figure was calculated. Because, it highlights one simple fact; increasing the use of shared resources results in a degeneration of system responsiveness.

The moral of the story? For good responsiveness minimize resource sharing. And just to repeat a piece of advice: the way to do this is to minimize the number of tasks in your design.

(b) Exercise 11.2.

As mentioned earlier, this exercise is essentially a recap operation: the elimination of resource contention by using access control of shared resources.

For this example:

1. Run it as a two-task design, the Red and Green tasks
2. Suspend the Red task immediately after it's started for a short period of time (to allow the lower-priority Green task to run until it is preempted).

Thus, just for this exercise, the program structure of the Red Led flashing task is:

Start of code:
   1. Suspend for one second to allow the Green task to start running. A simple way to do this is to use osDelay(1000)
   2. Access shared data.
   3. Flash Led for four seconds at a 10 Hz. rate.
   4. Suspend this task.
End of code

Re-run the code by resetting the processor until you have correctly noted the actual Led flashing sequence. You should find it corresponds with that of figure 3.10.

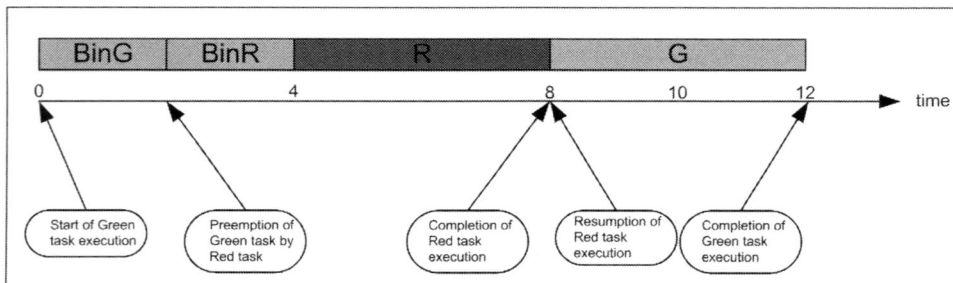

Figure 3.10 Led flashing sequence and timing for exercise 11.2

Explain precisely what's happening in the target system.

(Note: BinG means that the Blue Led is flashing, but that the code is running within the context of the Green task. Similar comments apply to BinR.

(c) Exercise 11.3.

This example demonstrates quite clearly what priority inversion is. Two important points:

1. Run all three tasks in this exercise.
2. For the Red and Orange tasks: immediately after they've started suspend them for a one-second period. This will enable the lowest-priority Green task to run and lock the semaphore (of the protected object) before it is subsequently preempted.

As before, re-run the code by resetting the processor until you have correctly noted the actual Led flashing sequence. You should find this to be the same as that of figure 3.11. Once more make sure you understand precisely what's happening in the target system (especially during the time periods 0-1, 5-6 and 6-8 seconds). Also explain the significance of this result vis-a-vis the temporal performance of the Red task (compare with figure 3.9).

(d) Exercise 11.4.

First, a very important note: figure 3.4 shows when the Leds are *flashing,* something that's important when observing the Blue Led. Modify your code to show whether the Blue Led is flashing in the context of the Green task or the Red task.
  Another important note: when the Red task starts it preempts the Green task, which then goes into the *ready* queue. At preemption time the the Blue Led could either be on or off; it just depends on precisely when preemption occurs. This Led state will persist until the Red task once more becomes the active task.

3.7.3 Exercise 11 comment and review.

As you can see:

- In exercises 11.1 and 11.2 the time taken for the Red task to complete (from the moment of activation) is six seconds.
- In exercise 11.3 the time taken for the Red task to go from being made active (at t = 1second) to completion (t = 12 seconds) is 11 seconds.
- The completion time of the Green task (in a three-task design) is:
     Exercise 11.1 — 16 seconds, as a single execution run of six seconds.
     Exercise 11.3 — 16 seconds, as three non-contiguous execution periods.
- Exercise 11.3 clearly shows the execution of lower-priority tasks in the time frame 1-to-6 seconds, even though the Red (highest priority) task was activated at t = 1 seconds. This is a classic case of priority inversion. Quite clearly this implies that during the 1-to-6 second time frame it (the Red task) cannot be in the ready state. Ergo, it must be in suspension.

You should be able to deduce that:

- There is no connection between mutual exclusion and task switching. The system scheduling policy determines *when* and *why* tasks should be readied/dispatched; contention for shared resources depends both on the code of the tasks *and* precisely when the tasks use these resources.
- Shared items are passive code units ('objects') that execute when called on by tasks. Thus during execution they can be considered to be part of the calling tasks.
- All objects in a multitasking design should be shared units (think about it!).
- Using shared resources usually affects the temporal behaviour of multitasking designs.
- We can accurately predict the time behaviour of multitasking systems only in very simple cases (a 'deterministic' response).

- The temporal behaviour of the more general multitasking designs (those consisting of both periodic and non-periodic tasks) is almost always unpredictable or 'non-deterministic'.
- Increasing the number of tasks and objects in multitasking designs leads to greater and greater uncertainty in the behaviour and responsiveness of tasks.
- For fast-hard robust multitasking systems we should always aim to minimize the number of tasks and objects within our designs.

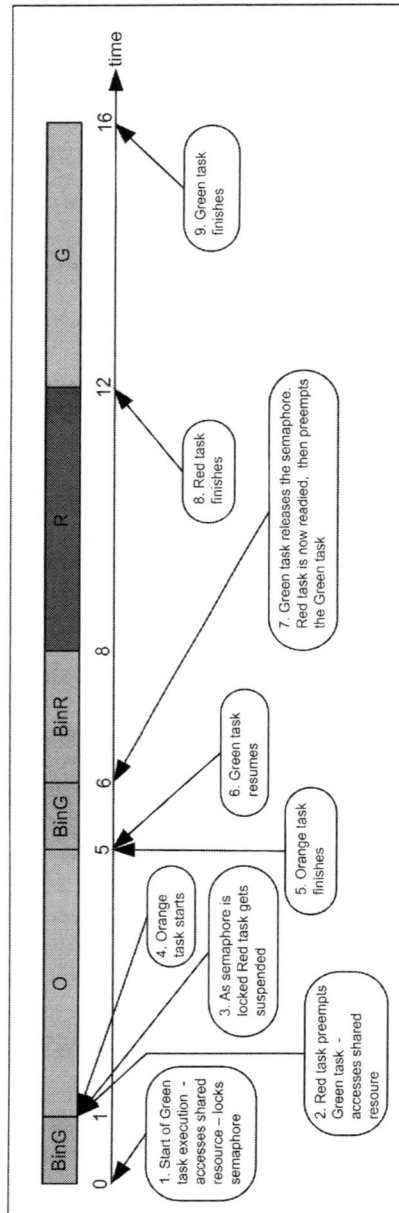

Figure 3.11 Led flashing sequence and timing for exercise 11.3

3.8 Exercise 12 - Eliminate priority inversion by using priority inheritance.

Fundamental purpose of the exercise: to demonstrate that priority inversion of tasks can be eliminated by using priority inheritance techniques.

3.8.1 Introduction.

You have earlier seen that tasks must *never* share resources simultaneously; access must be done in a mutually-exclusive manner. In our exercises we have, so far, implemented this using semaphore protection methods. As a result, if (say two) tasks do contend for a resource, only one can use it; the other is queued, suspended on the semaphore entry queue.

Now, that's fine. Unfortunately the task that gets suspended has its execution process and timing disrupted (the price to be paid for safety and robustness). This is unavoidable, so potential disruptions *must* be taken into account when designing systems. Fortunately, in such cases we can usually calculate worst-case scenarios, putting upper bounds on performance unpredictability. Where things come unstuck for us, however, is when task priority inversion occurs. As you saw from exercise 11 this can produce further disruption to task execution patterns and timings. Moreover, this disruption can be quite unpredictable because it depends entirely on the run-time state of the system. So if your aim is to produce reliable and robust software systems, this problem *must* be eliminated.

Book 1 describes theoretically how priority inheritance techniques prevent priority inversion; we'll now look at how this can be implemented in practice.

3.8.2 Problem overview.

FreeRTOS provides a priority inheritance mechanism as part of the mutex construct. This is automatically invoked and doesn't need any additional programming to activate it. The symbol used here for the mutex, and its application within a protected object, is shown in figure 3.12.

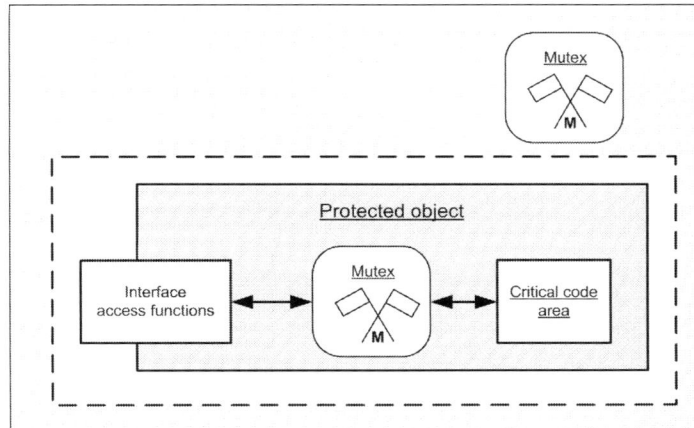

Figure 3.12 Mutex symbol and use within a protected object

What we'll do in this exercise is to repeat that of exercise 11, but using a mutex in place of the semaphore, figure 3.13. If necessary refresh your memory of the mutex APIs and their use from exercise 9. And, before you do any practical work, predict the expected flashing patterns of the Leds.

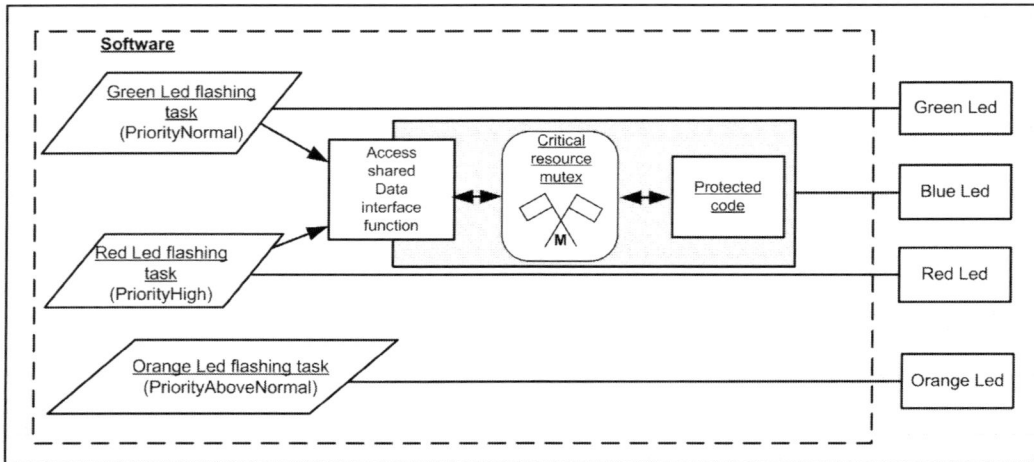

Figure 3.13 System task diagram

Update the program of exercise 11 to change the semaphore to a mutex, then run the system. If you've done this correctly you should produce the following Led flashing pattern (figure 3.14):

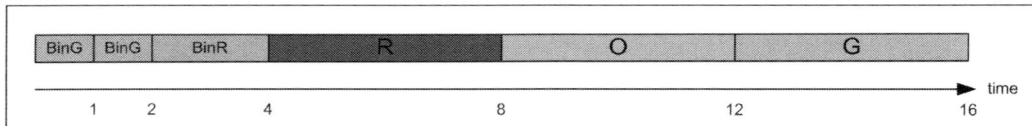

Figure 3.14 Led flashing pattern for exercise 12.

As before, make sure that you understand precisely what's happening in the target system.

3.8.3 Exercise 12 comment and review.

The key comparison is that of figures 3.11 (no priority inheritance) and 3.14 (priority inheritance used). Without priority inheritance the Red task completes ('delivers its results') at t=12 seconds; with priority inheritance it completes at t=8 seconds. Given that we need to control access to the shared resource (only one task at a time), that's the best we can do.

In view of this you should *always* use the mutex instead of the semaphore as an access control (mutual exclusion) mechanism. Later we'll see how the semaphore can be effectively employed in multitasking designs.

Chapter 4

Supporting task intercommunication.

4.1 Exercise 13 - Use flags to coordinate activities.

Fundamental purpose of the exercise: to show how flags can be used to coordinate activities.

4.1.1 Introduction.

A regular operational requirement for sequencing and logic controllers is to deal with combinational logic problems. Some examples:

'The shaft brake is to be released when the engine is running AND the throttle is moved past the idle position'.
'The master hydraulic alarm is to be activated if either pump 1 OR pump 2 fails'.

In software-based controllers flags can be used to coordinate such logical operations in a simple and straightforward manner. And that is the topic of the current exercise.

4.1.2 Problem overview.

The task diagram for this problem is shown in figure 4.1, comprising three tasks and two flags. Please note there isn't a standard symbol for a flag; this is our preferred representation.

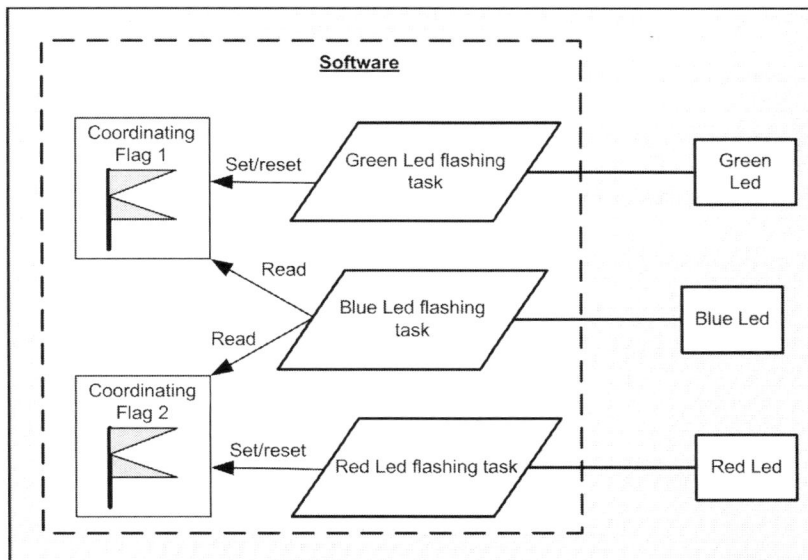

Figure 4.1 System task diagram

The flags:

- Are used as signalling mechanisms to coordinate the Blue task actions with those of the Green and Red ones and
- Have two states: Set and Reset.

CoordinatingFlag1 can be set and reset by the Green task. Likewise, CoordinatingFlag2 can be set and reset by the Red task. The Blue task can only read the states of the flags.

A key point of this exercise is to illustrate clearly what we mean by *task coordination*. The Green and Red tasks use the flags to signal information; the Blue task acts on this to set *its* mode of operation. With this approach there is no direct task-to-task communication; the flags act as a decoupling mechanism. Also, there is no concept a of task waiting at a flag for something to happen (although you *could* choose to do this if you so wish). Note well that coordination does *not* involve transference of data.
   The overall details of the exercise are given below. Timing isn't critical here, feel free to experiment.

Default condition - all flags to be reset on start-up.

The Green task runs to completion, as follows:
1. Flash Led at 10 Hz. for 10 seconds.
2. Set Flag 1.
3. Flash Led at 1Hz. for 10 seconds.
4. Reset Flag 1.
5. Flash Led at 10Hz. for 10 seconds.
6. End task.

The Red task runs to completion, as follows:
1. Flash Led at 10 Hz. for 15 seconds.
2. Set Flag 2.
3. Flash Led at 1Hz. for 10 seconds.
4. Reset Flag 2
5. Flash Led at 10 Hz. for 5 seconds.
6. End task.

The Blue task runs continuously, as follows:
1. At start-up flash Led at 10 Hz.
2. When both flags are Set flash Led at 1Hz.
3. When both flags are next Reset flash Led at 10Hz.
4. Loop to stage 2.

Sketch out a timeline for each task, noting the important time markers and the related flashing rates.

4.1.3 Problem detailed points.

Each flag (or 'flag object') should be constructed as shown in figure 4.2, using a combination of .h and .c files. This provides excellent encapsulation for the flag and hides it from the outside world. In this particular case there isn't a need to include access protection mechanisms (but these can always be incorporated if required).
   The interface access functions should be:

- Set flag.
- Reset flag.
- Check flag status.

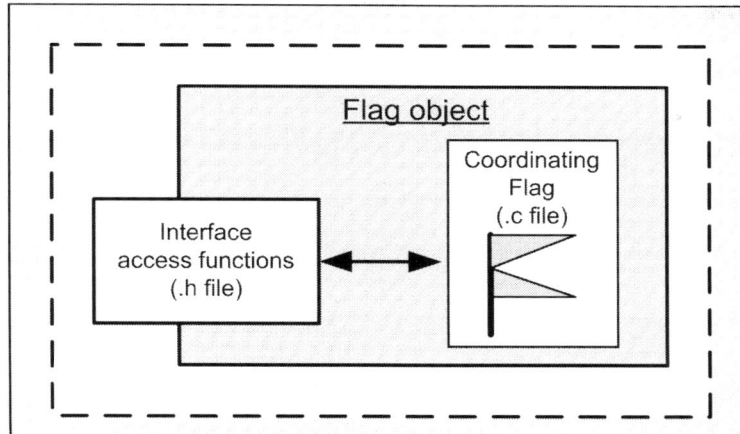

Figure 4.2 Flag construction - file structure

You *could* have a .h/.c file combination for each flag. Alternatively you could build both flags within a single .c file, with the corresponding .h file housing all access functions (this is merely a matter of taste in a problem as simple as this one).

It is recommended that a flag data type should be defined, as for example:

```
typedef enum {Set, Reset} Flag;
```

The type definition should be made public by placing it in the .h file.

We recommend that you use the osDelay API to provide the correct flashing rates. As a result the tasks spend most of their time in a timed suspension state, giving a very low processor utilization. This means that we can set all tasks to have the same priority without concern for possible task interference effects.

4.1.4 Exercise 13 comment and review.

This exercise, at the conceptual level, is very straightforward: just requires careful thinking about the code implementation. But there's more to it than a simple demonstration of inter-task signalling; it holds two important lessons for us. First, it demonstrates the use of a well-defined task communication object; second it shows how task behaviours can be decoupled.

The result of building the flag object in the specified manner is that:

- We avoid the use of global items.
- It (the flag object) has excellent encapsulation and information hiding properties.
- It is very easy to create named flags, so making it simple to map the task model to code.

The decoupling of tasks behaviours can be seen by observing the Led flashing actions, as follows:

- The Green and Red tasks merely set or reset flags, then carry on doing their own thing without having to wait..
- The Blue task regularly checks the flags but continues executing irrespective of the flag states.
- After 30 seconds the Green and Red tasks have completed but Blue continues to run indefinitely (until power is turned off or the processor is reset).

Just a piece of helpful advice: always minimize task coupling in your designs.

4.2 Exercise 14 - Use event flags to provide unilateral synchronization.

Fundamental purpose of the exercise: to show how event flags can be used to provide unilateral synchronization of tasks.

4.2.1 Introduction.

The basic requirement here is to implement the type of synchronization similar to that shown in figure 4.3.

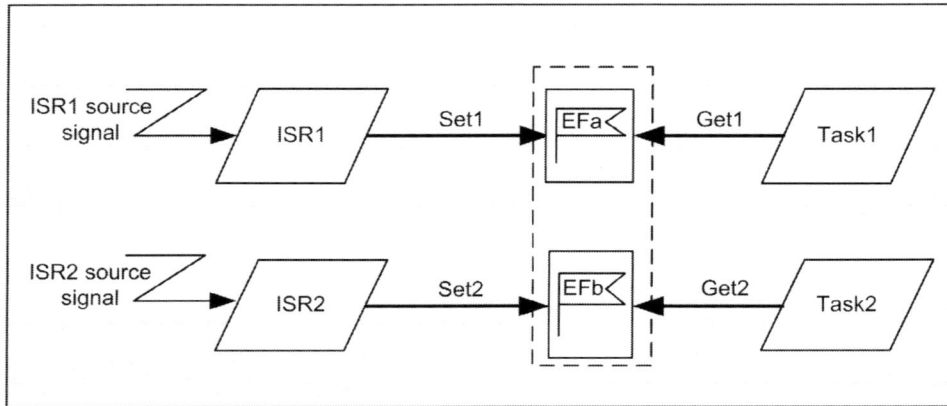

Figure 4.3 Unilateral synchronisation for a deferred server application

Here tasks 1 and 2 are aperiodic ones, to be activated by external interrupt signals. These interrupt signals, however, do not directly activate the tasks; this is an indirect process that uses ISRs in combination with event flags.

   Each task is designed to send a 'Get' signal to its flag at the start of its program. Provided the flag is correctly preset the task will stop at this point, waiting for its flag to be set (it is now in a suspended state). When an external interrupt signal arrives its corresponding ISR is invoked, resulting in the generation of a 'Set' signal. This readies the waiting task, which is now moved from the suspended to the ready queue, and then run under scheduler control.

   For many applications (e.g. handling keyboard switch signals) a task like this runs in an infinite loop. After being woken up it performs its specified processing, then returns to the point at which it once again generates a Get signal to its event flag. As before, the task now suspends, waiting until it is re-awakened.

4.2.2 Event flags, signals and FreeRTOS/CMSIS.

In the RTOS world we are bedevilled by a lack of agreed/specified definitions and diagram symbols. Thus, to avoid total confusion, it's necessary to look at how FreeRTOS deals with event flags. There seems to be some difference between 'standard' FreeRTOS and that ported for use with the STM CubeMX tool (although it may just be the way that information is presented), viz:

From STM UM1722 Developing Applications on STM32Cube with RTOS:
Signals: are flags that may be used to signal specific conditions to a thread.

From http://www.freertos.org/FreeRTOS-Event-Groups.html
Event bits are used to indicate if an event has occurred or not. Event bits are often referred to as event flags.

We, however, will use the following terms:

1. Flags: defined as being Signal or Event flags (use these as having synonymous meanings).
2. Calls on the flags: defined to be Signals.
3. Types of Signal and their corresponding FreeRTOS APIs:
    *   Set — *osSignalSet*.
    *   Wait — *osSignalWait*.
    *   Clear — *osSignalClear*.

Another factor to take into account is that Signal flags are conceptually part of a task structure, as depicted in figure 4.4.

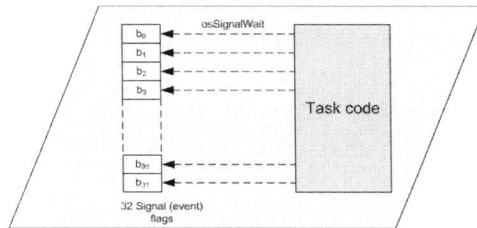

Figure 4.4 Signal (event) flags as part of a task structure.

Each task has a set of flags assigned to it (possible maximum is 32), *and are identified by number only*. Hence they are not explicitly-defined items but may be thought of as an implicit part of the task construct.
    The *actual* maximum flags per task (thread) is specified in the file cmsis_os.h, as for example:

*   #define osFeature_Signals 8

To use an individual flag (e.g. set, wait or clear) the API calls must include the number of that flag. Take, for example, the following wait operations:

*   General form: Wait (FlagNumber, WaitingTime);
*   For flag 0 — FreeRTOS API: osSignalWait (0x0, 10000); // waiting time of 10 seconds.
*   For flag 1 —   osSignalWait (0x1, 0); // no waiting.
*   For flag 2 —   osSignalWait (0x10, osWaitForever); // self-explanatory.
*   Etc.

It can be seen that the task code can only send a wait signal to one of the flags *assigned to that task*. As a result there is no need to identify the calling task in the API.
    If a task sends a wait signal to a 'cleared' flag it suspends at that point; it remains there until it is woken up by *another* task setting that flag, figure 4.5.

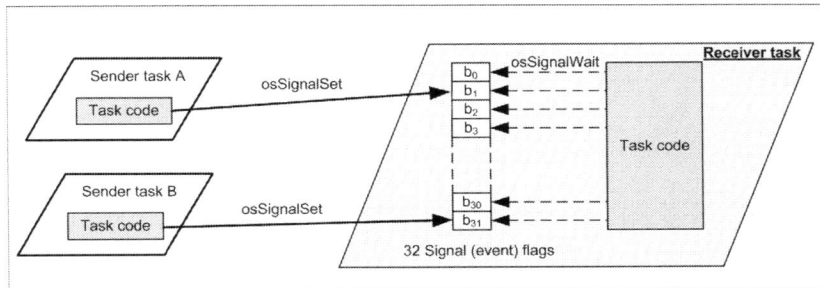

Figure 4.5 Signalling between tasks

From this it is clear that the sending task must specify *two* pieces of information: the task it's sending to and the specific flag 'in' that task. The general form is:

osSignalSet (DestinationTaskName, DestinationFlagNumber);

For example: assume that Sender task A wishes to set flag 1 of the Receiver task. To do this it calls the following API in its task code:
   osSignalSet (ReceiverTaskHandle, 0x01);

Finally, to clear a flag, use: osSignalClear(DestinationTaskHandle, FlagNumber);

These APIs have return values that can be used to control subsequent operations. We, in this exercise, won't employ this aspect of the APIs; however full details can be found in the file cmsis_os.h

4.2.3 Exercise details.

The task diagram for this problem is shown in figure 4.6, comprising one sending task (Blue) and two receiver tasks (Green and Red).

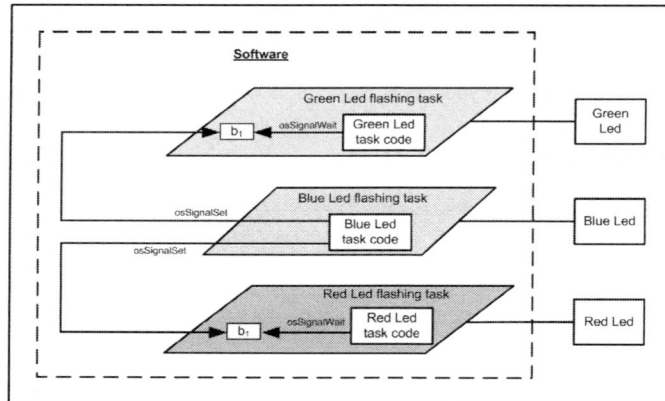

Figure 4.6 System task diagram

The purpose of the Blue task is to mimic the action of an ISR task. The other two tasks are designed to be deferred server (in this case a 'deferred interrupt server') aperiodic ones. Design your software to comply with the processing defined in the program structure (activity) diagram of figure 4.7. Set all tasks to have equal priority and note that timing isn't critical. Predict the behaviour of your software, run the system and check reality against expectations.

4.2.4 Exercise 14 comment and review.

First, note that each receiver task uses its flag 1 for synchronization purposes. Here (in this example) it is a completely arbitrary choice; any flag would do. Second, the exercise also highlights the point that even though the flags aren't named, there isn't any confusion in using them.
   From a programming point of view, the implementation of unidirectional synchronization using signal flags is quite straightforward. Essentially it's a mechanism that allows a task (or tasks) to control the running activities of others. A particularly useful application of this is to define the start-up order of tasks (something that can be very important in many embedded systems).

If you do decide to employ this technique in real applications think carefully about the issue of design traceability and program debugging. In very simple examples such as this one it is easy to see pretty-clearly how the tasks interact. But when designs are more complex this isn't always the case; it becomes increasingly difficult to understand what happens at run-time. For example, take the following program statement in your receiver task:

osSignalWait (0x0100, osWaitForever);

What can you deduce from this? Only that, when the receiver task sends a wait signal to flag 0x0100 then, if this flag isn't set, the task will wait forever. What we can't deduce is which task is responsible for setting the flag; the code isn't self-documenting. So, to improve things and bring clarity to the situation: try something like the following where an ADC sending task is to synchronize with a Control task?

1. On your *task diagram* name the flag 0x0100 in the Control task as 'ADC2ControlFlag'.

2. Implement this in code as a global comms item (say in a Comms.h file):
   const int32_t   ADC2ControlFlag = 0x100;

3. Use the following API in the receiving Control task.
   osSignalWait (ADC2ControlFlag, osWaitForever);

4. Use the following API in the sending ADC task:
   osSignalSet (ControlTaskHandle, ADC2ControlFlag);

You can achieve the same ends in many different ways; just use whatever suits you best. But please, do employ good naming.

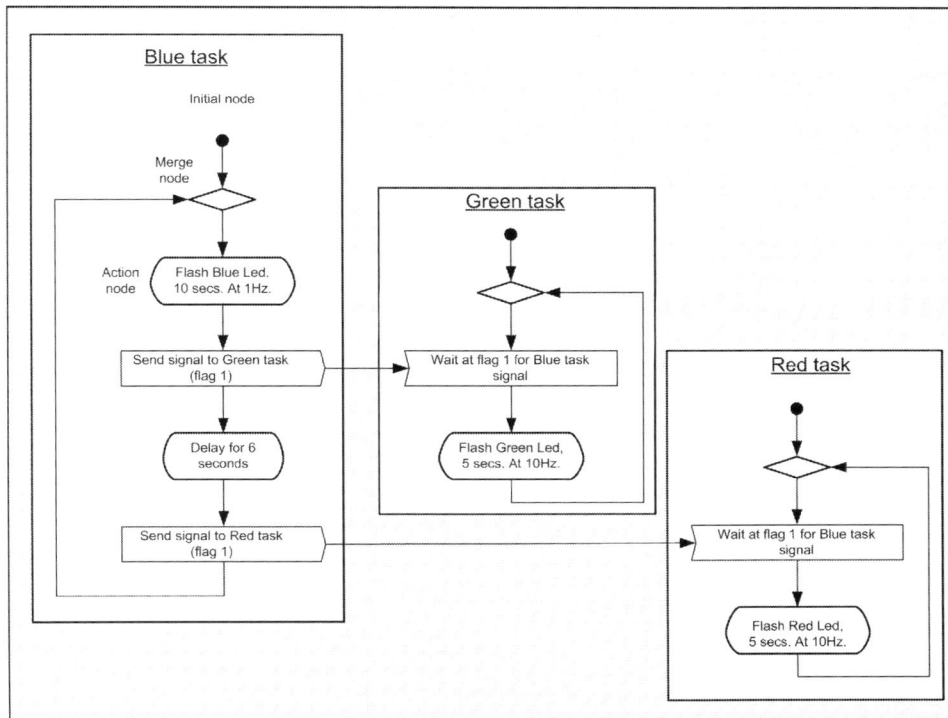

Figure 4.7 Problem program structure diagram.

4.3 Exercise 15 - Use semaphores to provide unilateral synchronization.

Fundamental purpose of the exercise: to show how semaphores can be used as event flags for unilateral synchronization purposes.

4.3.1 Introduction and problem outline.

You saw in the previous exercise how easy it is to implement unilateral synchronization using the standard signal flags.   However, this approach has one (potential) drawback; the technique is specific to FreeRTOS.   If you never intend to change your RTOS then it's a non-problem. However, if you *do* think changes might be made in the future then something more portable is needed.   It is better to use a standard RTOS component.   So, in our case we'll employ the semaphore as an event flag building block (but see comments at the end of this book regarding portability of RTOS code).

   The problem here is exactly the same as that of the previous one, as shown in the task diagram of figure 4.6 and program structure diagram of figure 4.7.

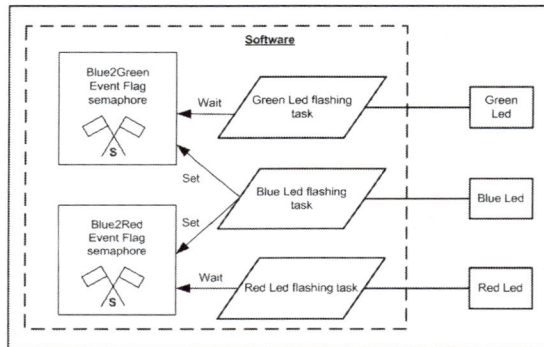

Figure 4.6 System task diagram

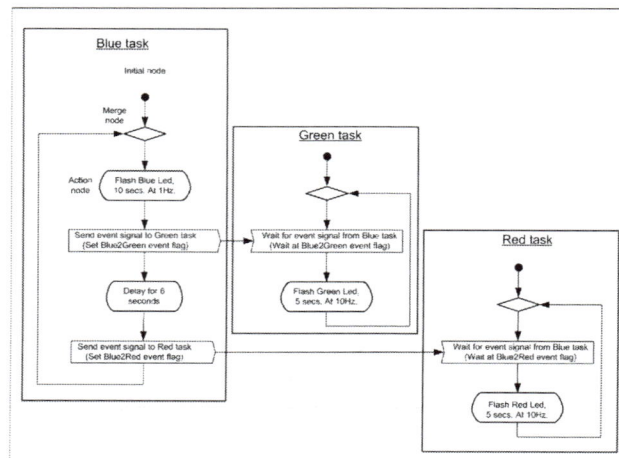

Figure 4.7 Problem program structure diagram

As before, the purpose of the event flags is to provide a unilateral task synchronization mechanism, but now based on semaphore techniques.

4.3.2 Exercise details.

This is quite a straightforward exercise which is simple to carry out. Its requirements have already been spelt out clearly and don't need any further elaboration. Now for just a few reference points and suggestions:

1. Create two semaphores using the RTOS configuration feature of CubeMX. Name these as event flags (EF), to indicate to (future) readers of the code that you're using these for unilateral synchronization: not for mutual exclusion.

        Blue2GreenEF
        Blue2RedEF

2. When accessing these use the following APIs:

        osSemaphoreRelease (SemaphoreHandle);
        osSemaphoreWait (SemaphoreHandle, WaitingTime);

3. To wait indefinitely use the following waiting time value: portMAX_DELAY

4. Make sure that you initialize the semaphores to the blocked state before you use them (remember that semaphores are, by default, initialized to the released (pass) state).

4.3.3 Exercise 15 comment and review.

This exercise demonstrates a method of providing unilateral task synchronization that can be implemented in most, if not all, RTOSs (the semaphore is a truly a fundamental building block). Also, this method is pretty-well a universal one, unlike the event flag/signal technique. Although most RTOSs provide some type of event signal these often differ in detail, sometimes significantly.
    You should have been able to reason out why the semaphores had to be initialized to the blocked state. This is one important difference between using a semaphore for access control and using it for synchronization. However, there is another difference (and a very important one at that). For access control the task that locks the semaphore is also the one that releases it. For synchronization, one task locks the semaphore whereas a different one releases it. This has two significant consequences:

• A mutex cannot be used in place of the semaphore (think about it) and
• It is essential to easily and clearly see where (in your source code) you make the semaphore calls.

Remember, the semaphore is a global item, visible to all tasks. This means that it can be locked/ released by any task at any time. All it takes is a bit of sloppy programming to destroy the correctness of a program (and, in concurrent software, it can be very difficult to track down problems like this). So consider carefully how you could improve the visibility of operations, especially for future maintenance. Just a few ideas for your contemplation (although hardened programmers will probably dismiss these as unworthy of consideration):

```
#define Blue2GreenEF      Blue2GreenEFHandle
#define Blue2RedEF        Blue2RedEFHandle
#define WaitForever       portMAX_DELAY
#define NoWait            0
#define WaitEventFlag     osSemaphoreWait
#define SetEventFlag      osSemaphoreRelease
#define BlockEventFlag    osSemaphoreWait
```

```
/* Set the semaphore to a blocked state */
BlockEventFlag (Blue2RedEF, NoWait);
BlockEventFlag (Blue2GreenEF, NoWait);

/* Waiting for a synchronization signal */
WaitEventFlag (Blue2GreenEF, WaitForever);
WaitEventFlag (Blue2RedEF, WaitForever);

/* Setting a synchronization signal */
SetEventFlag (Blue2GreenEF);
SetEventFlag (Blue2RedEF);
```

These provide unambiguous mapping from the task diagram to the source code and clear design traceability. But how you choose to do things is a very personal call; there is no single 'right' way. However, I do recommend that you read the chapter 'The power of variable names' in Steve McConnell's book 'Code Complete - a practical handbook of software construction'.

4.4 Exercise 16 - Use semaphores to provide bilateral synchronization.

Fundamental purpose of the exercise: to show how semaphores can be used to provide bilateral synchronization of tasks.

4.4.1 Problem overview.

Unilateral synchronization is used as a one-way signalling method, mainly to trigger task execution. Bilateral synchronization, in contrast, synchronizes task activities to ensure that they work together in an controlled manner. The problem here is relatively straightforward: to provide bilateral synchronization of two tasks, using semaphores to build the synchronization mechanism, figure 4.8.

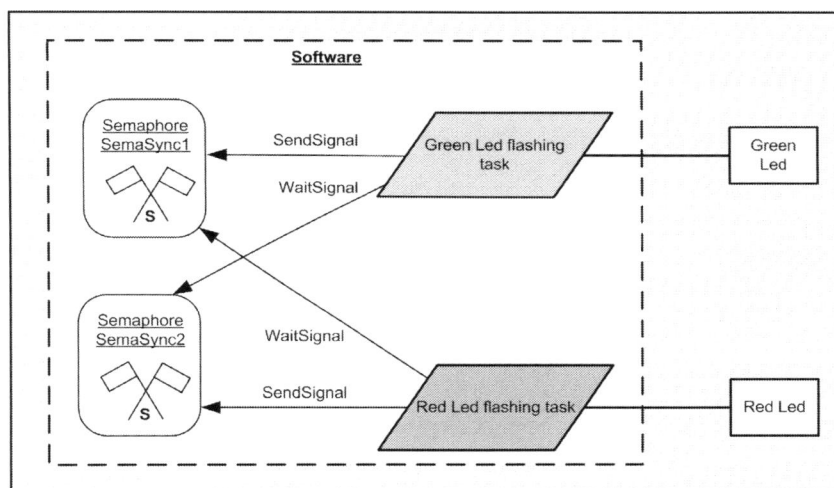

Figure 4.8 Problem task diagram

This construct requires two semaphores (as described in book 1) because, in general, we can't predict the rendezvous order of the tasks. Create these semaphores using the CubeMX tool.

4.4.2 The problem in detail.

Both tasks are to run as continuous loops using the timing values suggested below (though these aren't critical). The desired run-time behaviour (see figure 4.9) is as follows:

1. Both tasks start 'simultaneously'.
2. After the Red task starts it runs for 10 seconds, flashing its Led at a 1Hz. rate.
3. After the Green task starts it runs for five seconds, flashing its Led at a 10Hz. rate, then issues a synchronizing call. At this point it should automatically suspend.
4. The Red task issues the corresponding synchronizing call at the 10 second point, and then runs for a further five seconds, flashing the Led at a 10Hz. rate.
5. As a result of the Red task synchronizing call the Green task restarts execution. It runs for 10 seconds, flashing the Led at a 1Hz. rate.
6. At 15 seconds into the run the Red task makes a synchronizing call, causing it to suspend.
7. At 20 seconds into the run the Green task makes a synchronizing call, re-awakening the Red task.

8. At this point the whole process is repeated.

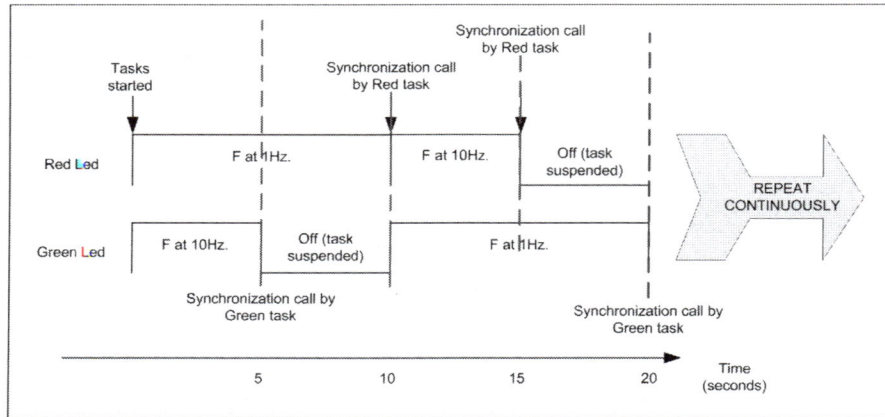

Figure 4.9 Task execution - behaviour and timing

For *WaitSignal* use   osSemaphoreWait
For *SendSignal* use   osSemaphoreRelease

Once again, make sure that the semaphores are correctly initialized.

4.4.3 Exercise 16 comment and review.

This exercise shouldn't have presented you with any real difficulties: just needs clear thinking. As a result you should be capable of implementing the rendezvous (bilateral) synchronization of two tasks in your multitasking designs.

The simplest and easiest way of coding this design has one undesirable consequence; the semaphores are likely to be global items. This aspect has been discussed earlier and, in real projects, should be avoided wherever possible. Consider how you would go about developing a simple monitor object as shown in figure 4.10. A very practical solution would be to:

- Provide encapsulation and access control similar to that of exercise 10.
- Use the native FreeRTOS constructs for semaphore building/handling instead of the CubeMX ones, namely:

    - vSemaphoreCreateBinary
    - xSemaphoreGive
    - xSemaphoreTake

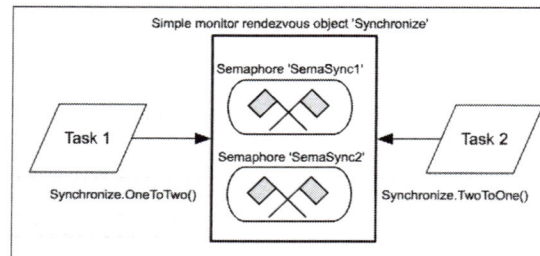

Figure 4.10 Monitor object with protected semaphores

4.5 Exercise 17 - Use semaphores to synchronize multiple tasks.

Fundamental purpose of the exercise: to show how semaphores can be used to provide synchronization of multiple tasks - the 'Rendezvous Barrier'.

4.5.1 Problem overview.

The synchronizing mechanism of exercise 16, although perfectly fit for purpose, is somewhat limited; it handles bilateral synchronization of two tasks only. In reality this meets most embedded design requirements, but there are times when we *do* need to synchronize multiple tasks. That's the topic of this exercise, where we'll look at two different ways to do this.

First, let's go back to to the technique used in exercise 16. There is, in fact, a variation on that method for the building of bilateral synchronization components. The key components are a *single* semaphore together with a counter of synchronizing calls. The outline code for this is contained in a function (here called *SynchronizeTasks*) as follows:
///

```
/* Code of function SynchronizeTasks */
if (TaskCount < MaxNumTasks)
{
     ++TaskCount;
     WaitSignal(SemaSync1, WaitForever);
}
else if (TaskCount == MaxNumTasks)
{
     for (LoopCount=1; LoopCount< MaxNumTasks; LoopCount++)
     {
        SendSignal(SemaSync1);
        osDelay(10); // important: see comment in notes
     }
     TaskCount = 1;
}
else
{ ; //error handler if required}
```

///
Please note: this is written for ease of understanding, not 'efficiency'.

In each task the synchronizing call is *SynchronizeTasks*. Also, just to reiterate a point; the semaphore must be initialized to blocked. Thus the first task to make the call will get suspended on the semaphore SemaSync1. When *MaxNumTasks* is set to 2 the next call awakens the suspended task (but the semaphore, of course, remains blocked), and both tasks then proceed to execute 'simultaneously'.

You can see that if MaxNumTasks is set to 3 then three tasks can be synchronized; setting it to 4 allows for the synchronization of four tasks, and so on.

There isn't a standard name for this construct, but we'll define it to be a *Rendezvous Barrier*. It is similar to the classical computer science barrier synchronization technique, used for synchronizing multiple threads. However, while the classical form uses busy-wait mechanisms, here we have suspend-wait operations (essential where high performance is required).

In this exercise we'll also look at the use of a slightly different approach to that described above: the *N-semaphore* method. The reason for using this technique is that we hit problems when using a FreeRTOS implementation of the one-semaphore technique. This is unlikely to be a design flaw, but may be due to rescheduling operations during execution of the release sequence. Such problems, we have found, can be eliminated by using a suspend-delay between individual releases (using osDelay, see code fragment above). Also, changing task priorities and tick times in an existing design *may* have some impact on the run-time behaviour.

Treat this as a work-in-progress problem.

4.5.2 The problem in detail.

The purpose of this exercise is to provide synchronization of multiple tasks, specifically the three tasks of figure 17.1. Here the synchronizing component (the *Rendezvous Barrier*) houses a semaphore(s) and a task counter. The required task behaviour and timing for this problem is given in figure 4.11. Note: set all task priorities to normal.

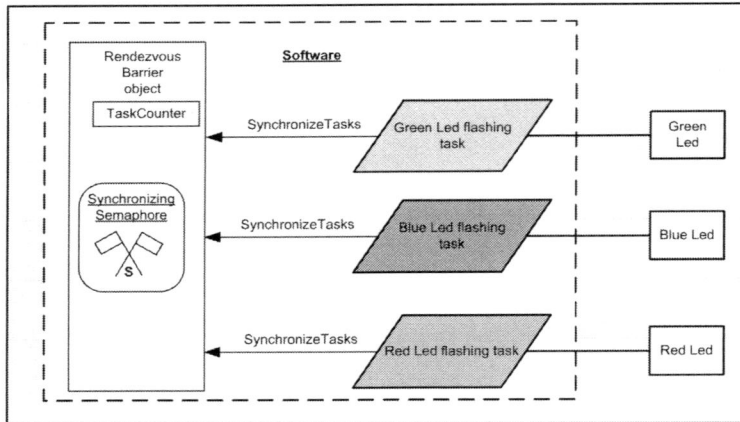

Figure 4.11 System task diagram

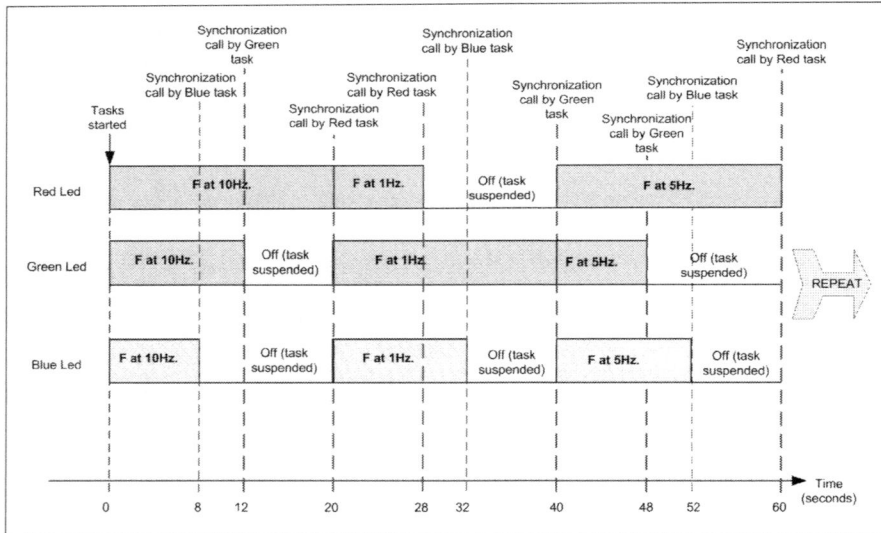

Figure 4.12 Task execution - behaviour and timing

All tasks are to run as continuous loops using the timing values shown in figure 4.12 (though these aren't critical, the timings are long enough for you to clearly observe the Led flashing pattern). The processing model of operation is given in figure 4.13, using an activity diagram to show details of program operations.

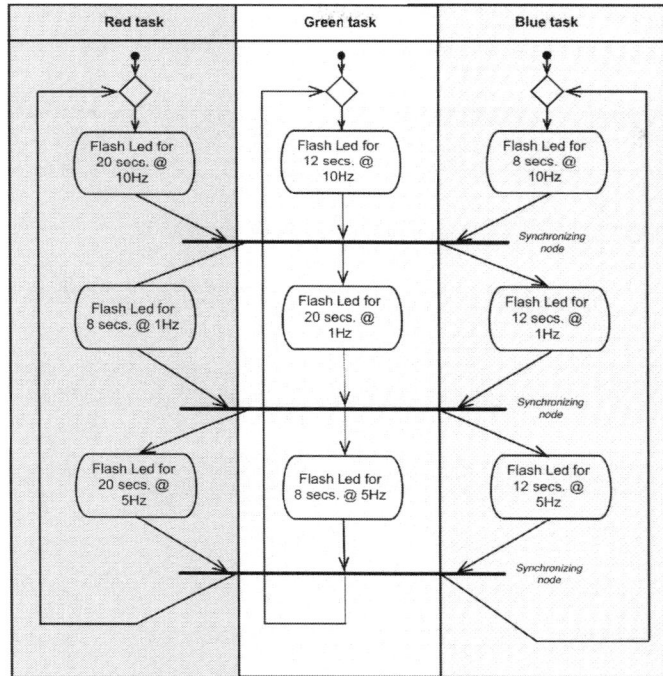

Figure 4.13 Activity diagram - rendezvous barrier synchronization

Note that the Synchronizing node represents a synchronization point; it does not define any particular implementation technique.

Study the details of figures 4.12 and 4.13 until you completely understand the exercise requirements.   And (very important), now predict the expected Led flashing pattern.

4.5.3 One-semaphore implementation of the Rendezvous Barrier.

Complete the exercise for a one-semaphore implementation of the Rendezvous Barrier. Just as a recap, the essential aspects of the rendezvous process are as follows:

1. Before the final task arrives (say Tmax) each task is queued FIFO in the semaphore suspended queue.
2. When Tmax arrives there are *(MaxNumberOfTasks - 1)* in this queue. Note that each arrival increments the task counter by one (1), from 1 to *(MaxNumberOfTasks - 1)*.
3. At this point the counter is reset and *(MaxNumberOfTasks - 1)* send signals are sent to the semaphore.
4. The effect of this is release all queued tasks but leave the semaphore locked (ready for the next rendezvous operation).

4.5.4 N-semaphore implementation of the Rendezvous Barrier.

Complete the exercise for a 3-semaphore implementation of the Rendezvous Barrier. Just as a recap, the essential aspects of the rendezvous process are as follows:

- First, the number of semaphores used (N) is [N = (MaxNumberOfTasks - 1)].
- Second, each semaphore is locked by a specific task (e.g. first task arrival locks semaphore 1, second locks semaphore 2, and so on).
- Third, all suspended tasks are released by the issuing of send signals to all the locked semaphores.
- Fourth, after the release actions are completed all semaphores are left in the locked state, ready for the next rendezvous operation.

4.5.5 Exercise 17 comment and review.

You should now appreciate that it's quite simple to synchronize multiple tasks using a Rendezvous Barrier. The N-semaphore operation can be considered to be reliable, robust and secure, a 'bullet-proof' approach. Unfortunately it is inferior to the single semaphore solution (if/when that works reliably, of course) for a number of reasons:

- First, it requires extra semaphores, resulting in increased memory store requirements (not a major issue).
- Second, the one-semaphore implementation is highly flexible and can be readily configured to handle different synchronization requirements.
- Third, the N-semaphore method is a 'hard-coded' one which requires significant reworking if the number of tasks changes.

I hope by now you're beginning to understand why it can be difficult to correctly predict the run-time behaviour in complex systems. Trying to work out *what* the system does and *when* it does it can be a formidable job because you have to consider:

- The collective behaviour of the tasks and
- The behaviour of each individual task.

This can be doubly-difficult if the only design documentation is source code. So once again it's worth pointing out that diagrams significantly improve our ability to grasp all aspects of the design. And *that* is a really important message for you to take away from this exercise!

4.6 Exercise 18 - Use pools to provide a data sharing mechanism.

Fundamental purpose of the exercise: To show how the pool is used to support data transfer between tasks without any synchronizing actions.

4.6.1 Introduction to the problem.

(a) The pool.

The pool is a mechanism that enables tasks to share data, being built as a read-write random access structure. Following our rules of good design it is constructed as a protected object, figure 4.14

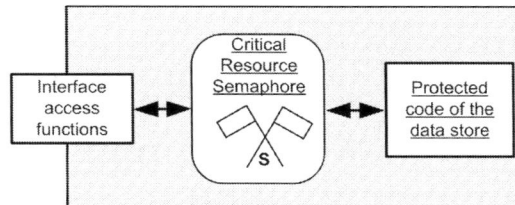

Figure 4.14 A protected pool object

This looks much the same as figure 3.6, the 'simple monitor'. In fact the essential difference is that the pool normally holds multiple pieces of data, often of different types (e.g. integer, floating point, boolean, etc.). Consequently, as far as the tasks themselves are concerned, there really isn't anything new here. But what *is* new (and is the central aspect of this exercise) are the construction details of the protected pool. Strictly speaking, the data store itself is the 'pool of data'. But our designs will *always* provide protection against resource contention; hence 'pool' is short for 'protected pool'.

(b) Constructing the Pool.

As mentioned above, data stores may in general hold items that differ in type (i.e. are heterogeneous). In C the standard type of heterogeneous read-write data store is the struct; hence this will be the core building block of the Pool.

In exercise 10 a C function was used as the encapsulating mechanism. This provided good encapsulation and information hiding, but not 100%; the semaphores were still global items. So we need a different approach: one that provides complete encapsulation and hiding both of the data store *and* the protection semaphore.

This is fine in theory but raises practical problems when programming in C ; the language just doesn't have proper modular structures (equivalent to the Java Module or Ada Package). Fortunately we can mimic the module construct using files, as shown in figure 4.15. The protected object, conceptually a single module, is actually a combination of .h and .c files, where:

- The .h file 'exports' the access function for use by clients (the tasks) and
- The .c file contains the executable code.

The exercise covered here is very much about building and using a C 'module'.

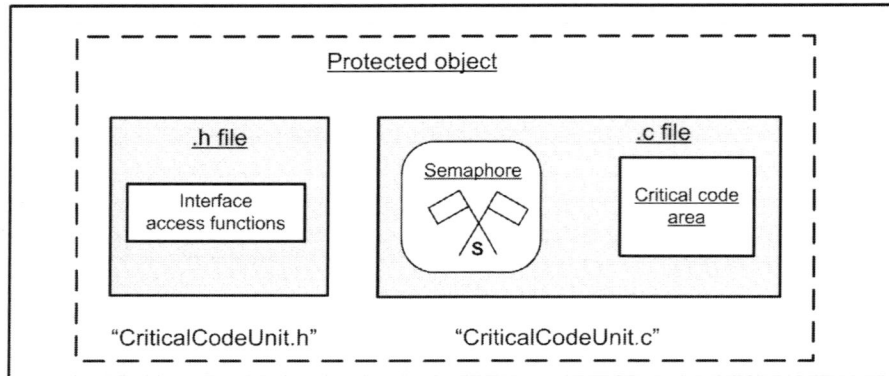

Figure 4.15 Protected object - a C-based modular construct

(c) Important implementation factors - using native FreeRTOS code.

Our intention to create a semaphore in a separate file may raise problems (relating to program scope) when using the CubeMX creation method. There are a number of work-arounds, but the one recommended here is straightforward, easy to understand and extends your knowledge of FreeRTOS.

Sometimes it is more flexible to use native FreeRTOS APIs instead of CubeMX-generated code. So, don't specify the semaphore in the CubeMX configuration data; instead implement it using FreeRTOS constructs, as described below.

Step 1 - Create a semaphore object reference (handle).
    SemaphoreHandle_t xSemaphore;

Step 2 - Create a semaphore:
    xSemaphore = xSemaphoreCreateBinary().
    http://www.freertos.org/xSemaphoreCreateBinary.html

Step 3 - Use the semaphore.
  (a) Release the semaphore:
    xSemaphoreGive(SemaphoreHandle_t   xSemaphore);
    http://www.freertos.org/a00123.html
  (b) Wait for the semaphore
    xSemaphoreTake(SemaphoreHandle_t   xSemaphore,   TickType_t   xTicksToWait);
    http://www.freertos.org/a00122.html

Note that the following information is just for guidance; adapt this as you wish.

Use these constructs to build the protected object of figure 4.16, as for example:

(i) The .c file — create a file *PoolObject.c.*
    1. Create the data store as a struct type. This should be global to the file.
    2. Create the semaphore which also should be global to the file.
        SemaphoreHandle_t CriticalResourceSemaphore
        CriticalResourceSemaphore = xSemaphoreCreateBinary();

3. Create access functions as required (see exercise details).
4. Hide the following semaphore calls in your access functions.
    xSemaphoreTake (CriticalResourceSemaphore, WaitTime);
    xSemaphoreGive (CriticalResourceSemaphore);

(ii) The .h file — create a file *PoolObject.h.*
Insert the declaration of the access functions here. This makes them public to importers (clients) of the file.

When tasks wish to access the shared data they merely call the access function. Of course, to be able to do this, they must first import the *PoolObject.h.* file into the CubeMX-generated file *main.c,* as follows:

```
//////////////////////////////////////
/* USER CODE BEGIN Includes

        #include "PoolObject.h"

/* USER CODE END Includes */
//////////////////////////////////////
```

4.6.2 The problem details.

(a) Overall aspects.

Figure 4.16 shows the task diagram for this problem.

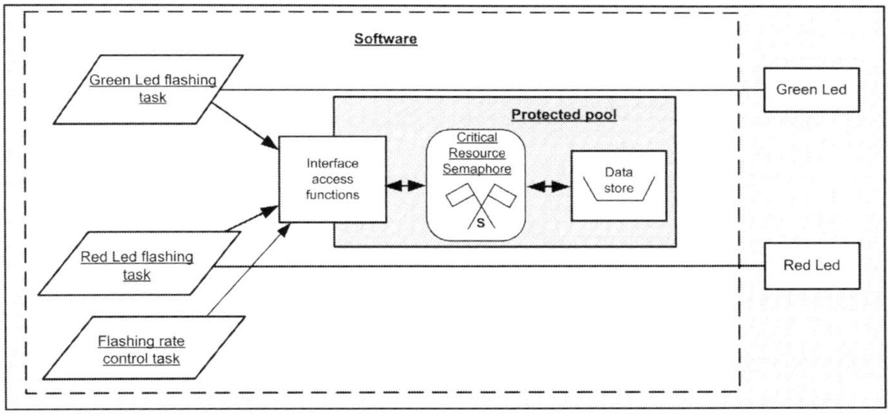

Figure 4.16 System task diagram

The purpose of the Flashing rate control task is to dynamically set the flashing rates of the Red and Green Leds. It does this by periodically writing new values into the data pool. The other tasks read these at regular intervals, and set their Led flashing rates accordingly.
    Construct a store to hold the two separate pieces of data (i.e. the set flashing rates of the Green task and Red tasks). This can be modelled as shown in figure 4.17.
    The pool object should provide access functions to:

• Set the flashing rate values.
• Get the flashing rate values.

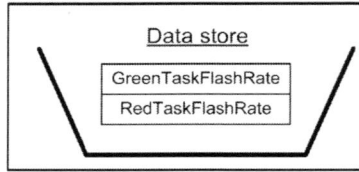

Figure 4.17 Data store structure

The initialized flashing rate values are to be 10Hz for the Green task, 1 Hz. for the Red task.

All details of the data store and the protecting semaphore are to be internal (private) to the pool object. The actual data store itself can be built using the C struct, as for example:

```
typedef struct
{
  int GreenTaskFlashRate;
  int RedTaskFlashRate;
}
FlashingRate;
FlashingRate  FlashingDataPool = {10, 1};  // default flashing rates.
```

(b) Exercise timing details.

(i) Flashing rate control task: Update the two *TaskFlashRate* values every 8 seconds, as follows:

```
/////////////////////////////////////////////////////////////////////////////
        LOOP:
        Delay for 8 seconds.
        Set GreenTaskFlashRate value to 1 Hz.
        Set RedTaskFlashRate value set 10 Hz.
        Delay for 8 seconds.
        Set GreenTaskFlashRate value to 10 Hz.
        Set RedTaskFlashRate value set 1 Hz.
        END LOOP.
/////////////////////////////////////////////////////////////////////////////
```

(ii) Green task: Check the current *TaskFlashRate* value in the pool each **10** seconds. Set the Green Led flashing rate to correspond to this.
(iii) Red task: Check the current *TaskFlashRate* value in the pool each **6** seconds. Set the Red Led flashing rate to correspond to this.

(c) Exercise - detailed points.

First, run the Green and Red tasks individually to check that your timings are correct. When you are satisfied run the full three-task system and observe/check the Led behaviour/timings.   Note specifically the system behaviour over the first 22 seconds of execution. You should find that you get results similar to that shown in figure 4.18.

Important note: there's nothing critical (or especially important) about these timings. The main points of this exercise are to show:

- How a pool is built and used and
- That using pools allows you to construct very loosely coupled task structures.

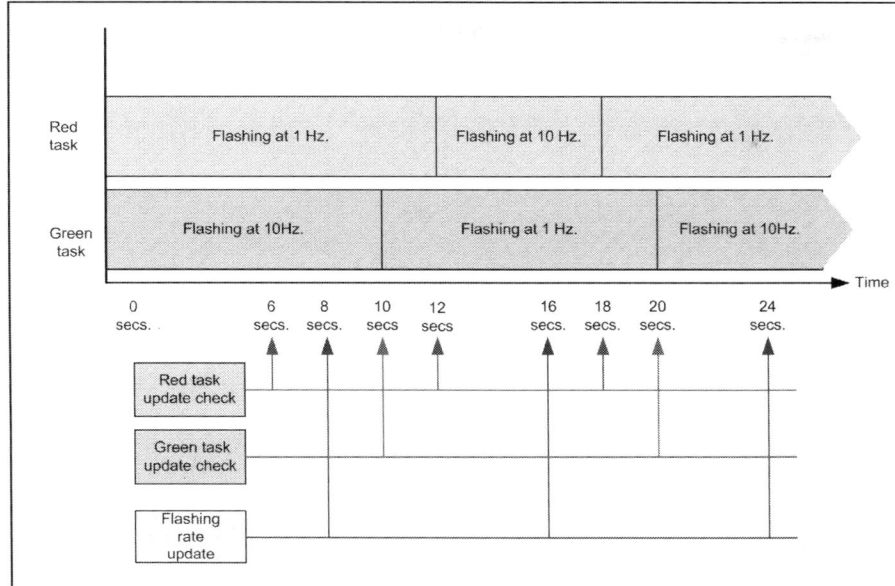

Figure 4.18 Led flashing behaviour

4.6.3 Exercise 18 review.

If you've successfully completed this exercise: excellent. You will have seen that:

- There is no sign of the semaphore in the code of the tasks.
- The semaphore is hidden in the .c file; it is a private item.
- The protected code is also private.
- Application code (i.e. the task code) cannot in any way control or misuse the semaphores.
- Application code cannot directly use the protected code.
- The only way for application code to manipulate the protected code is to use the functions declared in the .h file. This is a public item.
- The 'module' (the combination of the .h and .c files) is safe, secure, robust, portable and potentially reusable.

4.7 Exercise 19 - Use queues for data transfer with task synchronization.

Fundamental purpose of the exercise: To show how the queue is used to support data transfer between tasks without any synchronizing actions.

4.7.1 Introduction to the queue.

The queue is a mechanism that allows tasks to communicate by sending and receiving sequential data messages. It is built as a first-in first-out store structure, shown symbolically in figure 4.18:

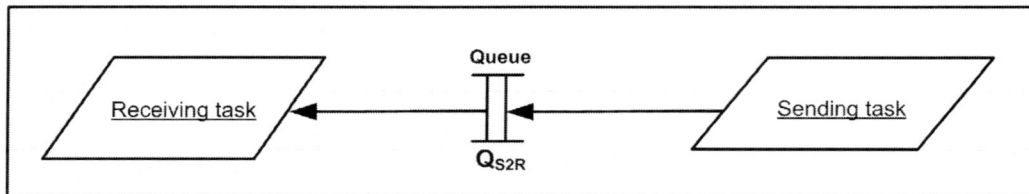

Figure 4.18 Queue symbol

When using CubeMx all queue management is carried out using the following three CMSIS-RTOS APIs:

1. Define and initialize a message queue:
   osMessageCreate
   General format: osMessageCreate (QueueName, QueueLength, ItemSize).

   - *QueueLength* - defines the maximum number of data items that the queue can hold at any one time.
   - *ItemSize* - defines the size in bytes of each data item.

     Note that if you use the facilities of CubeMX, there isn't a need to create the queues; this is done automatically when the source code is generated.

2. Put a message into a message queue:
   osMessagePut
   General format: osMessagePut (QueueName, ItemToSend, SendTimeout).

3. Get a message or suspend task execution until the message arrives:
   osMessageGet
   General format: osMessageGet (QueueName, ReceiveTimeout).

4.7.2 Exercise details - overall.

The system task diagram is shown in figure 4.19, containing two tasks and a single queue. This is intended to mimic the action of an alarm detection system that operates as follows:

- The sensor monitoring task checks to see if any parameters have gone into an alarm state. If an alarm is detected this is signalled to an alarming task, transferring the data via a queue. That is the sole function of the monitoring task.
- All alarm handling and processing actions are carried out by the alarming task.
- Interrupts aren't permitted (hence preventing the use of a deferred server).

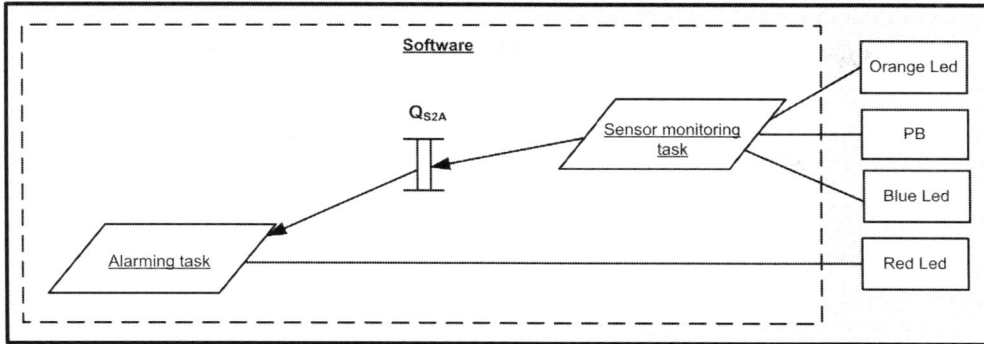

Figure 4.19 System task diagram

For this section of the exercise use the Cube tool to configure the system so that it has one queue, figure 4.20.

Figure 4.20 Queue listing and details in the CubeMX tool.

The queue parameters *Queue Size* and *Item Size* (together with queue name) are set up at configuration time, as shown in figure 4.21. The default values can be changed as required; for this exercise set the queue size to hold one (1) item.

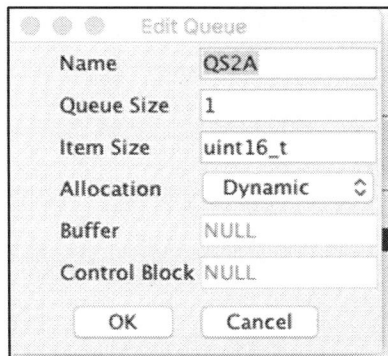

Figure 4.21 Setting up the queue information.

4.7.3 Exercise details - specific aspects.

(a) The queue — detailed features and handling operations.

///

(i) Create a queue.

For our particular example the CubeMX auto-generated code for the queue is:
```
/* Create the queue(s) */
/* definition and creation of QS2A */

osMessageQDef(QS2A, 1, uint16_t);
QS2AHandle = osMessageCreate(osMessageQ(QS2A), NULL);
```

///

(ii) Put a Message to a Queue.

General form: osMessagePut (QueueName, ItemToSend, SendTimeout).
Code form:
osStatus osMessagePut (osMessageQId queue_id, uint32_t info, uint32_t millisec);

```
// param[in]    queue_id    message queue ID obtained with osMessageCreate.
// param[in]    info        message information.
// param[in]    millisec    timeout value or 0 in case of no time-out.
/* return status code that indicates the execution status of the function.   If function is
completed successfully message event occurred, returned value is 0x10 (see the list of
Status and Error codes at the end of this section, specifically osEventMessage).
*/
```

Example:
```
        int         SensorStateMessage = SensorNotInAlarm;
        osStatus    SensorSendState;

        SensorSendState = osMessagePut(QS2AHandle, SensorStateMessage, 1000);
```

///

(iii) Get a Message or Wait for a Message from a Queue.

General form: osMessageGet (QueueName, ReceiveTimeout).
Code form:
osEvent osMessageGet (osMessageQId queue_id, uint32_t millisec);

```
// param[in]    queue_id    message queue ID obtained with osMessageCreate.
// param[in]    millisec    timeout value or 0 in case of no time-out.
// return event information that includes the transmitted data and the message status
code.
```

Example:
```
        osEvent     QreadState;
        int         SensorStateMesssage = SensorNotInAlarm;

        QreadState = osMessageGet(QS2AHandle, 0);
```

///

(iv) Handling the data obtained from the queue.

The handling received data in the Cube-based FreeRTOS implementation is quite different to that of native FreeRTOS work. As such it is _essential_ that you understand the structure of the osEvent variable (in the example above, _QreadState_), as shown below:

typedef struct

```
{
        osStatus            status;     //status value: either an event or an error code

        union
        {
                uint32_t            v;              // message as 32-bit value
                void                *p;             //message or mail as void pointer
                int32_t             signals;        // signal flags
        } value;                                    // event value

        union
        {
                osMailQId           mail_id;    //mail id obtained by osMailCreate
                osMessageQId    message_id;     // message id obtained by osMessageCreate
        } def;

}   osEvent;
```

We can call _osMessageGet_ any time but there's no guarantee that a message will be ready for collection at that time. Thus the first thing to do is to determine that one is actually present. This is performed by checking the value of the _status_ item. When a message is loaded this is automatically set to 0x10 (the CMSIS predefined status code for this is _osEventMessage_), being used as follows:

```
// Check if data is present and action the result of the check
if (QreadState.status == osEventMessage)
{
        /* Code */
}
```

Assuming success, we access the data item _value_ to extract the _actual_ message content. Note that in a union, only _one_ member can hold a value at a time (thus in union _value_ it would be v or *p or _signals_), all being extracted in a similar manner, e.g.:

```
SensorStateMessage = QreadState.value.v;
```

//

(b) Important implementation factors.

Please implement the exercise to conform to the specifications detailed below. Both tasks are to run within infinite loops, having equal priorities.
    Here the LEDs are used to indicate the current operational state of the system.

Blue LED:
• When off, denotes that the push button is _released_.
• When on, denotes that the push button is _pressed_.

Orange LED:
• When off, denotes that the sensor is _Not In Alarm_.
• When on, denotes that the sensor is _In Alarm_.

Red LED:
- Initially turned off, denoting that the Alarming task is in a non-alarm state.
- Is turned on when an *In Alarm* signal is received from the Sensor task.
- Is next turned off when a Not *In Alarm* signal is received from the Sensor task.

(i) Sensor monitoring task.
The key points are as follows:

- A change in the sensor alarm state is mimicked by depressing the push button (*depress* — press followed by release).
- The alarm default state is *Not In Alarm*.
- The first depressing action sets the alarm state to *In Alarm*. This state information is sent as a message to the queue and the Orange Led is turned on.
- The next depressing action sets the alarm state back to *Not In Alarm*. Again, this information is sent to the queue and the Orange Led is turned off.
- The next depressing action once again sets the alarm state to I*n Alarm,* which is then sent to the queue, and so on repeatedly.
- When the PB is pressed the Blue Led is turned on; when released the Led is turned off.
- After a PB press is detected and actioned there is a 250 ms delay before checking the button status again.
- After a PB release is detected and actioned there is a 250 ms delay before checking the button status again.

(ii) Alarming task.
- This gets messages from the queue every 500 ms.
- When an *In Alarm* message is received the Red Led is turned on.
- When a *Not In Alarm* message is received the Red Led is turned off.

4.7.4 Exercise 19 review.

If you've successfully completed this exercise you will:

- See that the queue is easy to implement and straightforward to use.
- Recognize that problems can arise if there are message production/consumption timing mismatches.
- Understand that any unforeseen production/consumption problems must be dealt with safely and securely.
- See that it necessary to specify clearly the system behaviour in the following situations:
  - Sending messages to a full queue.
  - Reading from an empty queue.
- Realize that it is *essential* to define the message sending and receiving requirements of the intercommunicating tasks before implementing the design.
- Appreciate that to ensure reliable, robust queue operations access control (i.e. mutual exclusion) should be included as part of the construct.

4.7.5 CMSIS-RTOS API — List of Status and Error Codes

Status and Error Codes returned by CMSIS-RTOS API functions.

```
enum  osStatus {
  osOK = 0,
  osEventSignal = 0x08,
  osEventMessage = 0x10,
  osEventMail = 0x20,
  osEventTimeout = 0x40,
  osErrorParameter = 0x80,
```

```
  osErrorResource = 0x81,
  osErrorTimeoutResource = 0xC1,
  osErrorISR = 0x82,
  osErrorISRRecursive = 0x83,
  osErrorPriority = 0x84,
  osErrorNoMemory = 0x85,
  osErrorValue = 0x86,
  osErrorOS = 0xFF,
  os_status_reserved = 0x7FFFFFFF
}
```

Description

The Status and Error Codes section lists all the return values that the CMSIS-RTOS functions will return.

Enumeration Type Documentation

enum osStatus

Note

MUST REMAIN UNCHANGED: **osStatus** shall be consistent in every CMSIS-RTOS.

The osStatus enumeration defines the event status and error codes that are returned by the CMSIS-RTOS functions.

Enumerator	
osOK	function completed; no error or event occurred.
osEventSignal	function completed; signal event occurred.
osEventMessage	function completed; message event occurred.
osEventMail	function completed; mail event occurred.
osEventTimeout	function completed; timeout occurred.
osErrorParameter	parameter error: a mandatory parameter was missing or specified an incorrect object.
osErrorResource	resource not available. a specified resource was not available.
osErrorTimeoutResource	resource not available within given time: a specified resource was not available within the timeout period.
osErrorISR	not allowed in ISR context: the function cannot be called from interrupt service routines.
osErrorISRRecursive	function called multiple times from ISR with same object.
osErrorPriority	system cannot determine priority or thread has illegal priority.
osErrorNoMemory	system is out of memory: it was impossible to allocate or reserve memory for the operation.
osErrorValue	value of a parameter is out of range.
osErrorOS	unspecified RTOS error: run-time error but no other error message fits.
os_status_reserved	prevent from enum down-size compiler optimization.

4.8 Exercise 20 - Use mailboxes for data transfer with task synchronization.

Fundamental purpose of the exercise: To show how the mailbox is used to support data transfer between tasks at designated synchronization points.

4.8.1 Introduction to the mailbox.

The mailbox is a mechanism that allows tasks to communicate by sending and receiving sequential data messages at predefined synchronization points.

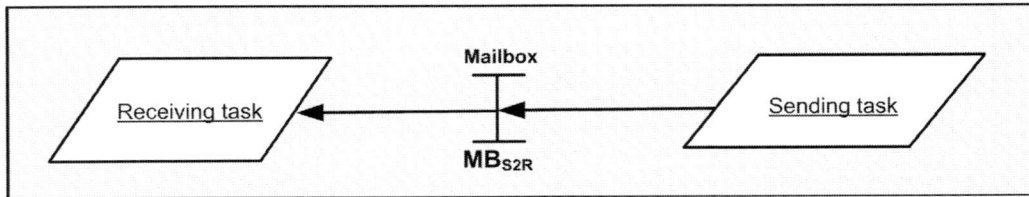

Figure 4.22 Mailbox symbol

The symbol used in figure 4.22 indicates that message transfer is unilateral (which takes place during task synchronization). A mailbox can also be constructed to support bilateral data transfer during synchronization (though in practice this isn't met very often).
    The key components of the mailbox (for a two-task interaction) are shown in figure 4.23, consisting of:

- A queue to handle the messages (for this exercise set the queue size to 1).
- A mutex, used to provide access protection (mutual exclusion) for the queue.
- Two semaphores, used to support bilateral task synchronization.

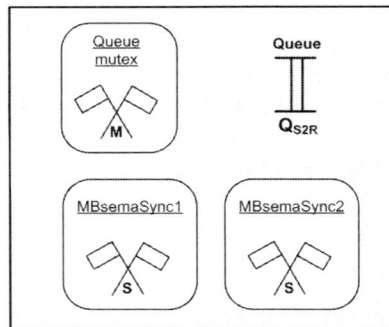

Figure 4.23 Mailbox components

Two APIs are needed by the tasks in order to use the mailbox:

- Post (data) - in the task sending the data.
- Pend (data) - in the task receiving the data.

Synchronization and data transfer actions are shown in the activity diagram of figure 4.24.

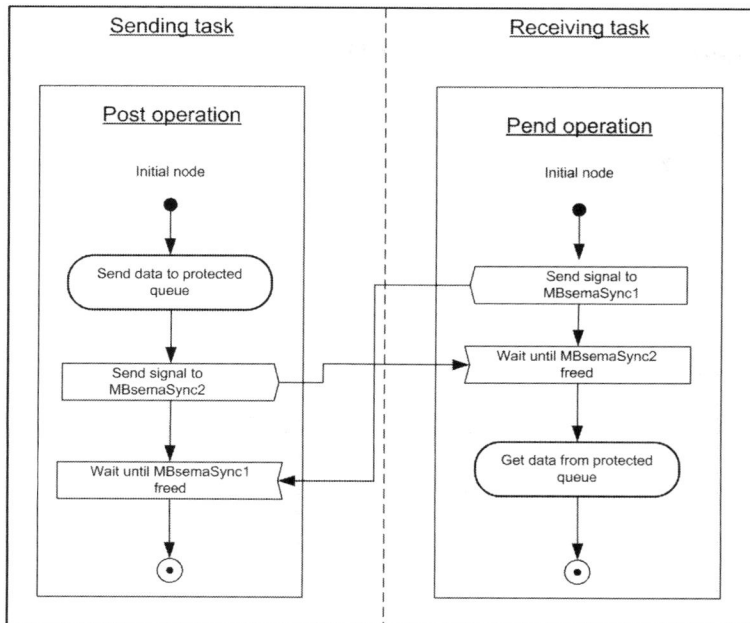

Figure 4.24 Activity diagram showing the mailbox operation

The term 'protected queue' denotes that (in this case) access to the queue is controlled by a mutex.
    For this exercise _you_ have to design all the software that implements the access APIs.

4.8.2 Building the mailbox.

Build the mailbox as a distinct modular component (as per exercise 18) consisting of two files: a .h and a corresponding .c. The operations listed below must be encapsulated in the .c file:

(a) Mutex.
  • Mutex definition.
  • Mutex creation.
  • Mutex acquisition and release.
(b) Semaphore.
  • Semaphore definition.
  • Semaphore creation.
  • Semaphore wait and release.
(c) Queue.
  • Queue definition.
  • Queue creation.
  • Queue message put and get.

All these functions, and their use, have already been covered in earlier exercises.
    The .h file is used to export your own design Post and Pend functions for use by the tasks.

If you wish to experiment with FreeRTOS native constructs see the appendix to this exercise for a listing of relevant items.

4.8.3 Exercise details.

The software system consists of two tasks and one mailbox, figure 4.25.

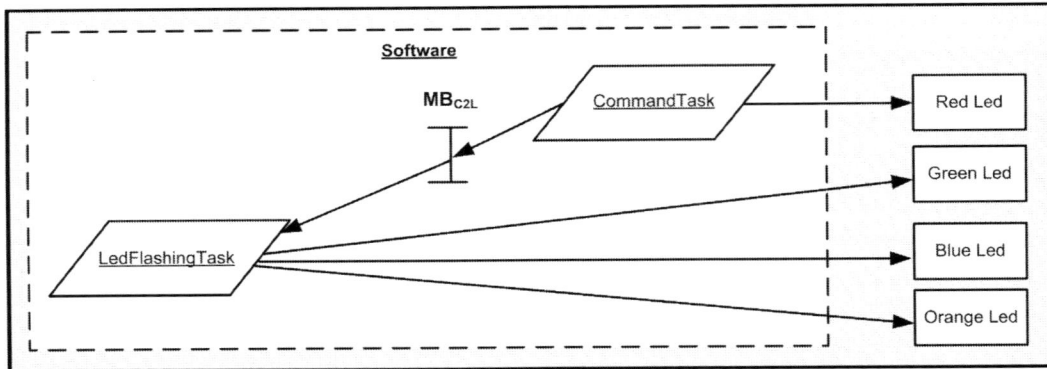

Figure 4.25 System task diagram

Here the LedFlashingTask controls the four Leds, specific operations being set by messages received from the command task.
 The overall required behaviour of the software is as follows:

1. Command task.
Loop forever:
        Flash the Red Led for 10 seconds at a 1Hz. rate.
        Post command to the mailbox (call this 'sync1').
        Flash the Red Led for 5 seconds at a 10Hz. rate.
        Post command to the mailbox (call this 'sync2').
End loop.

2. Led flashing task.
Loop forever:
        Flash the Green Led for 5 seconds at a 10Hz. rate.
        Pend on mailbox.
        Act on message.
        Flash the Green Led for 10 seconds at a 1Hz. rate.
        Pend on mailbox.
        Act on message.
End loop.

3. Response by the Led flashing task to the incoming message.
If the message is sync1 then:
        TurnOrangeLedOn;
        TurnBlueLedOff;
Else if the message is sync2 then:
        TurnBlueLedOn;
        TurnOrangeLedOff;

This will produce a loop periodic time of 20 seconds. The resulting Led operations are as shown in figure 4.26, after the loop has been executed for the first time. A useful check: before you run the software for the first time predict what you expect to see on this first loop.

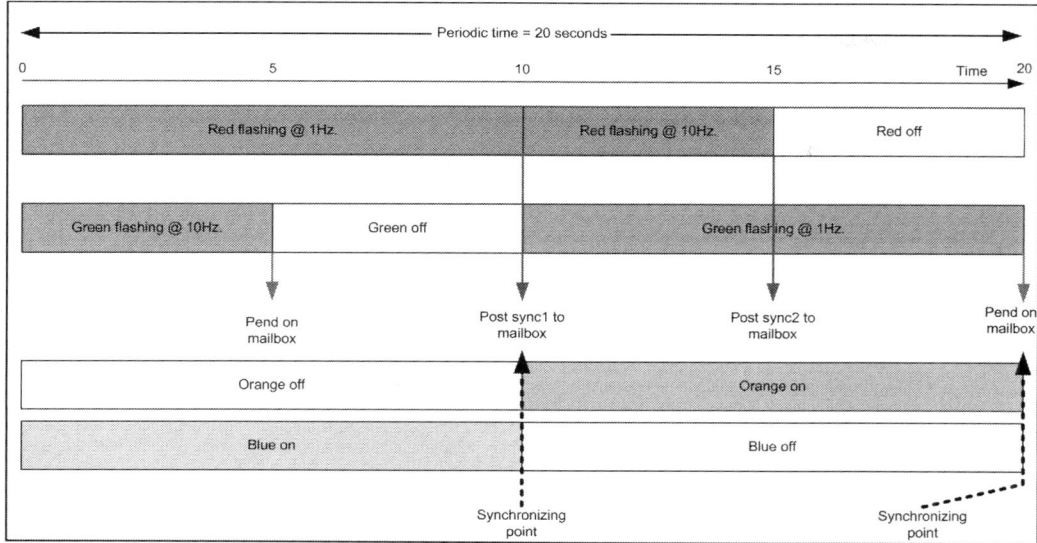

Figure 4.26 Timing diagram of Led operations

4.8.4 Exercise 20 review.

This is a challenging exercise in that it requires you to build a component that uses the major basic inter-task communication constructs: semaphore, mutex and queue. If you've successfully completed it you will:

- See precisely how the mailbox is intended to work.
- Realize that in the 0-10 second run the LedFlashingTask reaches the synchronization point first ('Pend') and then waits for the other task ('Post'). In the 10-20 second run the CommandTask reaches the synchronization point first ('Post') and then waits for the LedFlashingTask ('Pend').
- Have acquired a very good understanding of the core communication constructs of multitasking designs.
- Be able to use this information to build mailboxes in other RTOSs.
- Appreciate that the 'modular' structure used here can form the basis of a reusable software component.
- See that the visibility of these components to tasks can be controlled via the use of include directives (i.e. if a task doesn't *include* the mailbox.h file it can't use that component). This can significantly increase the robustness of the software; unauthorised accesses can be completely eliminated.

Exercise 20 appendix - using FreeRTOS APIs to construct the mailbox.

//
MUTEX

```
/* Definition of the mutex */
xSemaphoreHandle   GlobalMBqueueMutex        = NULL;

/* Creation of the mutex */
GlobalMBqueueMutex = xSemaphoreCreateMutex();

/* Using the mutex  -  controlling access to the queue*/

xSemaphoreTake (GlobalMBqueueMutex, MutexWaitingTime);  // lock mutex
        Queue Send or Receive operation (see below)
xSemaphoreGive (GlobalMBqueueMutex ); // unlock mutex
```

//

//
QUEUE

```
/* Definition of the queue parameters */
const int GlobalMBqueueLength        = 1;
const int GlobalMBqueueItemSize   = 4;

/* Definition of the queue */
 xQueueHandle        GlobalMBqueue = NULL;

/* Creation of the queue */
GlobalMBqueue = xQueueCreate (GlobalMBqueueLength, GlobalMBqueueItemSize);

/* Using the queue  —  the sending operation */
        xQueueSendToBack (GlobalMBqueue, &OutgoingMessage, WaitingTime);

/* Using the queue  —  the receiving operation */
        QueueReadResult = xQueueReceive (GlobalMBqueue, &QueueData, WaitingTime);
```
//

//
SEMAPHORE

```
/* Definition of the semaphores */
xSemaphoreHandle   GlobalMBSemaSync1 = NULL;
xSemaphoreHandle   GlobalMBSemaSync2 = NULL;

/* Creation of the semaphores */
vSemaphoreCreateBinary (GlobalMBSemaSync1);
vSemaphoreCreateBinary (GlobalMBSemaSync2);

/* Using the semaphores in the posting task */
* Synchronize with the other task */
xSemaphoreGive (GlobalMBSemaSync2 );                // signal (release) semaphore 2
xSemaphoreTake (GlobalMBSemaSync1, SemaWaitingTime);      // wait on semaphore 1

/* Using the semaphores in the pending task */
/* Synchronize with the other task */
xSemaphoreGive (GlobalMBSemaSync1 );                // signal (release) semaphore 1
xSemaphoreTake (GlobalMBSemaSync2, SemaWaitingTime);      // wait on semaphore 2
```
//

4.9 Exercise 21 - Implement a push-button generated interrupt service routine.

Fundamental purposes of the exercise: to learn how to implement a push-button generated interrupt service routine (ISR).

4.9.1 Introduction to the problem.

Our objective with this exercise is to implement the system 'task' diagram of figure 4.27.

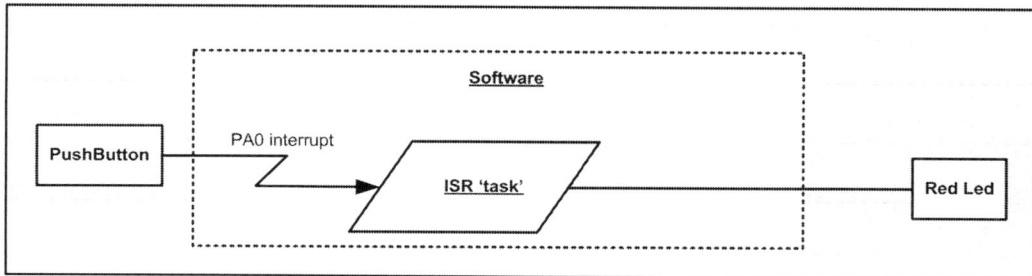

Figure 4.27 Basic ISR system task diagram

An ISR can be regarded as a task because, when invoked, it normally runs (quasi)concurrently with the rest of the software. In our example the ISR is activated by a signal generated when the on-board *User* push-button is pressed. This is fed to pin 23 (PA0) of the micro, which then raises a hardware interrupt request internally in the chip. The software of the ISR is launched automatically at this point — you don't have to write any code to start it. You do, of course, have to define exactly what the ISR does when it's invoked. This is done by inserting your own code into the body of a Cube-generated ISR code skeleton. Once this is completed (and all machine code has been downloaded to the target board) then a single press of the push-button starts the execution of your ISR code.

4.9.2 Using CubeMX to generate the ISR skeleton code.

Create a new Cube project in the usual way, but now configure PA0 to be 'GPIO-EXTI0', figure 4.28.

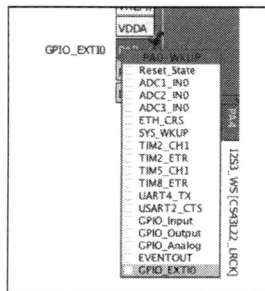

Figure 4.28 Setting of pin PA0

Check the configuration details are as shown in figure 4.29.

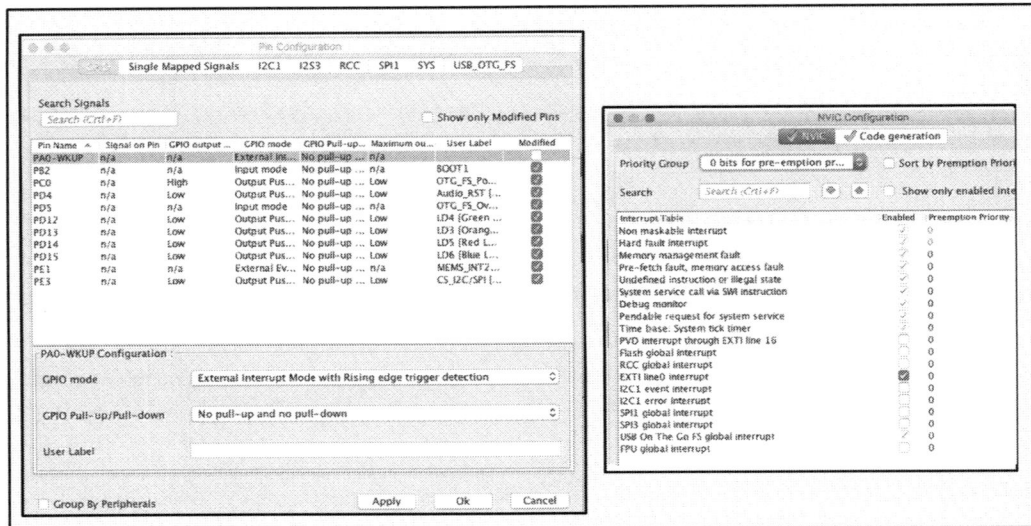

Figure 4.29 Project GPIO/NVIC pin configurations

Now generate the project code and find the stm32f4xx_it.C file. Open this file and search for the ISR skeleton code, figure 4.30.

```
72  /**
73   * @brief This function handles EXTI line0 interrupt.
74   */
75  void EXTI0_IRQHandler(void)
76  {
77    /* USER CODE BEGIN EXTI0_IRQn 0 */
78
79    /* USER CODE END EXTI0_IRQn 0 */
80    HAL_GPIO_EXTI_IRQHandler(GPIO_PIN_0);
81    /* USER CODE BEGIN EXTI0_IRQn 1 */
82
83    /* USER CODE END EXTI0_IRQn 1 */
84  }
85
```

Figure 4.30 ISR skeleton code

This shows clearly where you should insert your own ISR code.

4.9.3 Exercise details.

Embedded designers use interrupt service routines for two main reasons. First, such ISRs provide fast response to external real-world aperiodic events. Second, they can be used to emulate the periodic tasking of a simple time-driven RTOS. This, which I call 'poor-man's

Real-Time Operating Systems Book 2 - The Practice

concurrency', is where a timer routine fires off ISRs at predefined periodic times; each ISR represents a task.

In general, non-RTOS embedded designs consist of a set of ISRs and a background loop. This can be modelled as shown in figure 4.31.

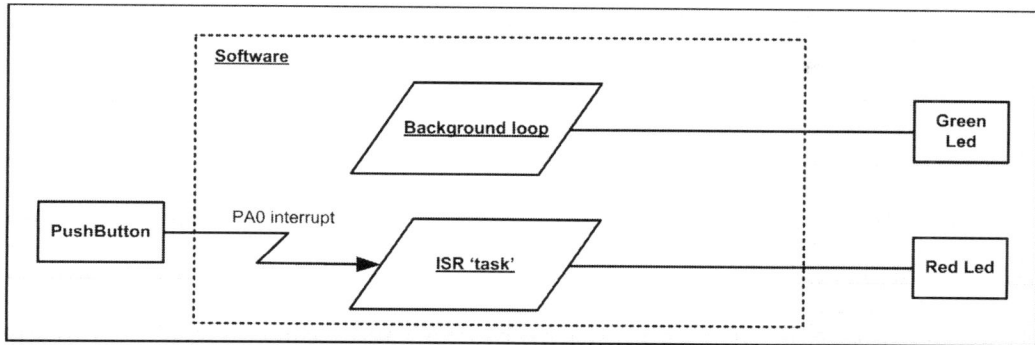

Figure 4.31 System 'tasking' diagram

The background loop software is, of course, that contained in the main function (in main.c).

This purpose of this exercise is to implement the task design of figure 4.31. To create the background loop insert code in main's infinite loop, in this case to toggle the Green Led (this will let you see that the loop is running correctly). For the ISR, insert your own code as shown below:

```
///////////////////////////////////////////////////////////////////////////////////
void EXTI0_IRQHandler(void)
{
  /* USER CODE BEGIN EXTI0_IRQn 0 */
        HAL_GPIO_TogglePin(GPIOD, GPIO_PIN_14);
  /* USER CODE END EXTI0_IRQn 0 */
  HAL_GPIO_EXTI_IRQHandler(GPIO_PIN_0);
  /* USER CODE BEGIN EXTI0_IRQn 1 */

  /* USER CODE END EXTI0_IRQn 1 */
}
///////////////////////////////////////////////////////////////////////////////////
```

When the resulting machine code is executed in the target you should find that:

• The Green Led flashes in accordance with your code of main.
• The Red Led toggles once for each press of the User push-button.

If you are concerned about the effects of switch bounce you can always add some debounce software to the ISR code.

A final point. Look through the code of main.c to find the following interrupt-related initialization code:

```
/* EXTI interrupt init*/
HAL_NVIC_SetPriority(EXTI0_IRQn, 0, 0);
HAL_NVIC_EnableIRQ(EXTI0_IRQn);
```

The first function (HAL_NVIC_SetPriority) sets the priority of the designated interrupt, the general form being:

HAL_NVIC_SetPriority(External_Interrupt_Number, Preemption_Priority, Sub_Priority);

There are two different kinds of priorities: preemption priorities (or just priorities) and sub priorities. The rules governing their operation are as follows:

- Normally the task with the highest priority gets executed first.
- When a number of interrupts have the same priority, then the one with the highest sub priority will be executed first.
- If all interrupts both have same priority *and* sub priority, then these are executed on a first-come first-served basis.

(i) The preemption priority for an IRQ channel:
- This parameter can be a value between 0 and 15
- A lower priority value indicates a higher priority

(ii) The sub priority level for an IRQ channel:
- This parameter can be a value between 0 and 15
- A lower priority value indicates a higher priority.

Observe that by default the EXTI0 interrupt is set to have the highest priority level (zero, 0).

4.9.4 Exercise 21 review.

You should now:

- See that the CubeMX facilities make it really very simple to implement interrupts.
- Know where to find the cube-generated code.
- Understand the nature and structure of this code.
- Realize that this code handles the ISR planting/vectoring aspects and also associates the ISR with a specific source signal.
- Appreciate the difference between the code needed to set up an ISR and that required to implement the actual response to the interrupt signal.

4.10 Exercise 22 - Demonstrate why ISRs should be as fast as possible.

Fundamental purposes of the exercise: to show that using lengthy interrupt-driven aperiodic tasks in multitasking designs can seriously affect system temporal behaviour

4.10.1 Exercise overview and timing details.

Implement the design of figure 4.32, which consists of two periodic tasks and an ISR-driven 'aperiodic' one.

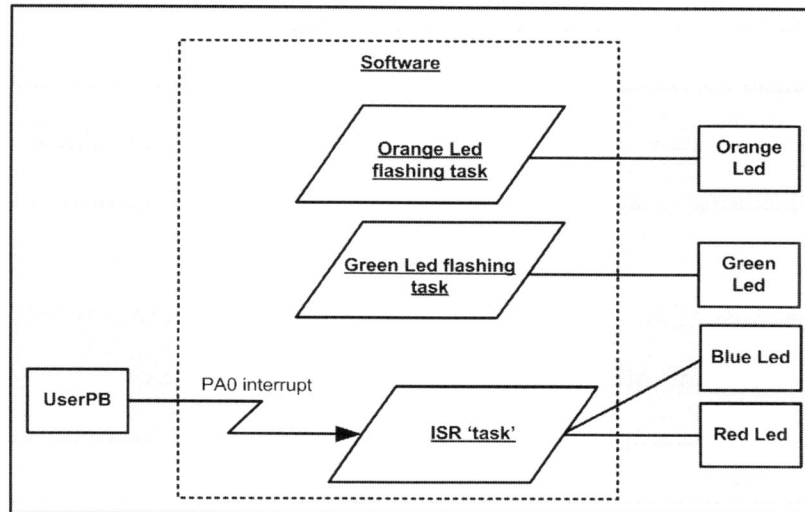

Figure 4.32 System tasking diagram

The Orange and Green Leds are activated by periodic tasks whilst the Blue and Red Leds are driven by the ISR aperiodic task. Normally we use interrupts to provide fast responses to specific signals (either hardware or software-generated); thus ISRs usually have higher priorities than the periodic tasks so that they can preempt them.

One of the great strengths of periodic tasks is that their temporal behaviour is reasonably predictable (depending on the implementation, of course). Unfortunately this is not the case for aperiodic tasks; one significant problem with interrupt signals is that their arrivals are pretty-well random. As a result the mixing of periodic and aperiodic tasks in a system produces behaviour that's highly unpredictable; everything depends on *what* is happening when the interrupt arrives. This would appear to be so self-evident that it hardly needs saying. If only! Too often designers of embedded systems use multiple interrupts in a very casual, almost unthinking, manner. But if you know that aperiodic tasking (the 'randoms') can play havoc with timing behaviour, you aren't likely to fall into that trap. This exercise sets out to reinforce this point by demonstrating just how much disruption can be produced by an interrupt-driven task.

The important timings for the tasks are as follows:

Orange Led flashing task: Period - 2 secs.   Duration - 500 ms   Normal priority
Green Led flashing task: Period - 4 secs.   Duration - 500 ms   Normal priority
ISR task: Aperiodic   Duration - 4 secs.

The periodic tasks are to run as shown in figure 4.33 where the flashing rate for each Led is to be 10Hz. It isn't necessary to have precise flashing timings for this exercise; good approximations are sufficient.

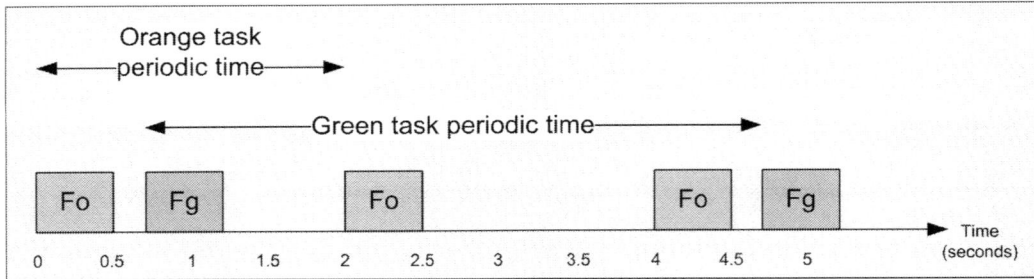

Figure 4.33 Timing diagram of Led flashing operations (periodic tasks)

Observe that the Green task is offset by 700 milliseconds relative to the Orange task. There are various ways to produce this offset; one very simple way is to have a 700 millisecond delay in the code of the Green task before entering its infinite loop.

The required operation of the ISR task (the aperiodic), when launched, is as shown in figure 4.34.

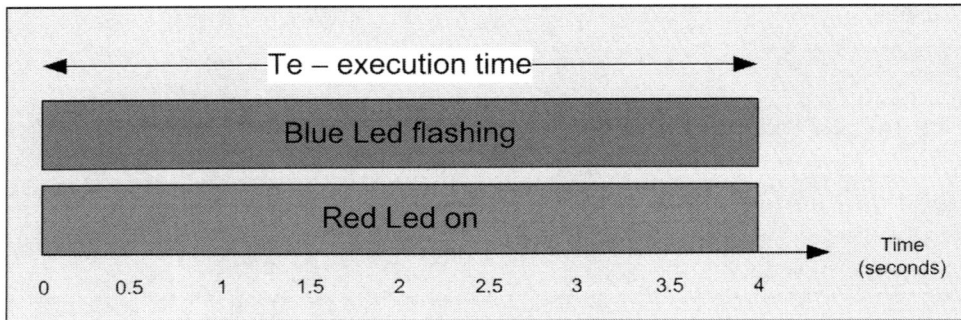

Figure 4.34 Timing diagram of Led operations (ISR-driven task)

When the user pushbutton is pressed the Red Led is to be turned on and the Blue Led is to start flashing at a 10 Hz. rate. After four seconds the Leds are to be turned off.

The Red Led operation mimics the action of giving visual feedback (to the user) that the button press has been accepted. Flashing the Blue Led mimics the execution of the code of an ISR.

Compile and downloaded the code to the board; then execute it to check out the correctness of the periodic task timing and operations. Next, invoke the interrupt operation using the pushbutton signal and observe the result. Repeat this numerous times to demonstrate variations in system behaviour (i.e. press during the flashing of the Orange Led, during the flashing of the Red Led, and when both Leds are off).

4.10.2 Some CubeMX issues.

There aren't any new CubeMX design features here; all aspects have been covered in earlier exercises. However, at the time of writing there is a bug in the tool; when the design contains both interrupts and periodic tasks it generates incorrect code. Check out the following items.

(a) Initialization code in main.c

Make sure that the following initialisation code is present in the file (if not, you can do a cut-and-paste job from the previous exercise):

```
/* EXTI interrupt init*/
HAL_NVIC_SetPriority(EXTI0_IRQn, 0, 0);
HAL_NVIC_EnableIRQ(EXTI0_IRQn);
}
```

(b) Task code in stm32f4xx-it.c

Check that the ISR function code skeleton is present in this file (if not do a cut-and-paste job as noted above).

```
void EXTI0_IRQHandler(void)
{
  /* USER CODE BEGIN EXTI0_IRQn 0 */

  /* USER CODE END EXTI0_IRQn 0 */
  HAL_GPIO_EXTI_IRQHandler(GPIO_PIN_0);
  /* USER CODE BEGIN EXTI0_IRQn 1 */

  /* USER CODE END EXTI0_IRQn 1 */
}
```

IMPORTANT NOTE: if you regenerate the source files from CubeMX these will be deleted unless you place them in a 'User Code' section!

4.10.3 Exercise 22 review.

Although the timing used for the various tasks may be unrealistic, it does allow you to see the extent of the problem. Changing the times (e.g. making them much shorter) does not make the problems go away; the effects can still be quite serious.
  The important lessons to take away from this exercise are as follows:

- When designs mix periodic and aperiodic tasks the temporal performance is unpredictable (in some situations best case/worst-case scenarios *can* be deduced).
- Specific effects due to launching an aperiodic task depend entirely on the state of the system at that time.
- Resulting timing variations can be described only in statistical, not deterministic, terms.
- If you use aperiodic tasks in your design you *should* always evaluate their possible effects on temporal performance.
- An increase in the number of interrupt-driven aperiodic tasks in your designs leads to greater uncertainty in system temporal behaviour.
- Any variation in the timing performance of the periodic tasks may lead to problems in the real world (e.g. late opening of a valve, jitter in a control loop, etc.).
- Where possible, the use of interrupt-driven tasks should be minimized. The alternative, polling for events, may be sufficient in many applications.

4.11 Exercise 23 - Minimize ISR disruptions by using deferred servers.

Fundamental purposes of the exercise: to show how to minimize the effects of interrupt-driven aperiodic tasks by using the deferred server technique.

4.11.1 Deferring responses to interrupt signals.

When an interrupt is generated by a critical function — fuel tank fire detection, vehicle crash, ground proximity warning, etc. — then it must be actioned as quickly as possible. All other software actions must be subordinated to this one.   Otherwise you're likely to end up in a catastrophic situation: major physical damage and perhaps loss of life. However, in many cases the initial response to an interrupt must be fast but the bulk of the work is much less critical. Take the case, for example, where a ship's navigating officer requests a display update of all navigation data.   Good HMI design calls for a fast acknowledgement of the request (we've all experienced the frustration of dealing with slow HMIs!).   But it doesn't mean that the display details have to be updated as quickly; it is likely that a slower rate is perfectly acceptable. Thus we can defer the bulk of the work, separating this out from the ISR itself. By keeping the ISR short and simple it can be very fast in operation, thus minimising its impact of system performance. The deferred work can be allocated to a separate task, run by the scheduler at an appropriate priority level.   And linking the two is a unilateral synchronization mechanism, figure 4.35.

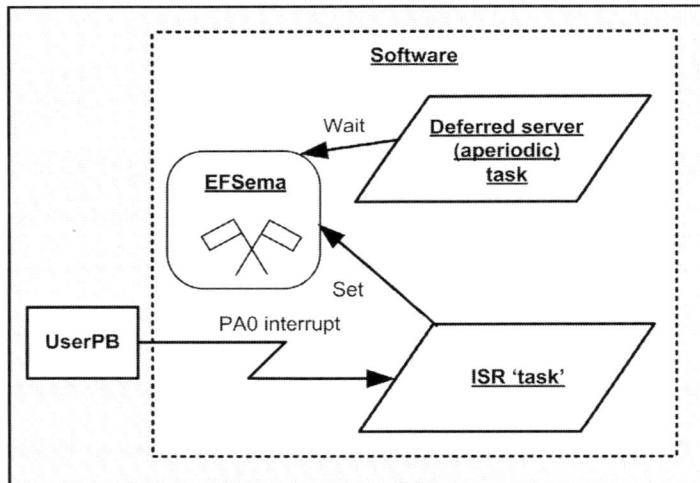

Figure 4.35 The deferred server structure

The deferred server task spends most of its time suspended, waiting for the semaphore to be released ('Set'). This happens when the interrupt activates its ISR, which then generates a *Set* call to the semaphore. This readies the server task and places it in the ready queue. The point at which it is dispatched depends on its defined priority, the current state of the ready queue and the RTOS scheduling policy.

4.11.2 Exercise overview and timing details.

Implement the design of figure 4.36, which consists of two periodic tasks, a single aperiodic server task and an interrupt-driven one.

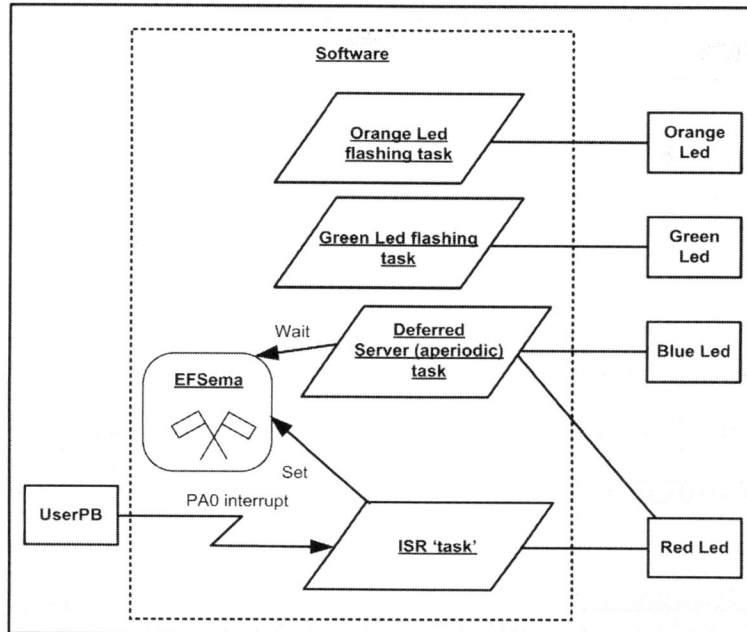

Figure 4.36 System tasking diagram

The important timings for the tasks are as follows:

Orange Led flashing task: Period - 2 secs. Flashing duration - 500 ms Normal priority
Green Led flashing task: Period - 4 secs. Flashing duration - 500 ms Normal priority
Deferred Server task: Aperiodic   Priority below normal.
ISR task: Aperiodic   Execution time - minimal. Priority: default to highest.

The Green and Orange tasks are to be executed exactly the same as they were in exercise 22 (repeated here, figure 4.37).

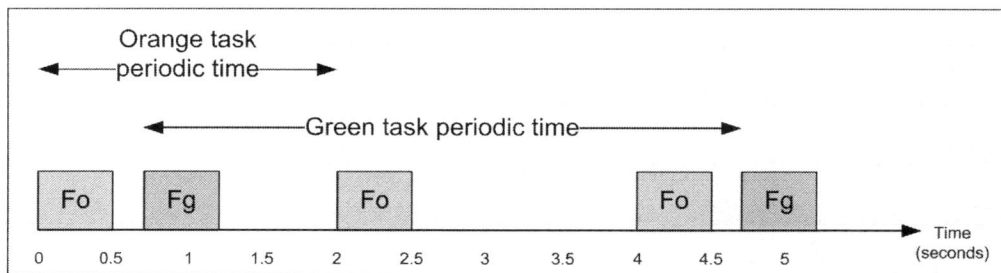

Figure 4.37 Timing information — Periodic tasks

The desired interaction between the ISR and the Deferred Server task (and their effects on the Red Led) is shown in figure 4.38:

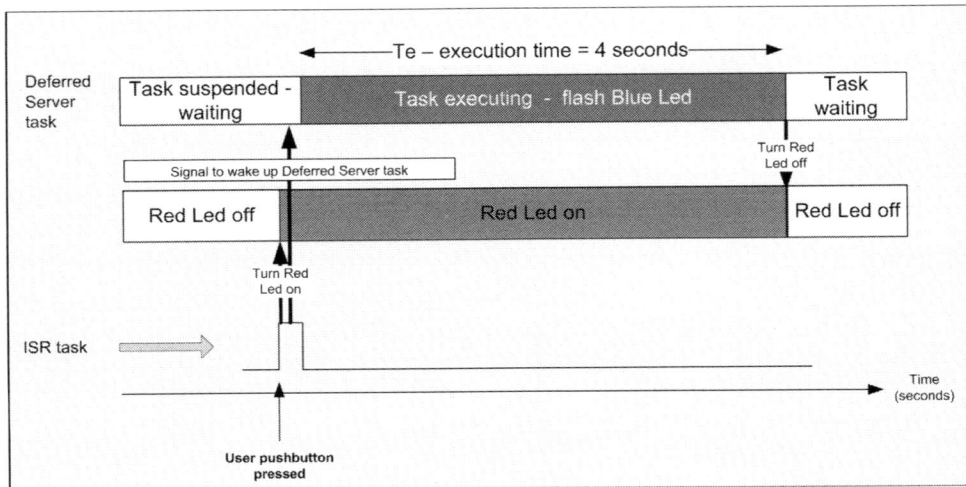

Figure 4.38 Basic interactions of the ISR and Deferred Server tasks.

This is the behaviour to be expected when the Green and Orange tasks are inhibited, the details being as follows:

- After the Deferred Server (DS) task is set running it immediately suspends at the defined synchronization point.
- When the user pushbutton is pressed it activates the ISR.
- As the ISR starts it turns the Red Led on, signals the DS task via the synchronization mechanism and then completes.
- The DS task gets readied but can't begin executing until the ISR finishes (owing to the priority settings).
- The DS task now runs back round to wait at the synchronization point, the last action being to turn the Red Led off.

Thus the Red Led is illuminated from the moment the ISR is activated to the completion of the DS task. We can use this as a measure the total execution time of the DS task.

Predict the behaviour of the system when the periodic (Orange and Green) tasks are active. Also, estimate the minimum and maximum actual total execution times of the server task. Then, when you've downloaded the machine code to the target, run the system and compare reality with predictions. Contrast the behaviour now with that of the previous exercise.

4.11.3 Code generation and run-time aspects.

You will have to modify your Cube-generated code as described in the previous exercise, a fairly straightforward change. Most implementation aspects have been covered in previous exercises, so you shouldn't have problems in producing the design. The exercise calls for the use of a unilateral synchronization mechanism (see exercise 14) to allow the ISR to control the Deferred Server task. Here we'll use a semaphore, not a mutex, to implement synchronization. The reason for using this approach is that it (the semaphore) is set by one task but cleared by a different one. Also, for reasons explained below, we choose to use FreeRTOS, not Cube-generated, APIs. Note the following implementation aspects:

1. When the semaphore is created it must be initialized to a blocked (Wait) state. The relevant APIs are *vSemaphoreCreateBinary* followed by *xSemaphoreTake* (with a block time set to portMAX_DELAY).
2. It is released ('Set') by the ISR 'task', using the FreeRTOS API *xSemaphoreGiveFromISR* (see http://www.freertos.org/a00124.html).
3. The Deferred Server task waits in a blocked state until the semaphore is released. It does this by issuing a 'Wait' call, *xSemaphoreTake,* the moment it begins to execute (should be the first code statement in the task's infinite loop).
4. When the Deferred Server task loops back and makes the next 'Wait' call it blocks, once more waiting to be released.

There isn't a unique design solution to these requirements. Our preferred method is to:

- Build the synchronizing component as a 'module', using a .h/.c file combination.
- Hide and protect all direct semaphore operations within this module.
- Provide interface functions for Create, Wait and Set operations.

This results in a robust, testable and reliable code structure.
  Using this approach, the following code would be placed in the ISR:

```
/* ===================================================== */
* @brief This function handles EXTI line0 interrupt.
*/

void EXTI0_IRQHandler(void)
{
  /* USER CODE BEGIN EXTI0_IRQn 0 */

        SetEFSema1(); // Releases the semaphore
.
./* Note: in this design SetEFSema() calls xSemaphoreGiveFromISR  */
.
/* ===================================================== */
```

Within the Deferred Server task:
```
/* ========================================== */

/* StartDeferredServerTask function */

void StartDeferredServerTask(void const * argument)
{

  /* USER CODE BEGIN 5 */
.
.
  /* Infinite loop */
  for(;;)
      {
              WaitEFSema1(); // Blocks on the semaphore
.

/* ========================================== */
```

4.11.4 Exercise 23 review.

The key points to take from the last two exercises are as follows:

- Aperiodic tasks activated by 'random' signals affect the normal temporal behaviour of the periodic tasks.

- Critical tasks must be actioned immediately the activating signal arrives.
- Their effect on system timing can be difficult to predict, especially when there are a number of such tasks.
- In such circumstances it is impossible to guarantee predictable behaviour.
- Less-critical tasks can have their execution deferred (as long as the overall system response is acceptable).
- By executing aperiodic tasks under the control of the scheduler, temporal unpredictability can be minimized.
- Systems that have high processor utilization are especially sensitive to the use of aperiodic tasking.

Part 3

Visualization of software behaviour using Tracealyzer

This section has just one objective; to show you the value of using run-time recording and analysis tools when developing RTOS-based software.

The material given here consists of a series of run-time recordings captured using the Percepio Tracealyzer tool (introduced in Book 1). These describe the behaviour of software in execution, covering all major aspects of multitasking elements.

Tracealyzer is, for this work, the tool of choice, for a number of reasons:

- It enables us to quickly and easily gather useful and meaningful behavioural aspects of multitasking software.
- It is easy and straightforward to integrate it into our existing development environment.
- A specific variant is available for use with FreeRTOS.
- Percepio have provided a raft of support material: videos, white papers, webinars, application notes, etc.

It is possible to get a time-limited copy of Tracealyzer for evaluation purposes. I recommend that you consider downloading this so that you can analyze your own exercise results in great detail. Also, a reduced-cost version is available for educational purposes.

Please be aware that this section does not set out to be a tool tutorial. You can find comprehensive guidance on all aspects of Tracealyzer on the Percepio website; make good use of it. However, what *is* given here is sufficient to demonstrate the key points of the various recordings.

The section begins with a guide to integrating Tracealyzer into your existing software/hardware environment. This has been provided to help you get up and running quickly. Following this is a set of exercises that cover the salient aspects of multitasking software in execution. Please (please!) carry out all these exercises, investigating them in detail; it will truly deepen your understanding of the subject. Moreover, I strongly urge you to also check out all exercises covered in part 2 of the book; I believe it will expand your grasp of the subject.

Important web site:

http://percepio.com/gettingstarted

Chapter 5

Tracealyzer integration and setup guide.

5.1 Trapealyzer exercise 1 - Introduction to Tracealyzer.

The purpose of this section is act as a guide for the installation, integration and configuration of Tracealyzer on STM32F4 microcontrollers running FreeRTOS. It includes just enough material to get your project working correctly.

However, if needed, you can find comprehensive details at:

https://percepio.com/docs/FreeRTOS/manual

Consider that to be <u>the</u> primary source of information and thus overrides anything written here (moreover, software updates to the Tracealyzer tool may also raise conflicts).
   You need to carry out four key actions in order to produce successful tool operation:

(a) Incorporate the Percepio Trace Recorder Library into your project.
(b) Integrate FreeRTOS with the Tracealyzer recorder.
(c) Configure the CubeMX project to meet the tool needs.
(d) Adapt the project source code to initialize/start trace recordings.

5.2. Incorporating the Trace Recorder Library.

5.2.1 Adding the recorder library to the project.

Overall details of the library can be found at:
       https://percepio.com/docs/FreeRTOS/manual/Recorder.html#
Download this from the Percepio site
       https://percepio.com/download/

The library is delivered as a single folder, figure 5.1:

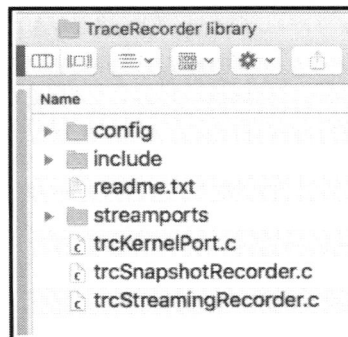

Figure 5.1 Trace recorder library contents

This view highlights the key source files that form part of the recorder library package. Two other important factors are the folder 'config' and 'include' (for the moment ignore the 'streamports' folder).
A more detailed view of its contents is shown in figure 5.2 below:

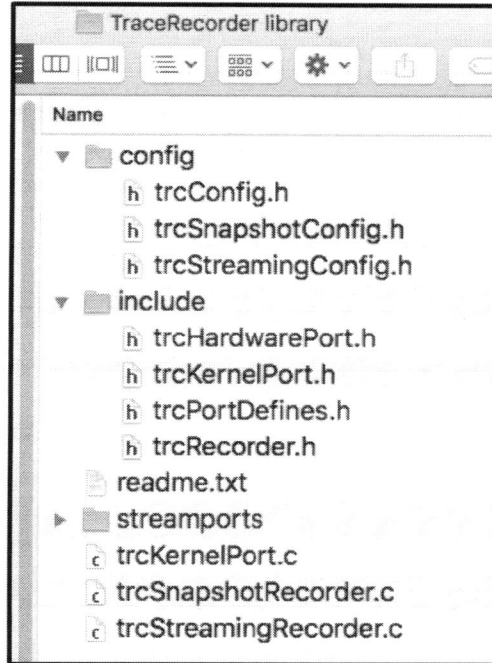

Figure 5.2 Trace recorder library contents - more detailed

The config, include and source files need to be added to your project, at suitable locations. There isn't a specific way of doing this as there are a variety of options (depending on both personal choices and the project IDE). However it is essential that the project 'sees' all the additional files. Again, techniques for doing this are project-specific, one example being that given in figure 5.3 for project 'Lab 2'.
This project uses the Keil μVision IDE.

5.2.2 Configuring the library files for your system.

There are three configuration files, as you can see from figure 5.2. In the first part of this work we'll use the 'snapshot' mode, so for present ignore 'trcStreamingConfig.h'. Now, please read the following documents and follow the configuration information given there:

https://percepio.com/docs/FreeRTOS/manual/Recorder.html#config
https://percepio.com/docs/FreeRTOS/manual/Recorder.html#tracedetails

For ARM Cortex-M devices the recorder needs the ARM's CMSIS library. To ensure this is accessible from the recorder code, we recommend including the processor's header file in **trcConfig.h,** as follows:

#include "stm32f407xx.h"

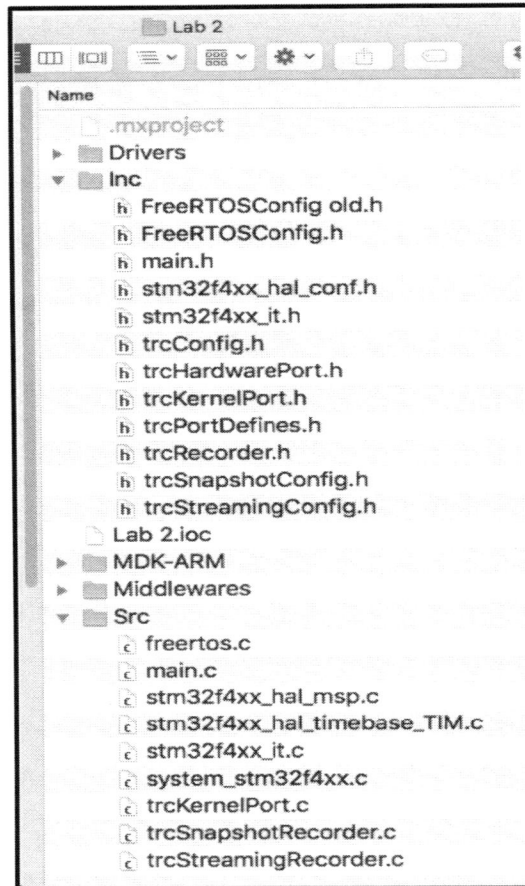

Figure 5.3 Example project files

5.2.3 Enabling the trace recorder.

In your *FreeRTOSConfig.h* file there is a "master switch" for the trace recorder. To make sure that the recorder is enabled, check that the it includes the following setting:

#define configUSE_TRACE_FACILITY 1

(Note: if you set this to 0 the trace recorder is completely disabled and excluded from the build).

5.3. Integrating FreeRTOS with the Tracealyzer recorder.

Insert the following in *FreeRTOSConfig.h*, at the end of the file in a user code defines section:

```
/* USER CODE BEGIN Defines */
/////////////////////////////////
/* Integrates the Tracealyzer recorder with FreeRTOS */
#if ( configUSE_TRACE_FACILITY == 1 )
#include "trcRecorder.h"
#endif
/////////////////////////////////
/* USER CODE END Defines */
```

5.4. Configuring the CubeMX project to meet the tool needs.

In the CubeMX FreeRTOS Config Parameters:

(1) Set each task minimal stack size to 512.
(2) Set total heap size to 32000.
(3) Set USE_TRACE_FACILITY to Enabled.

5.5. Adapting the project source code to initialize/start trace recordings.

Tracealyzer has two recording modes: Snapshot and Streaming.

https://percepio.com/docs/FreeRTOS/manual/
Recorder.html#Trace_Recorder_Library_Snapshot_Mode

https://percepio.com/docs/FreeRTOS/manual/
Recorder.html#Trace_Recorder_Library_Streaming_Mode

5.5.1 Adapting for the Snapshot mode of operation.

This section briefly explains how to adapt your source code for the Snapshot mode. The process is quite simple; first, initialize the system, then start the trace recorder.

(a) To initialize *and* start the recording.

Call *vTraceEnable(TRC_START);* in your main function

(b) To initialize the recorder and start tracing sometime later.

First, to initialize the recorder, Call *vTraceEnable(TRC_INIT);* in your main function. Then to start tracing call *vTraceEnable(TRC_START);* at the desired point in the code.
   Very important note: the call must be made *after* the initial hardware setup but *before* any RTOS objects (tasks etc.) have been created. as for example:

https://percepio.com/docs/FreeRTOS/manual/Recorder.html#vtraceenable

```
///////////////////////////////////////////////////////////////////////////////////////////////////////
int main(void)
{

 /* Reset of all peripherals, Initializes the Flash interface and the Systick. */
 HAL_Init();

/* Configure the system clock */
```

```
SystemClock_Config();

/* USER CODE BEGIN SysInit */
    vTraceEnable(TRC_INIT);
    vTraceEnable(TRC_START);
/* USER CODE END SysInit */

/* Initialize all configured peripherals */
 MX_GPIO_Init();

/* Create the thread(s) */
 /* definition and creation of LedFlashingTask */
 osThreadDef(LedFlashingTask, StartLedFlashingTask, osPriorityNormal, 0, 512);
 LedFlashingTaskHandle = osThreadCreate(osThread(LedFlashingTask), NULL);

 /* Start scheduler */
 osKernelStart();
///////////////////////////////////////////////////////////////////////////////////////////////////
```

If, during testing, you reset the board and then make a Tracealyzer recording, you will capture events that occur after the TraceEnable call. Whenever you wish to repeat recordings please remember to do the reset.

There are situations where you want to make recordings that start at selected points in your tasks. The recommended way to do this is to first initialize the recorder, then actually start recordings at a later point. This is shown in the following code fragment:

```
///////////////////////////////////////////////////////////////////////////////////////////////////
myBoardInit();

...
/* Init only, trace starts later...*/
vTraceEnable(TRC_INIT);

...
/* RTOS scheduler starts */
vTaskStartScheduler();

...
/* In a task or ISR */
vTraceEnable(TRC_START);
///////////////////////////////////////////////////////////////////////////////////////////////////
```


5.5.2 Adapting for the Streaming mode of operation.

Initialize the recorder and then wait for a start command:

```
vTraceEnable(TRC_START_AWAIT_HOST);
```

Example code fragment:

```
///////////////////////////////////////////////////////////////////////////////////////////////////

myBoardInit();
...
/* From startup - blocks until start from host */
vTraceEnable(TRC_START_AWAIT_HOST);
...
/* RTOS scheduler starts */
vTaskStartScheduler();
///////////////////////////////////////////////////////////////////////////////////////////////////
```

This topic will be discussed in more detail later, in exercise 6.

Chapter 6

Basic features and use of Tracealyzer.

6.1 Tracealyzer exercise 2 - Tracealyzer basics.

The purpose of this exercise is to help you understand the basics of the Tracealyzer tool.

To do this let us record and analyze the simplest of multitasking designs: a single periodic task such as:

```
/* StartDefaultTask function */
void StartDefaultTask(void const * argument)
{
  /* init code for USB_HOST */
  MX_USB_HOST_Init();
  /* USER CODE BEGIN 5 */
  /* Infinite loop */
  for(;;)
  {
      HAL_GPIO_WritePin(GPIOD, GPIO_PIN_13, GPIO_PIN_SET);
      osDelay(500);
      HAL_GPIO_WritePin(GPIOD, GPIO_PIN_13, GPIO_PIN_RESET);
      osDelay(500);
  }
  /* USER CODE END 5 */
}
```

The recordings are going to be made with the tool set to 'Snapshot' mode, so please first consult the following documents:

https://percepio.com/2016/10/05/rtos-tracing/
https://percepio.com/docs/FreeRTOS/manual/
    Recorder.html#Trace_Recorder_Library_Snapshot_Mode

Before going further confirm that the following configuration selection is made in the file trcConfig.h: *#define TRC_CFG_RECORDER_MODE TRC_RECORDER_MODE_SNAPSHOT*

Although this is the default setting it's always worth seeing that it's correct.

After you've compiled and downloaded the test program, reset the board. The next step is to activate Tracealyzer and execute the 'Read Trace (Snapshot)', figure 6.1.

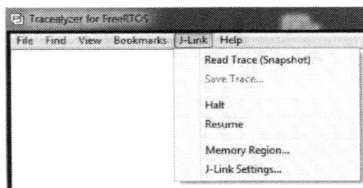

Figure 6.1 Selecting the Read Trace operation

Once the action has been completed you will be presented with the default Trace View of program execution, called the 'Gannt View Mode'. Detailed information can be found at:

https://percepio.com/docs/FreeRTOS/manual/MainView.html#Main_Window_Trace_View

We'll now work our way through various aspects of the recording.
    Figure 6.2 shows just part of the trace recording, concentrating on the task executions. Make sure that you understand what information is presented here and what it means. Cross-check this against your own recording.

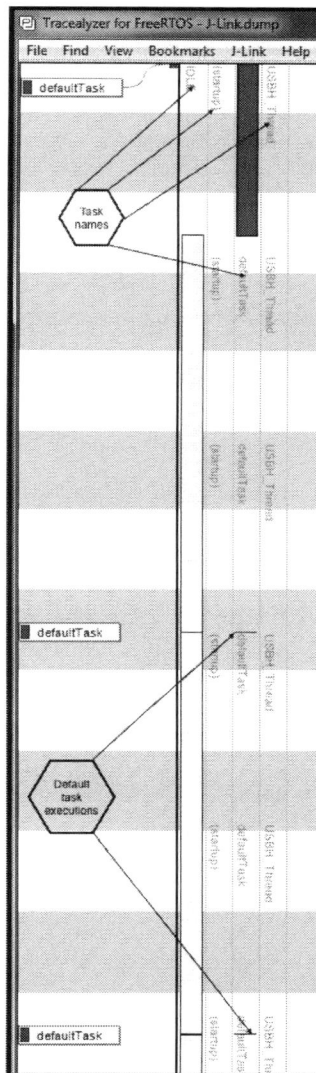

Figure 6.2 Trace recording - default Trace View

Here you can see that there are four trace columns: *IDLE*, (*startup*), *default task* and *USBH-Thread*. For us the trace of main interest is the default task; we'll return to this in a moment.

Both the (*startup*) and *USBH-Thread* columns are empty; there is no processor activity relating to these.   The IDLE task is a FreeRTOS-specific one, created automatically when the RTOS scheduler is started (to ensure there is always at least one task that is able to run).
If you wish to find more details about the idle task see:

      http://www.freertos.org/RTOS-idle-task.html

Returning to the default task: execution instances are shown as a set of colour-coded rectangles. From this you can see that first there is an initial execution instance. After this the display shows that the task executes periodically, as defined by its the source code.

This gives us a very good overview of task behaviour.   However, it isn't possible to extract meaningful timing information from the diagram itself; the scale is somewhat coarse. Fortunately Tracealyzer provides ways to get at such information, one example being that shown in figure 6.3.

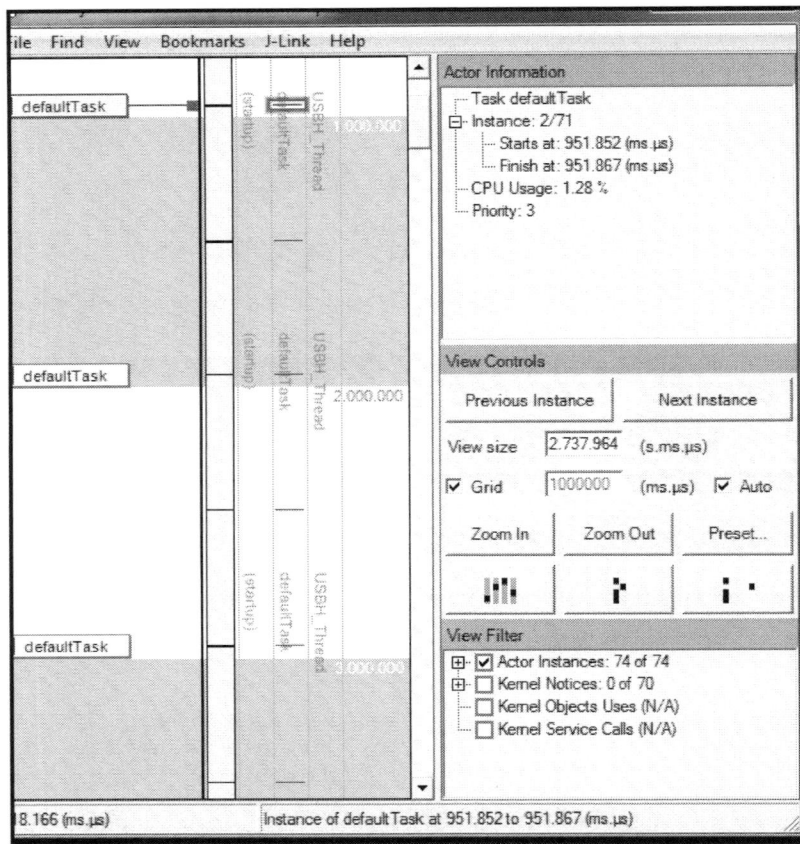

Figure 6.3 Task timing information - 1

This was produced by clicking on a specific execution rectangle (highlighted in figure 6.3), resulting in the 'Actor' timing information. Note that an *Actor* is defined to be 'a FreeRTOS task/ thread or ISR'; an *Actor Instance* is an execution of an Actor.

Information relating to the next execution occurrence is shown in figure 6.4. The timing data given here is self-explanatory, apart from one item; the value given at the bottom left of the window. This denotes the current time position of the cursor on the trace: useful as a navigation tool but not important to us at the moment.

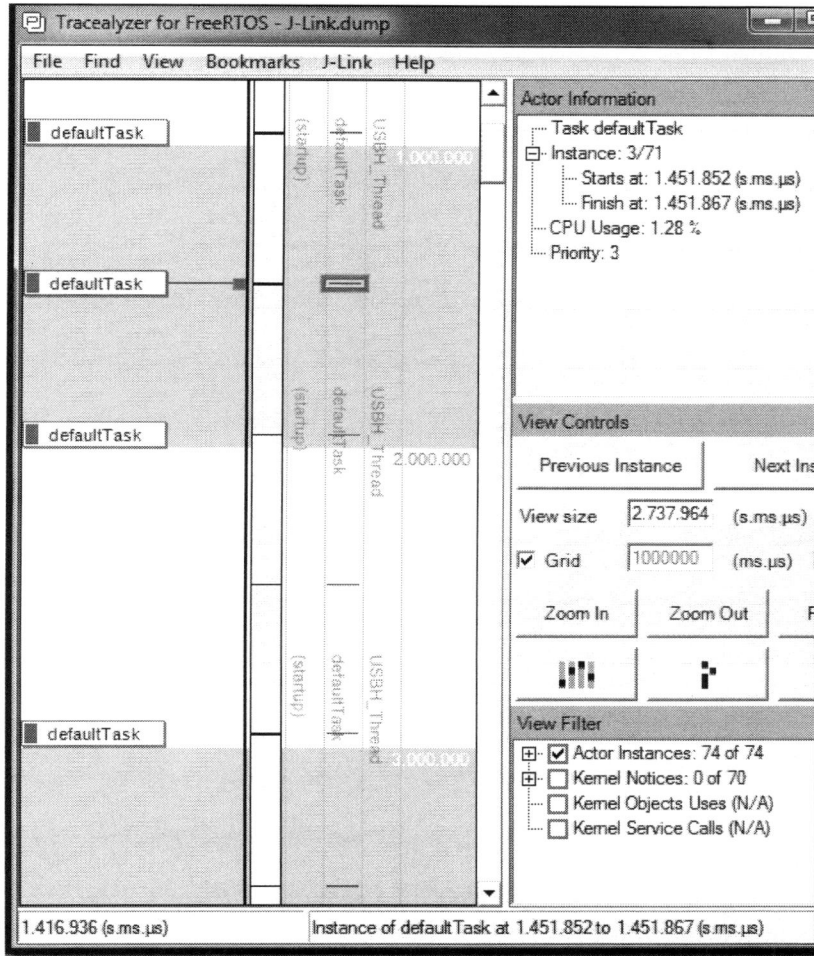

Figure 6.4 Task timing information - 2

Another way of presenting the recorded information is that shown in figure 6.5, the 'Horizontal Trace View'. Here all task event occurrences ('instances') are shown on a horizontal scale and, as before, can be individually selected to obtain timing data. As you can see a great deal more data is provided regarding task timing, processor utilization, etc. (see also figure 6.6, a zoomed-in trace recording of execution instance 3/71).   According to the Tracealyzer documentation the basic purpose of this view is that it *allows for correlating the detailed execution trace with other horizontal views*. More of this later.

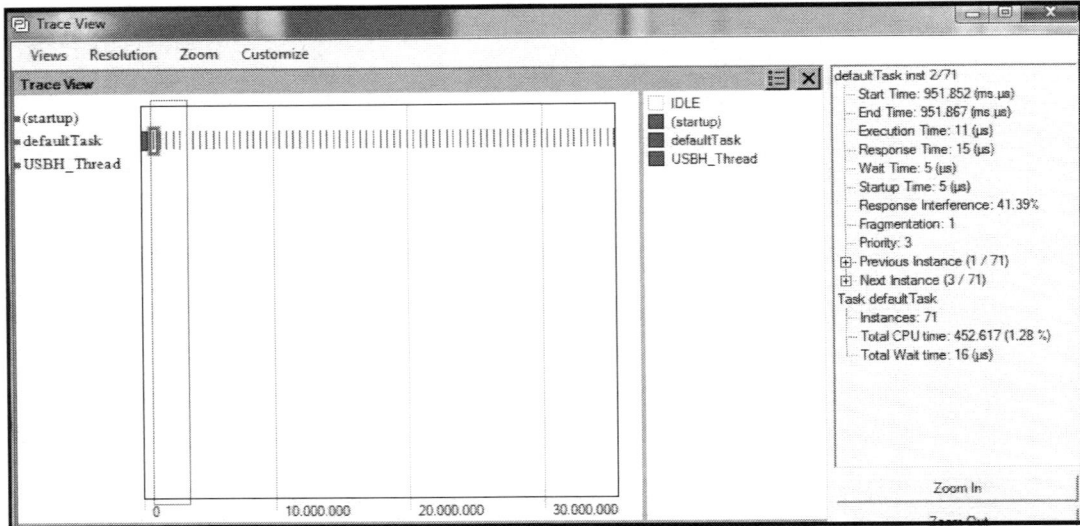

Figure 6.5 Trace recording - Horizontal Trace View - 1

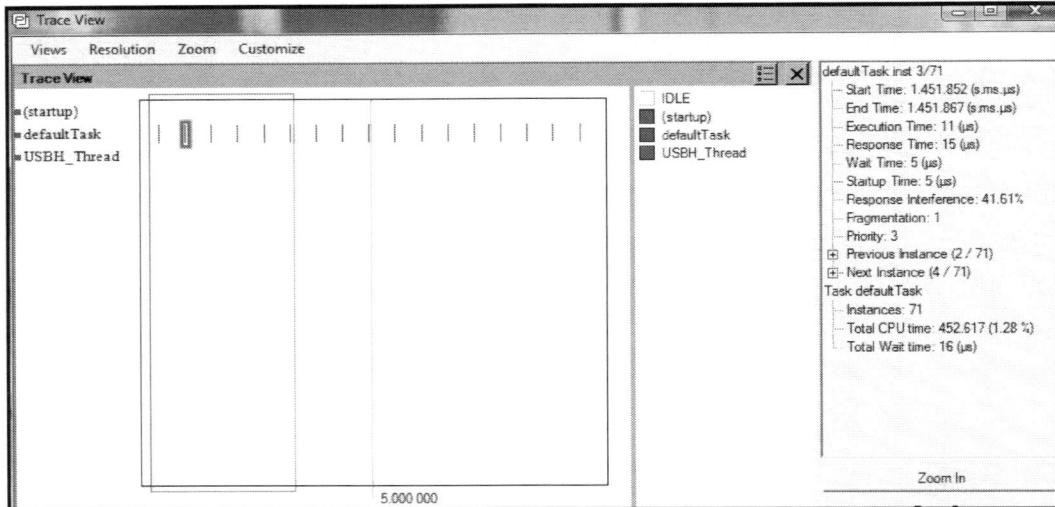

Figure 6.6 Trace recording - Horizontal Trace View - 2

The timing information given in figures 6.5 and 6.6 is defined in the Tracealyzer documentation

(https://percepio.com/docs/FreeRTOS/manual/Terminology.html#Terminology) as follows (see also figure 6.7):

- Start and End Times: Self-explanatory.

- Execution Time: The amount of CPU time used by an Actor Instance, excluding preemptions.

- Response Time: The time from the start of an actor instance until it finishes. More precisely: the response time for tasks is counted from the point when the task becomes ready to execute (i.e. the point where the kernel sets the task's scheduling status to *Ready*). Please note this is _not_ the same definition as that given in Book 1.

- Wait Time: This is the time within an instance when the actor is not actually executing, calculated as [(End time - Start time) - (Execution Time)].

- Startup Time: This is the time between ready and execution start.

- Response Interference: The relation between execution time and response time. A value of 30% means that the response time is 30% longer than the execution time, i.e., due to preempting tasks, interrupts or blocking. A value of 0% means that the response time is equal to the execution time (i.e. the actor instance executed to completion without context switches).

- Fragmentation: The number of fragments of execution within an Actor Instance (usually due to task preemption). If an Actor Instance executes in full without preemptions, the fragmentation of the instance is 1.

Note: when the Startup *and* Wait Times are zero then the Response Time is the same as the Execution Time.

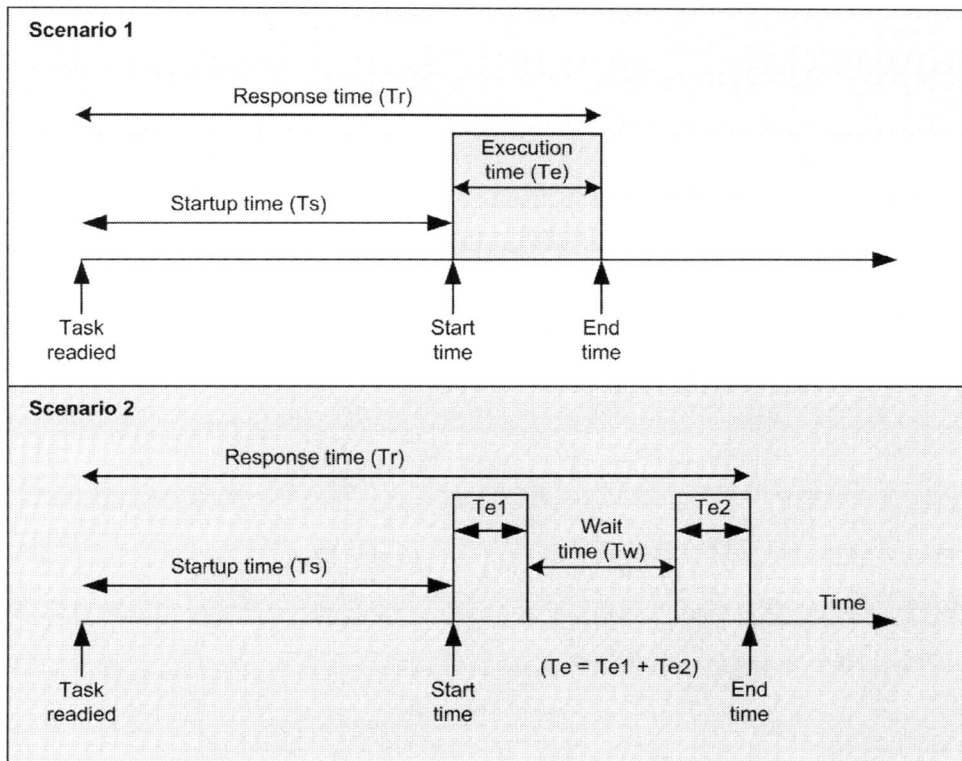

Figure 6.7 Tracealyzer timing definitions.

All collected information can be exported to files, as described in the Tracealyzer documentation:

- *The File menu also includes Save Current View as Image, and Export Actor Data.*

- *Save Current View as Image allows you to export the current trace view to an image, e.g., for documentation or for sharing an issue with colleagues.*

- *Export Actor Data allows you to export actor instance data to a text file. The exported data includes start time, execution time, response time and fragmentation of each instance of the selected actors.*

Images are saved as JPGs, while the exported actor data is copied to a text file, as for example:

==

**This file is generated using Tracealyzer for FreeRTOS,
using the "Export Actor Data" feature.**

Task defaultTask
  Instance count: 74
  Fragment count: 75
  Execution time
    Range: 11 to 451852 µs
    Average: 6117 µs
  Response time
    Range: 15 to 451867 µs
    Average: 6122 µs
  Periodicity
    Range: 500000 to 950999
    Average: 506178
  Separation
    Range: 499131 to 499985
    Average: 499973
  Fragmentation
    Range: 1 to 2
    Average: 1.014

==

Using the tool you can view the CPU loading, figure 6.8, and also obtain trace details, figure 6.9.

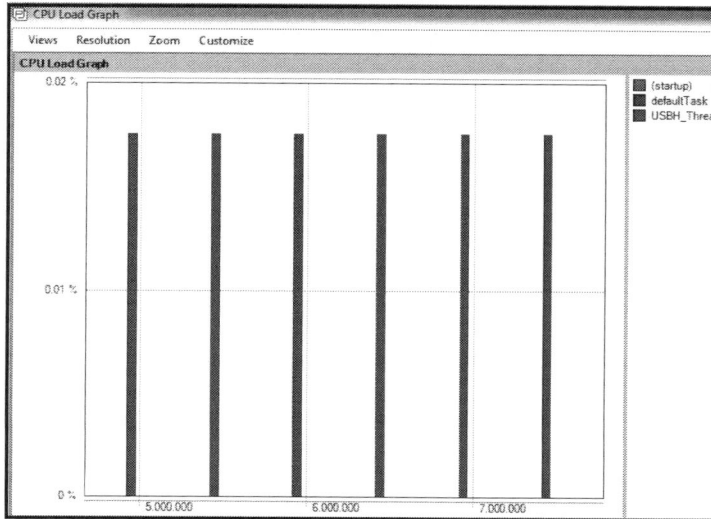

Figure 6.8 CPU Load Graph

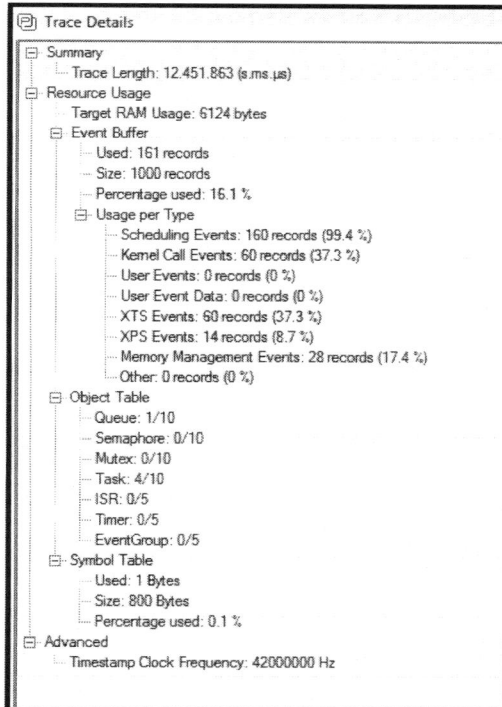

Figure 6.9 Trace details

6.2 Tracealyzer exercise 3 - Evaluating trace recordings.

The purpose of this exercise is to increase your understanding of the trace recordings.

Here we'll perform the recording and analysis of a slightly more complex single task having the following code structure:

LedFlashingTask.
Loop
    TurnLedOn
    Simulate task execution for 500 ms (software delay)
    TurnLedOff
    osDelayUntil(two seconds)

    TurnLedOn
    Simulate task execution for 1000 ms (software delay)
    TurnLedOff
    osDelayUntil(two seconds)
End Loop

It is designed to provide information that is visually more informative, so please implement a similar task and analyse the results.

For our example we can predict that the trace results should show a series of Actor instances, repeating at two second intervals. The pattern of execution should be a 500 ms instance followed by a 1000 ms instance, then another 500 ms instance etc. This prediction is confirmed by the results given in figure 6.10 below.

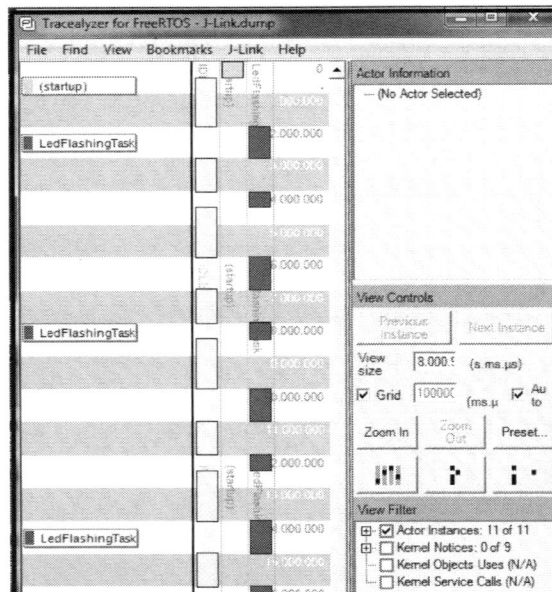

Figure 6.10 Trace recording - default Trace View

Please note that this exercise code contains two *osDelayUntil* function calls. This has been done purely for demonstration reasons; a normal periodic task would have only one such call. In such cases *periodicity* is defined as:

The time between two consecutive instances of an actor, counted from the start of the previous actor instance to the start of the current actor instance.

Moving on: to get detailed timing information, open the horizontal trace view for a one-second execution instance (figure 6.11).

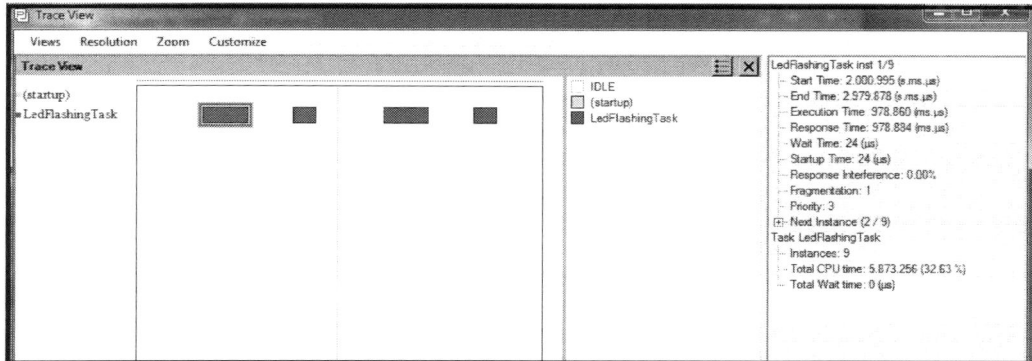

Figure 6.11 Horizontal trace view - one second Actor instance

Read through this, absorb the timing data and compare it with your own results.
   The same information for a 500 ms execution instance is shown in figure 6.12.

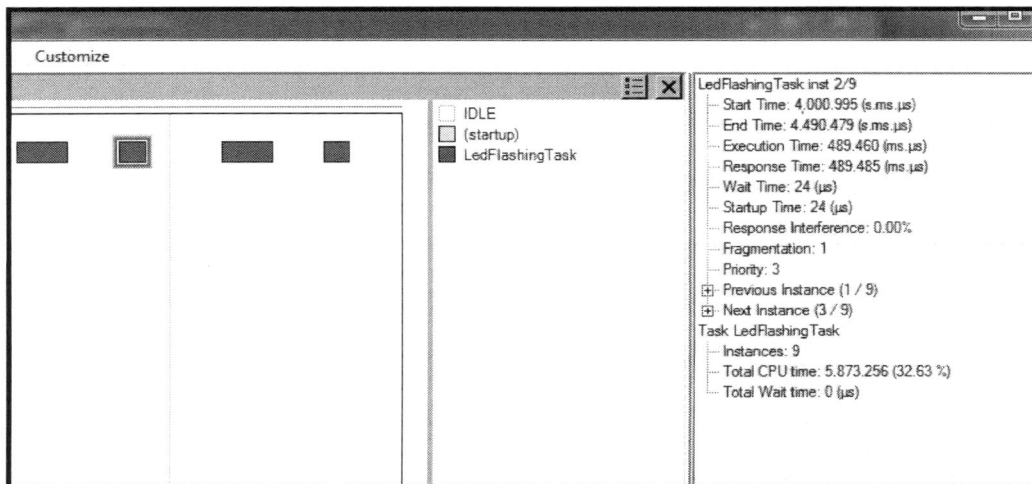

Figure 6.12 Task timing information - 0.5 second Actor instance

Just for completeness: the timing information of the next two instances is given in figure 6.13.

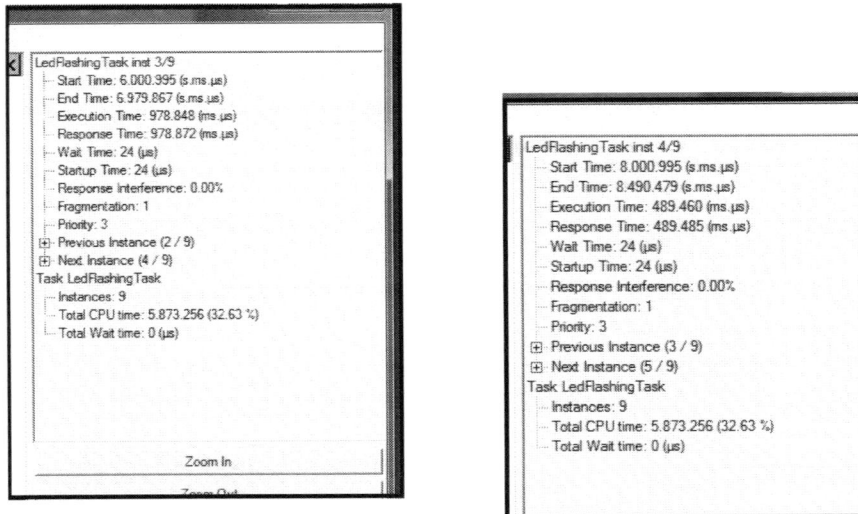

LedFlashing Task inst 3/9
- Start Time: 6.000.995 (s.ms.µs)
- End Time: 6.979.867 (s.ms.µs)
- Execution Time: 978.848 (ms.µs)
- Response Time: 978.872 (ms.µs)
- Wait Time: 24 (µs)
- Startup Time: 24 (µs)
- Response Interference: 0.00%
- Fragmentation: 1
- Priority: 3
- ⊞ Previous Instance (2 / 9)
- ⊞ Next Instance (4 / 9)
Task LedFlashing Task
- Instances: 9
- Total CPU time: 5.873.256 (32.63 %)
- Total Wait time: 0 (µs)

LedFlashing Task inst 4/9
- Start Time: 8.000.995 (s.ms.µs)
- End Time: 8.490.479 (s.ms.µs)
- Execution Time: 489.460 (ms.µs)
- Response Time: 489.485 (ms.µs)
- Wait Time: 24 (µs)
- Startup Time: 24 (µs)
- Response Interference: 0.00%
- Fragmentation: 1
- Priority: 3
- ⊞ Previous Instance (3 / 9)
- ⊞ Next Instance (5 / 9)
Task LedFlashing Task
- Instances: 9
- Total CPU time: 5.873.256 (32.63 %)
- Total Wait time: 0 (µs)

Figure 6.13 Timing information - instances 3 and 4

The next trace to consider is the 'CPU Load Graph', figure 6.14.

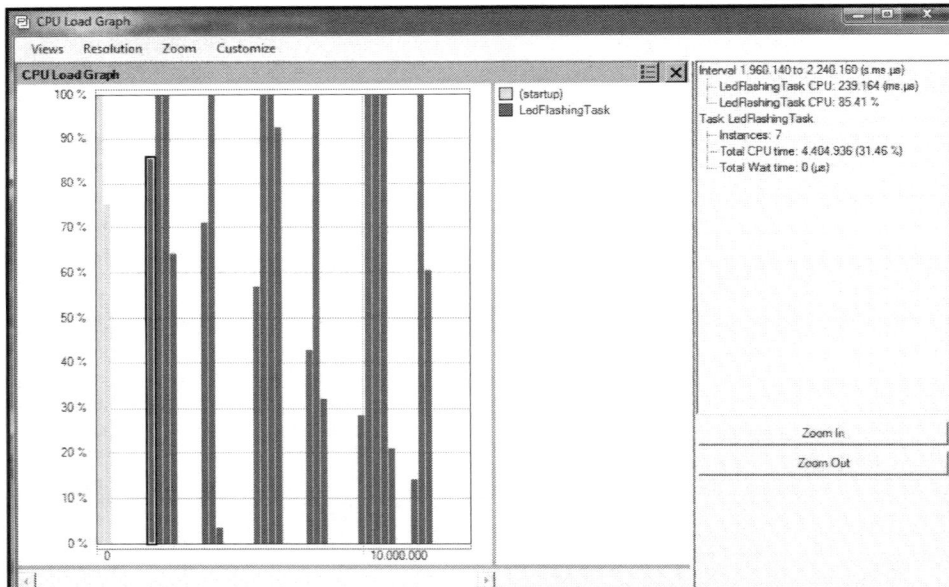

Figure 6.14 CPU Load Graph

A recap: this provides us with a useful visual indication of the CPU workload, the key aspects being that:

- The CPU Load Graph displays CPU usage over time, per actor and in total.
- The analysis works by dividing the trace into a number of intervals.
- The CPU usage for an actor in any interval is the amount of CPU time used by that actor within this interval divided by the length of the interval.
- The height of each actor's rectangle represents the CPU usage for that actor in that time interval.
- By default the graph shows all actors except the idle task.

Be careful when interpreting this graph, because the usage factor is a *calculated* one. If the CPU executes the task for the complete duration of an interval, the graph will show a loading of 100%. If, however, the CPU executes task code for only half a task interval the result will be 50% (even if the CPU is running flat out during the execution time).

Where this graph is really useful is in showing loadings for multiple tasks (the normal situation).

Lastly, we can review the trace details, figure 6.15.

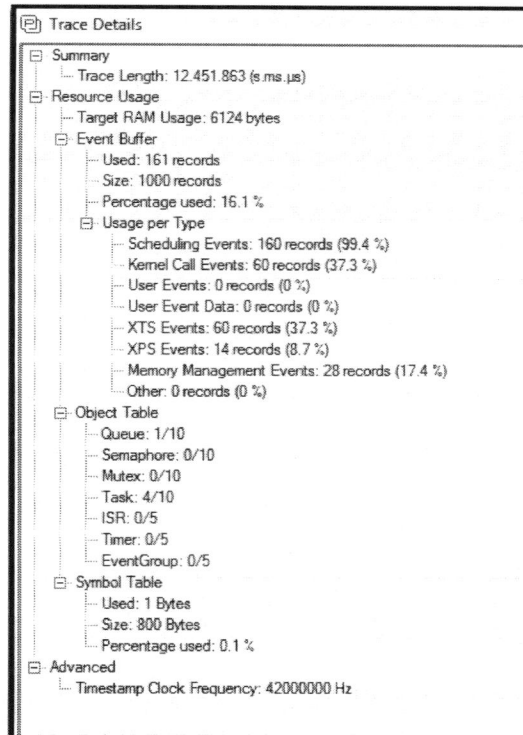

Figure 6.15 Trace details

6.3 Tracealyzer exercise 4 - Run-time analysis of a two-task design.

The purpose of this exercise is to use Tracealyzer to evaluate the run-time behaviour of a simple two-task design (similar to that specified in the original practical exercise 3).

Task outline details are as follows:

GreenLedFlashingTask: Execution time 500 ms, periodic time 2 seconds.
RedLedFlashingTask: Execution time 500 ms, periodic time 1 second
Tasks have equal priorities.

Within each task use a software delay function to simulate its executable code.   Use the *osDelayUntil* function to ensure that the periodic times will be correct.   Hence each task should have the following code structure:

Loop
    TurnLedOn
    Simulate task execution for 500 ms (software delay)
    TurnLedOff
    osDelayUntil(xx seconds)
End Loop

For the *GreenLedFlashingTask* xx is two seconds.
For the *RedLedFlashingTask* xx is one second.

For each task we can predict the trace timing values and patterns.   We cannot, however, predict the timing relationship *between* the tasks as these are executed under the control of FreeRTOS.
      Once the code is running correctly in the target you can use Tracealyzer to measure its behaviour.   Colour the recorded task events, Red and Green as appropriate, using the menu:

View —> Trace View Settings —> Set Colour Scheme —> Custom

This isn't necessary but is just good, sensible practice to help you understand what's in front of you.
      Compare your results with those shown in figures 6.16 to 6.20.   Carefully read through the details until you completely understand all the information presented in the recordings.

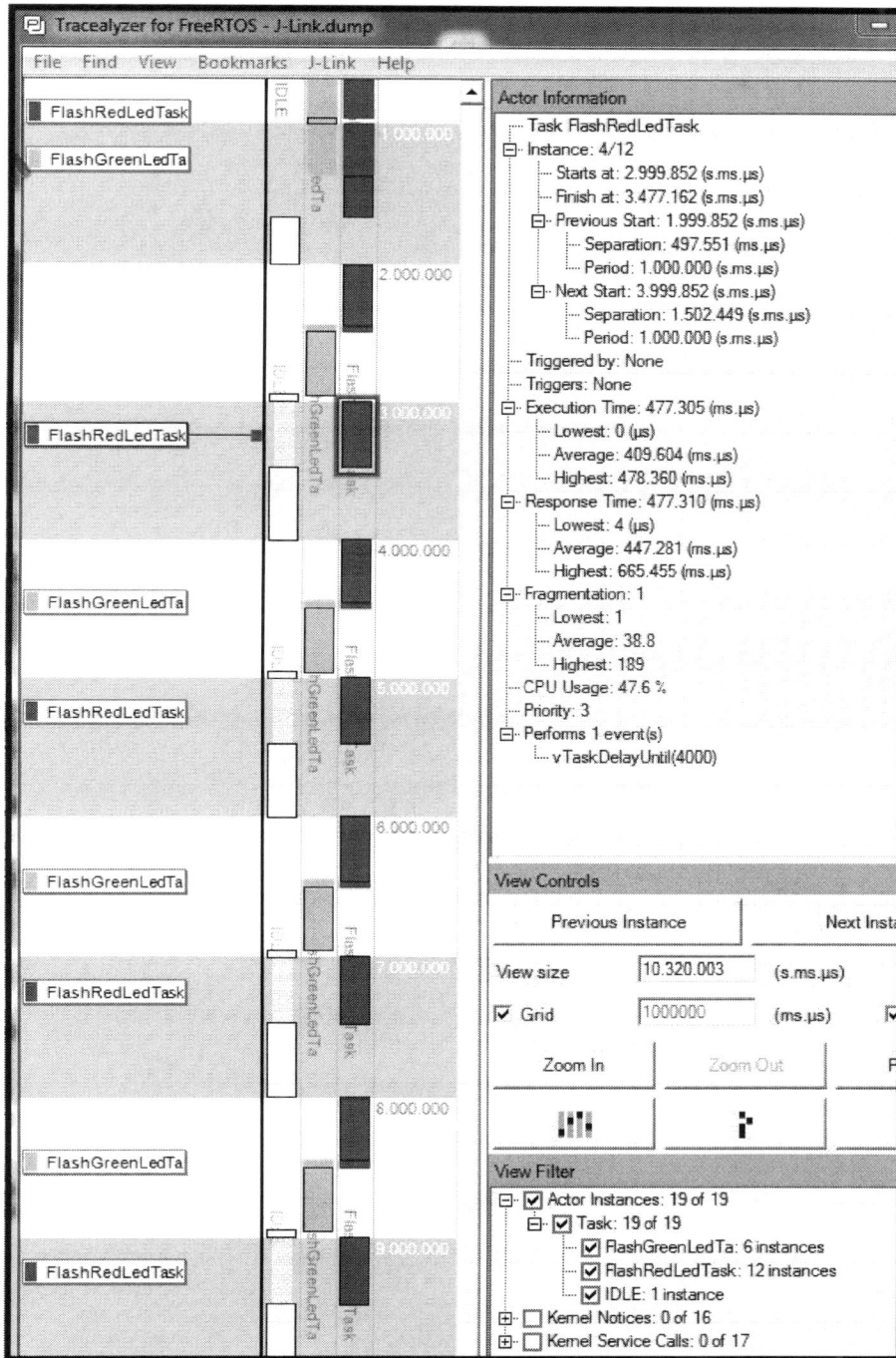

Figure 6.16 Trace recording - FlashRedLed default Trace View

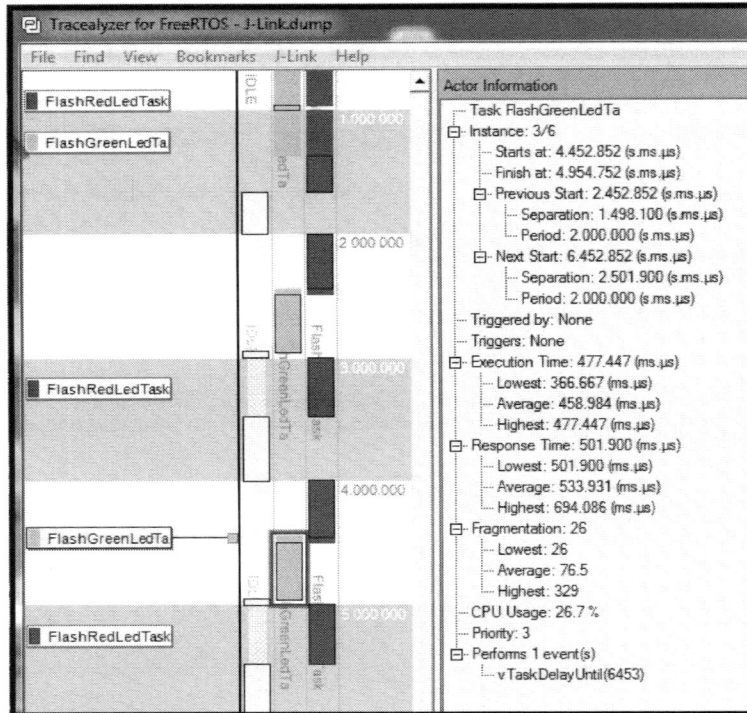

Figure 6.17 Trace recording - FlashGreenLed default Trace View

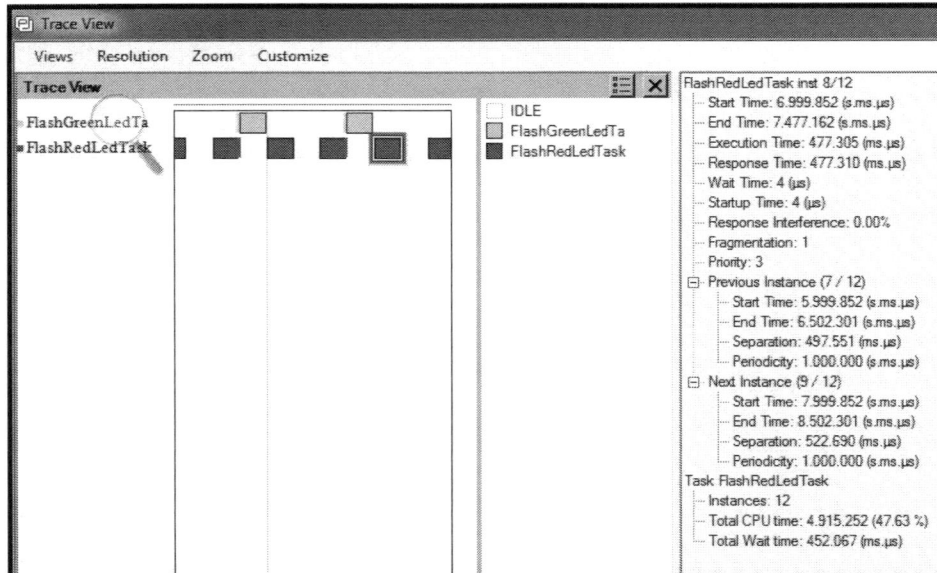

Figure 6.18 Horizontal Trace View - FlashRedLedTask timing data

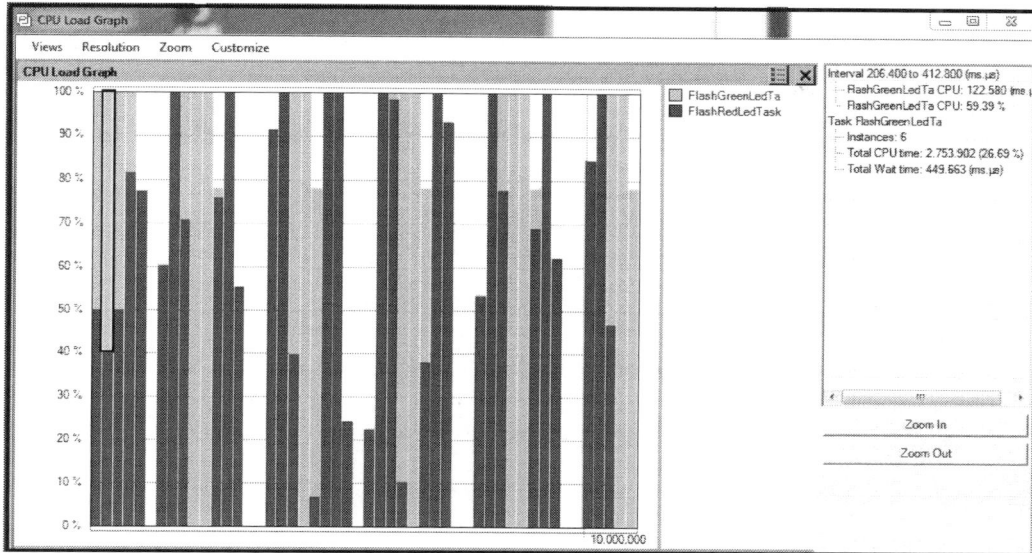

Figure 6.19 CPU Load Graph - FlashGreenLed data

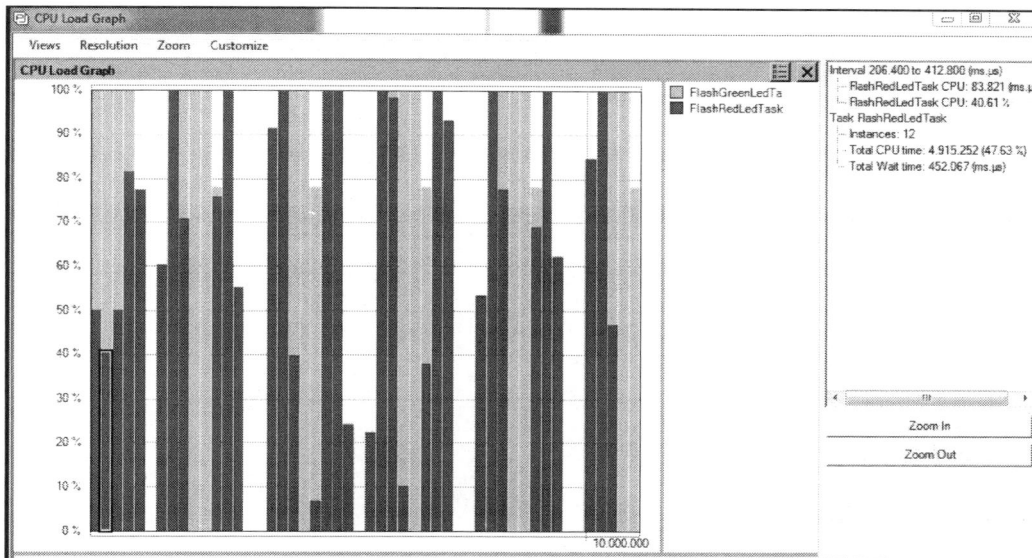

Figure 6.20 CPU Load Graph - FlashRedLed data

6.4 Tracealyzer exercise 5 - Investigating priority preemptive scheduling.

The aim of this exercise is to use Tracealyzer to observe the run-time behaviour of a two-task design that uses a priority preemptive scheduling policy. Use your own implementation of the original practical exercise 4 for this.

6.4.1 Exercise 5.1.

Review and revise the original practical exercise 4, then adapt it so that it is instrumented with Tracealyzer. Following this implement the original exercise 5.2, capturing and analyzing the run-time data using Tracealyzer.

   Compare your own results with those shown in figures 6.2 to 6.26. Carefully read through the details presented here until you understand its content and meaning.

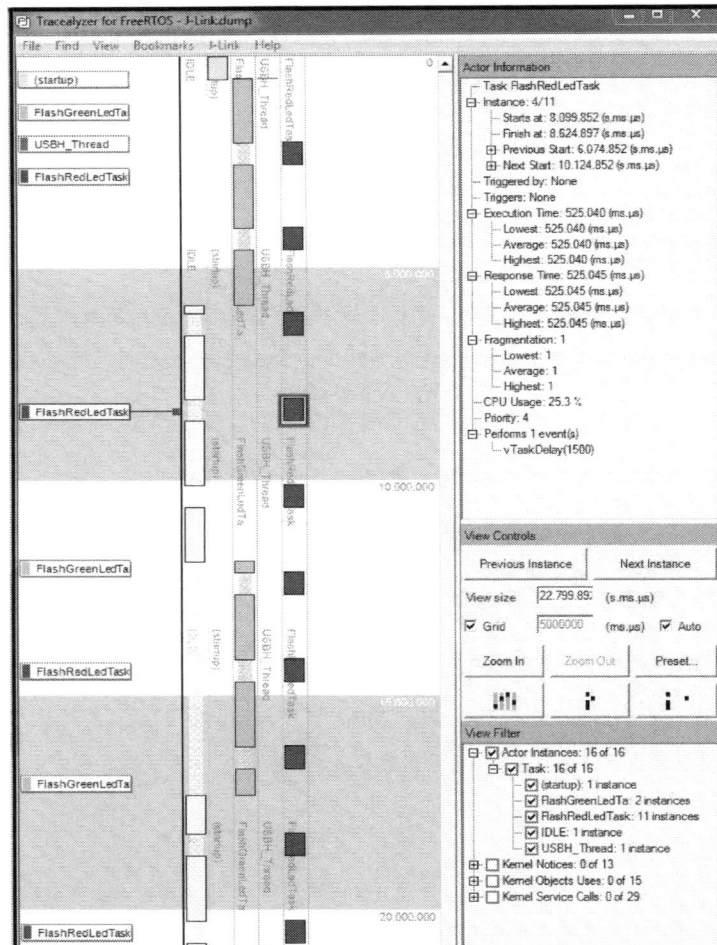

Figure 6.21 Trace recording - *FlashRedLed* task and actor information

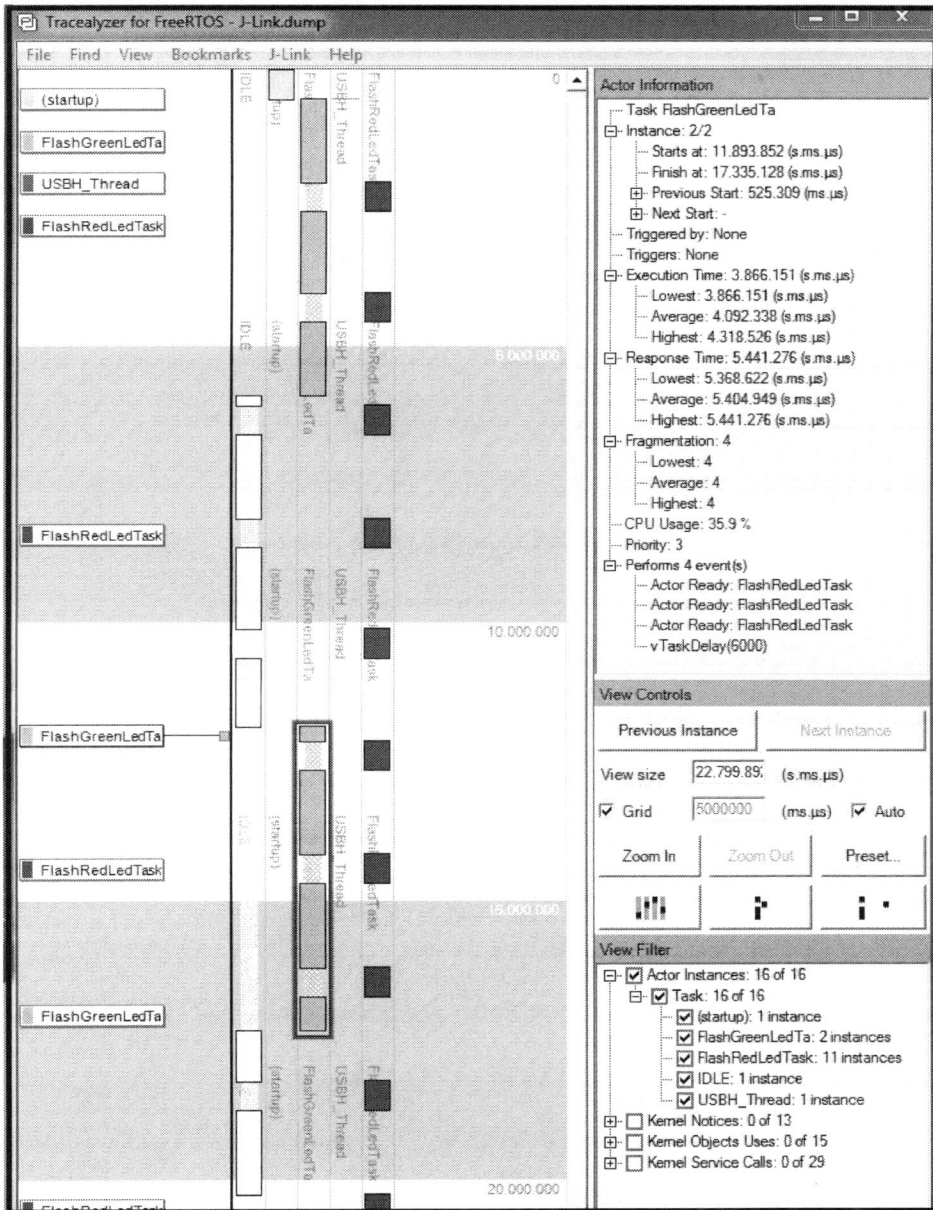

Figure 6.22 Trace recording - *FlashGreenLed* task and actor information

It is important to check your understanding of the information presented here (a form of consolidation exercise). So, referring to figure 6.22: sketch a timing diagram for the highlighted green trace. You can, remember, also obtain start and stop points of the various fragments using the cursor   Complete the timing diagram, showing all timing data.

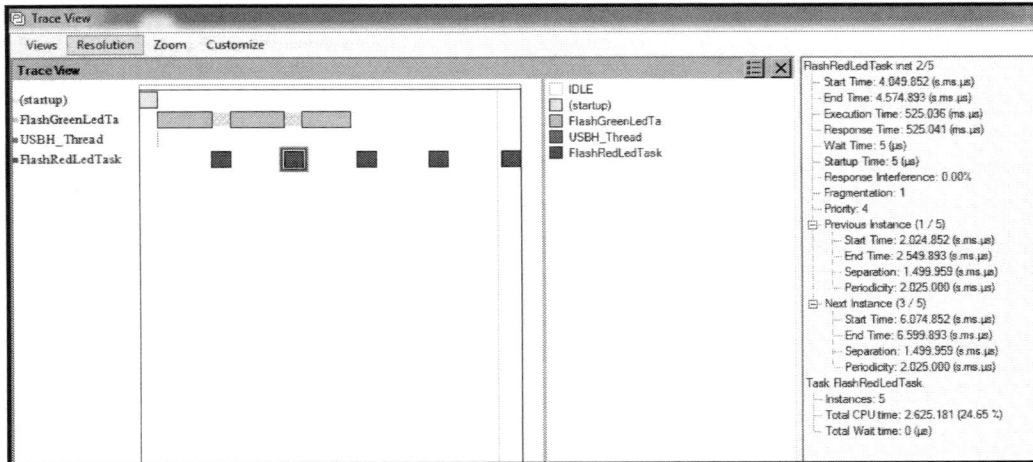

Figure 6.23 Horizontal Trace View - *FlashRedLedTask* timing data

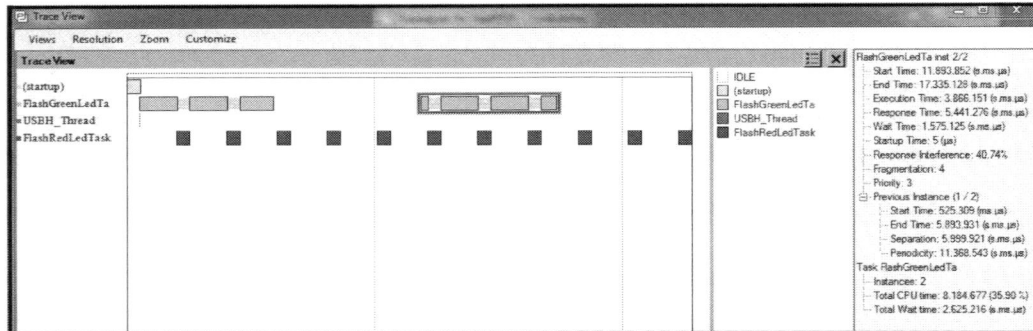

Figure 6.24 Horizontal Trace View - *FlashGreenLedTask* timing data

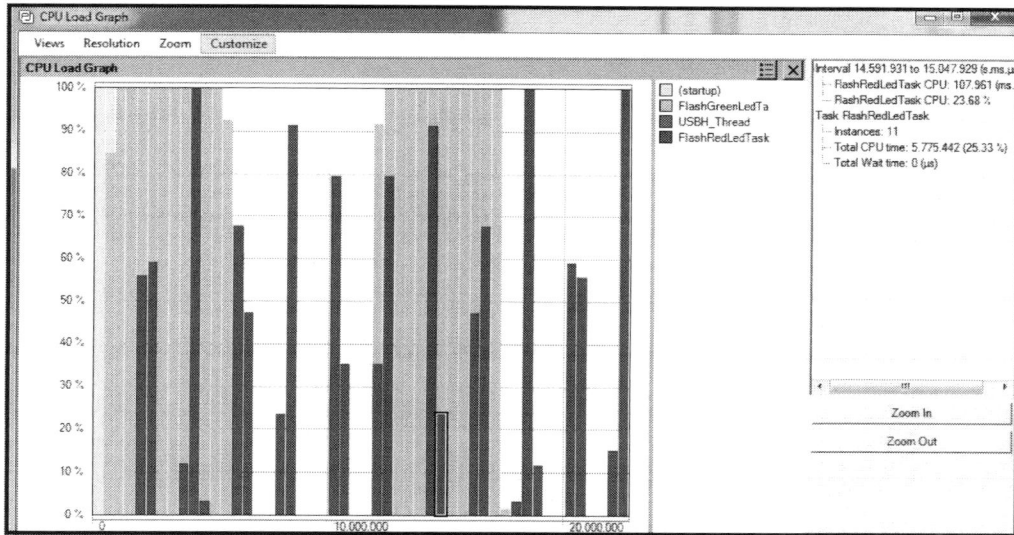

Figure 6.25 CPU Load Graph - *FlashRedLed* data

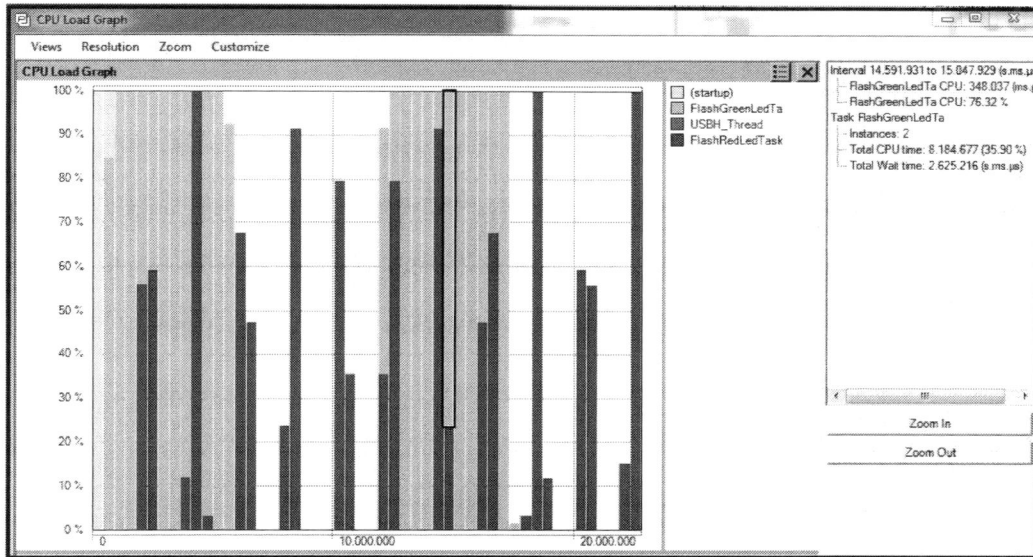

Figure 6.26 CPU Load Graph - *FlashGreenLed* data

6.4.2 Exercise 5.2.

Now modify your code to implement the original exercise 4.3. Further:

(a) Replace the call *vTraceEnable(TRC_START)* with *vTraceEnable(TRC_INIT)* and

(b) Insert the call *vTraceEnable(TRC_START)* at the start of the code for the *FlashGreenLed* task.

The result of doing this is that Tracealyzer starts collecting data on the first run of the *FlashGreenLed* task. You should get results similar to those shown in figures 6.27 and 6.28, where the preemption of the *FlashRedLed* task is clearly shown (as a 'hatched' trace section, indicating it is in the ready queue).

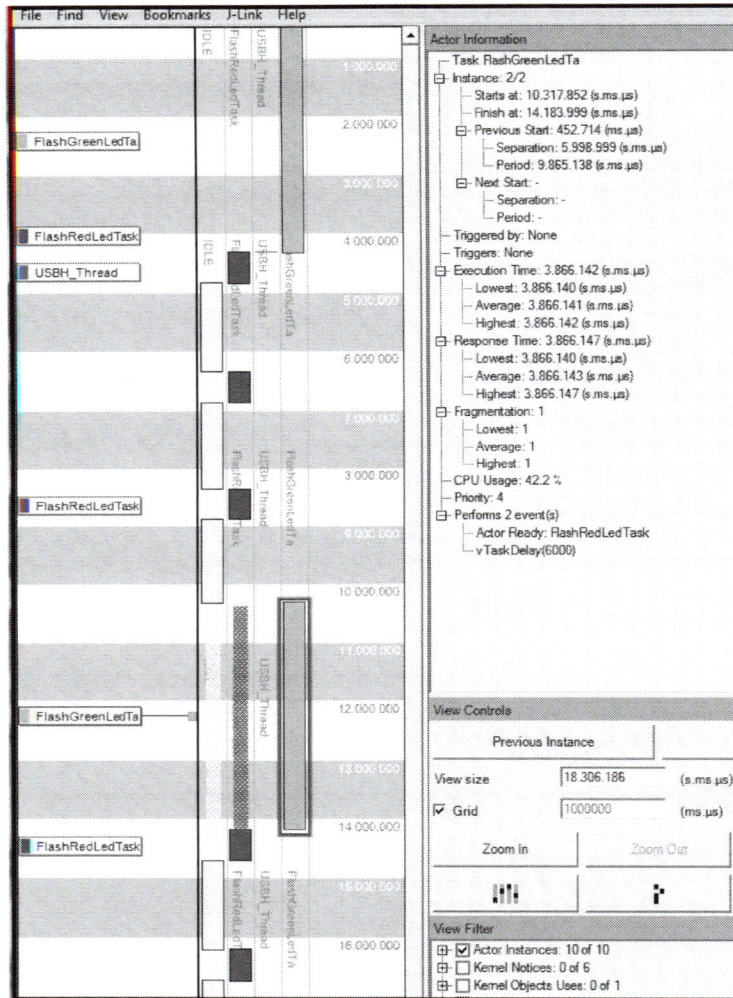

Figure 6.27 Trace recording - Default Trace View -original exercise 4.3

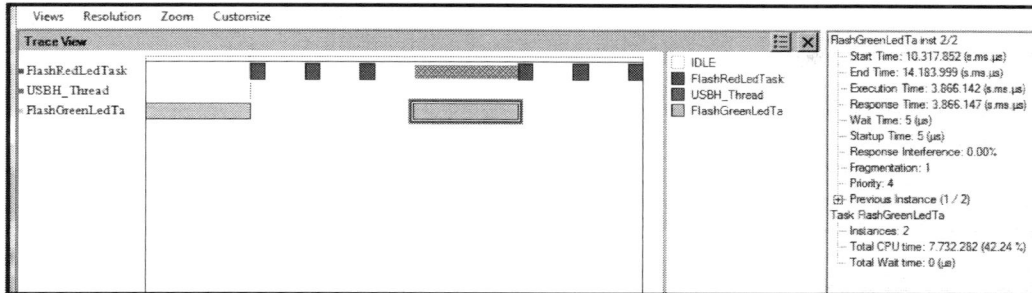

Figure 6.28 Horizontal trace view - original exercise 4.3

6.5 Tracealyzer exercise 6 - Evaluating the FreeRTOS delay functions.

The purposes of this exercise are to:

- *Investigate task behaviour when the osDelayUntil function is used.*
- *Investigate task behaviour when the osDelay function is used.*
- *Compare the two behaviours.*

6.5.1 Exercise 6.1.

The aim here is to record and evaluate task behaviour when the *osDelayUntil* function is used. The specification for this is a two-task (Green and Red) design, both tasks being periodic. Priority scheduling is to be used, the Green task having highest priority.

Task timing info - FlashGreenLedTask (for brevity, Green task).
    Execution time: 2 seconds (approximately).
    Periodic time: 3.7 seconds.
    Use *osDelayUntil* to set the timing.

Task timing info - FlashRedLedTask (Red task).
    Execution time: 0.5 seconds (approximately).
    Periodic time: 1.5 second.
    Use *osDelayUntil* to set the timing.

The general specification for the exercise, apart from timings, is exactly the same as Tracealyzer exercise 5.
   These timings may appear to be somewhat odd, but there is a good reason for using them. We wish to prevent the Green task preempting at exactly the same points in multiple runs of the Red task. This will let us check if variations in preemption points lead to variations in behaviour.
   Please note that your task execution times don't have to be *exactly* the same as those specified above; those are for guidance only.
   The first thing to do is to establish the behaviour of the Red task when it runs without preemptions. So now execute the code with only the Red task running. In our case the results gathered by Tracealyzer are shown in figure 6.29; yours should be similar.

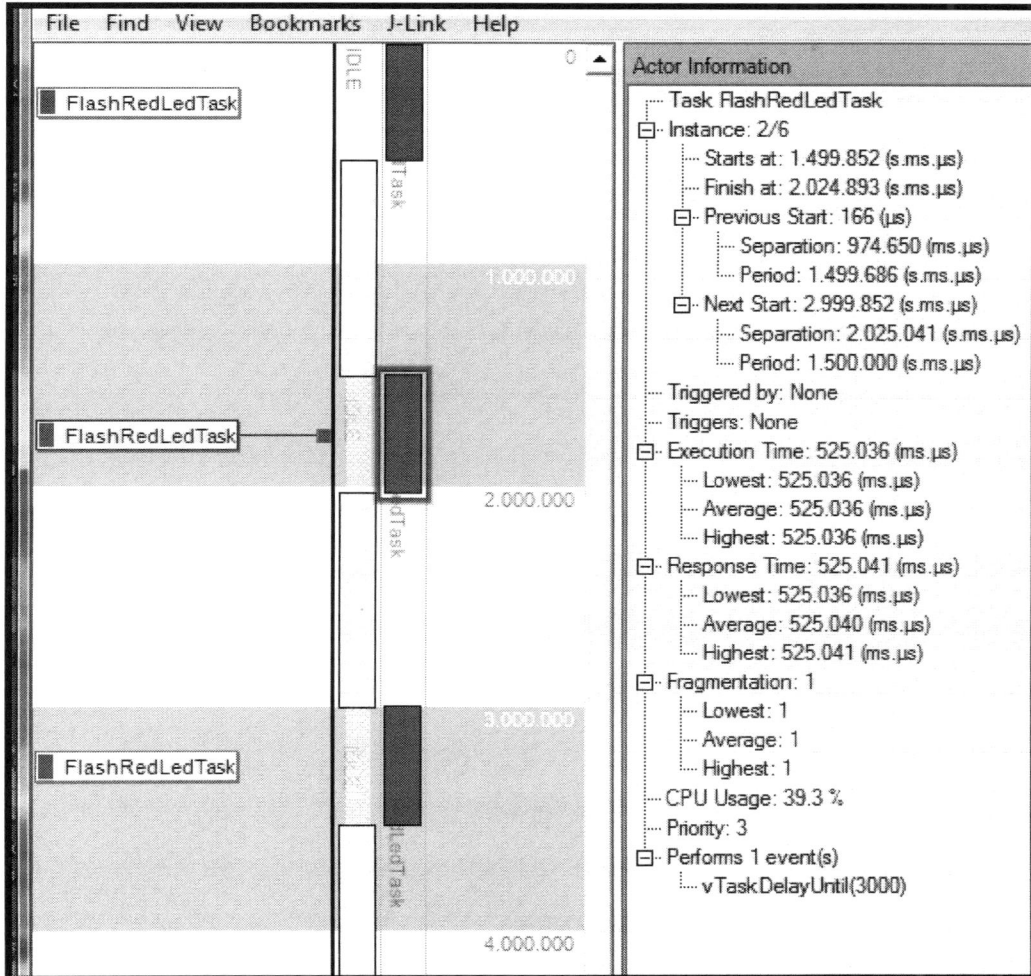

Figure 6.29 Run-time behaviour - Red task only executing

The run-time behaviour corresponds with that specified in the source code - no problems here. Now repeat the measurements with both tasks active; also observe the behaviour of the Leds. You will find that the behaviour of the Red task will be dramatically different, one particular instance being shown in figure 6.30:

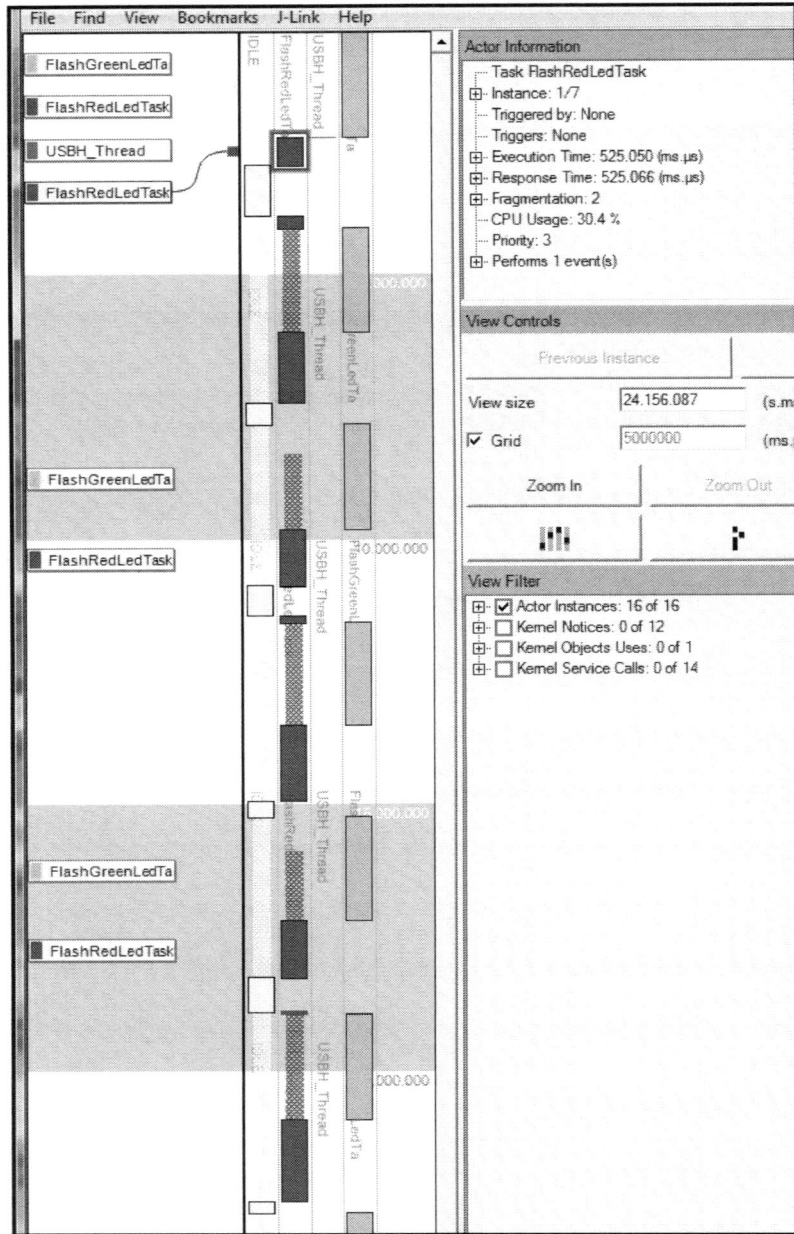

Figure 6.30 Run-time behaviour - both tasks active.

In this figure Actor information is shown for instance 1 of the Red task. This, you will see, performs as specified. Now look at figure 6.31, which provides details of instance 2.

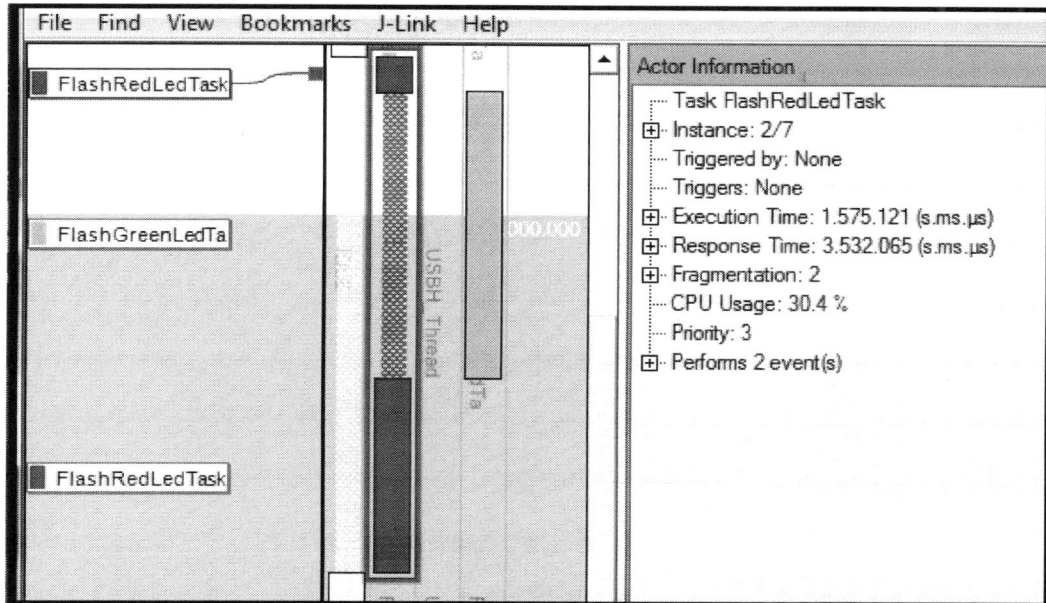

Figure 6.31 Run-time behaviour - Red task instance 2

Here the Green task, having the higher priority, preempts the run of the Red task; all seems to be correct. However, what isn't expected is the behaviour of the Red task when it restarts: it executes for an extended period of time. From the Execution Time value we can deduce that this is equivalent to two additional executions of the task. You can also see from figure 6.28 that, in our design, the task execution time is 0.525 seconds (to three DPs). The measured Execution Time in figure 6.31 is given as 1.573 seconds, three time the specified execution time. This, we believe, is due to the way the *osDelayUntil* function works (numerous extra tests, not shown here, were carried out to confirm this hypothesis).

   Figure 6.32 shows the run-time behaviour during instance 3 execution. From this you can see that the Red task was readied while the Green task was running. It is then correctly dispatched when Green completes. But note that now it too has an extended run-time, being twice the specified execution time.

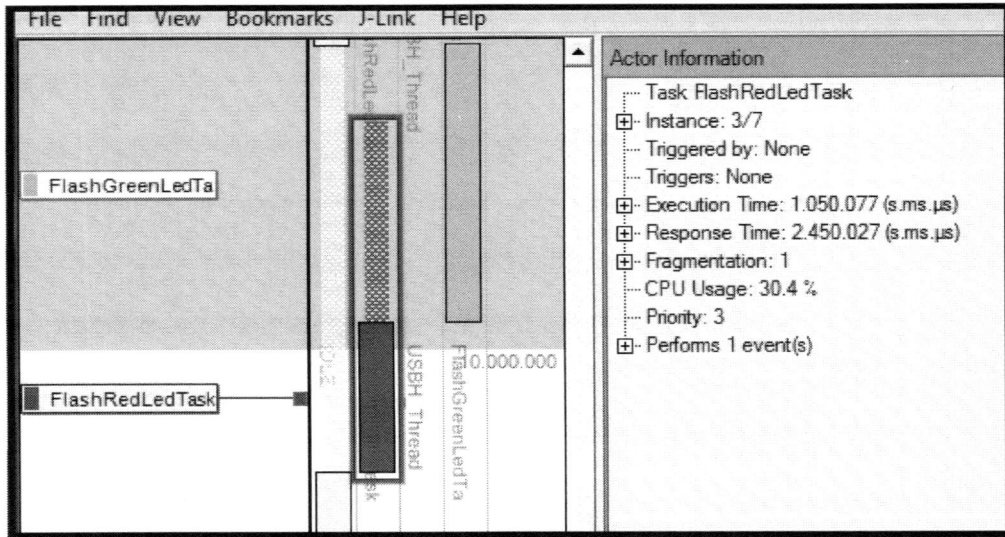

Figure 6.32 Run-time behaviour - Red task instance 3.

6.5.2 Exercise 6.2.

The objective here is to investigate task behaviour when the *osDelay* function is used instead of *osDelayUntil*. This will allow us to see how they differ in their effects on system run-time behaviour.

For the Green task:
     Replace *osDelayUntil(&TaskTimeStamp,3700);* with *osDelay(1700);*
     Task execution time is still to be 2 seconds.
Thus the predicted periodic time is approximately 3.7 seconds.

For the Red task:
     Replace *osDelayUntil(&TaskTimeStamp,1500);* with *osDelay(1000);*
     Task execution time is still to be 0.5 seconds.
Thus the predicted periodic time is approximately 1.5 seconds.

Now execute the modified code in the target system, where results should be similar to that shown in figure 6.33.

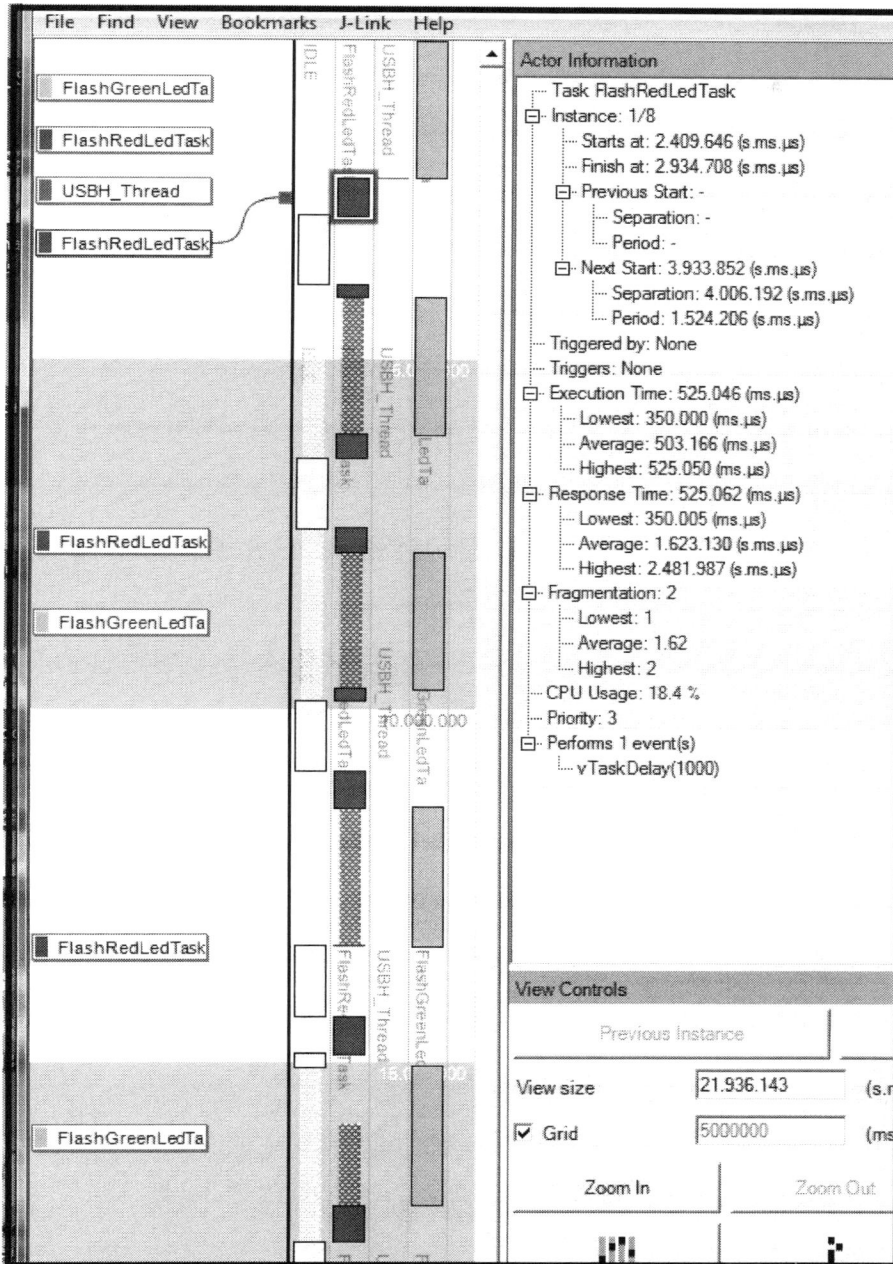

Figure 6.33 Both tasks active - using *osDelay*

Study this carefully until you understand exactly what it's telling you. In this particular case the Actor information relates to instance 1 execution of the Red task. You can see this is the only instance that hasn't been preempted, so timings should be as stipulated in the source code (which they are).

Moving on: let's look into instance 2 in more detail, figure 6.34.

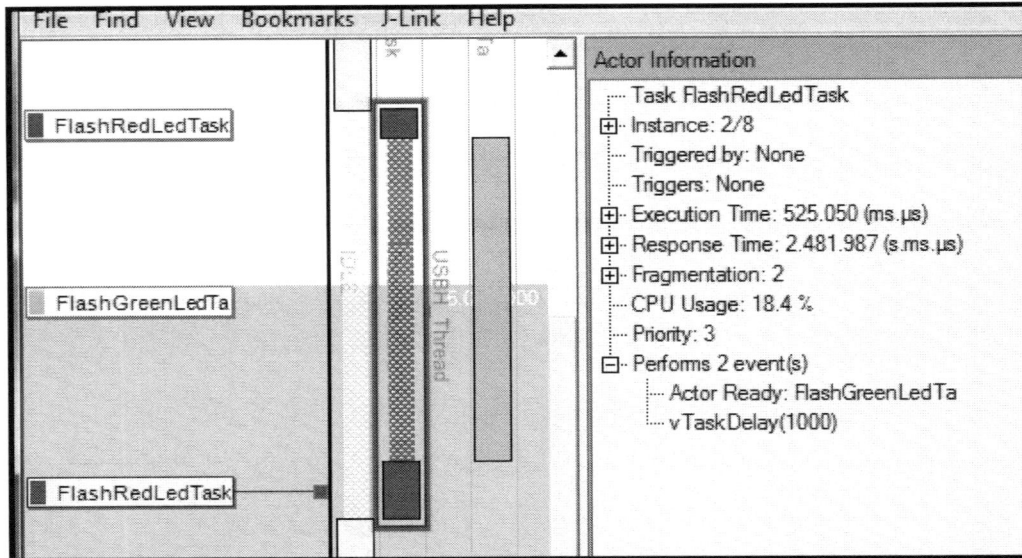

Figure 6.34 Red task instance 2 information

You can see that the Red task begins to execute, later being preempted by the Green task. At this point it goes into the ready state. When the Green task completes its work it (the Green task) goes into a timed-suspended state; the Red task is now restored, runs to completion and then enters a timed-suspended state. But note that, in spite of the preemption, the Red task Execution Time is correct.

Next, consider Instance 4, figure 6.35. Here the Red task begins to execute, later being preempted by Green before it complete its work. When the Green task relinquishes the processor Red is re-installed and runs to completion.

Once again you can see that the Execution Time is correct.

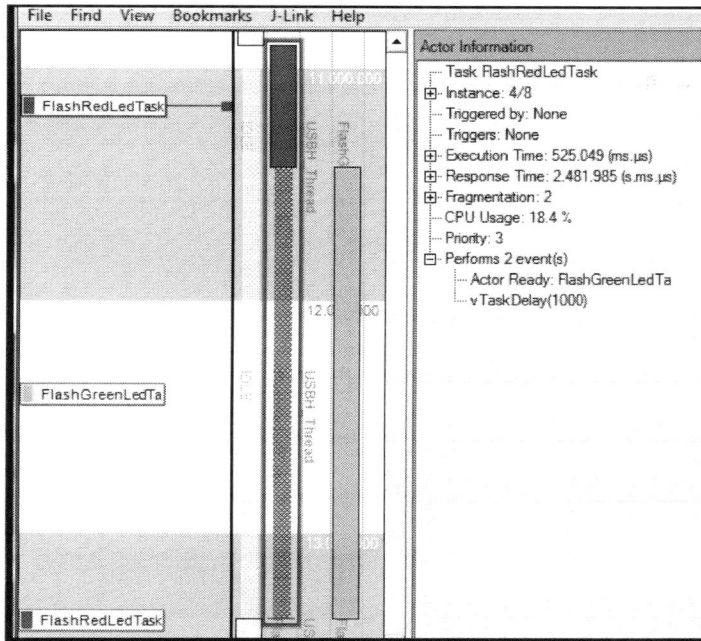

Figure 6.35 Red task instance 4 information

Lastly, the next uninterrupted execution of the Red task is shown in figure 6.36.

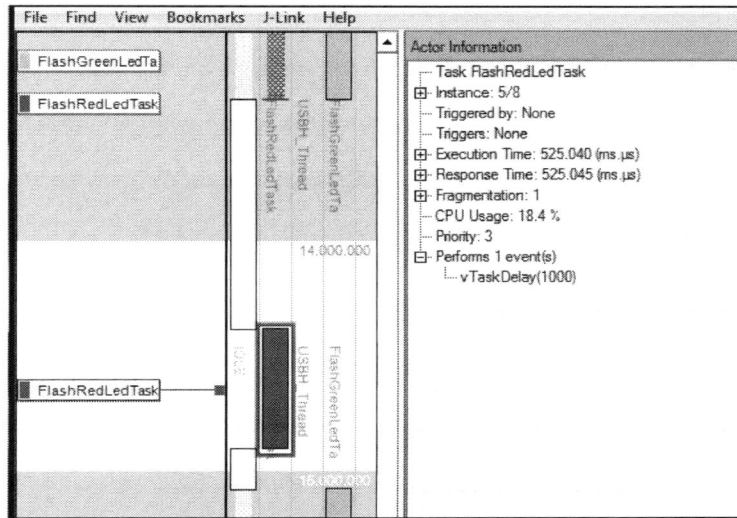

Figure 6.36 Red task instance 5 information

6.5.3 Comment and conclusions.

(a) Using the *osDelayUntil* function.

A key aspect of the *osDelayUntil* function is to allow us to implement periodic tasking. This works fine until such tasks can be preempted. However, when preemption can occur, behaviour becomes unpredictable and undesirable. This, it appears, is due to the wrapping of FreeRTOS APIs by the Cube tool, not a design flaw of FreeRTOS***. Best to check out your design if you intend to use this API.

(b) Using the *osDelay* function.

This performed exactly as expected, providing a very straightforward way to implement highly accurate time delays. It can also be used to provide support for periodic tasking in the following situations:

(i) Where task execution times are small compared with their periodic times *and* task preemptions aren't expected to be a problem. In this case any time jitter from run-to-run would be insignificant.
(ii) Where task execution times are significant compared with their periodic times *and* task preemptions aren't expected to be a problem but jitter *is* acceptable.

Lastly, a general comment: these exercises truly demonstrate the power of Tracealyzer as a recording/analysis tool. It has allowed us to obtain highly detailed timing data together with an excellent visual display of tasking operations.

*** Note that issues have been reported with the *osDelayUntil* function for some time now. http://www.freertos.org/FreeRTOS_Support_Forum_Archive/February_2015/ freertos_bug_in_cmsisOS_api_wrapper_for_FreeRTOS_28f2f402j.html

Chapter 7

Introduction to the streaming mode of operation.

7.1 Tracealyzer exercise 7 - Using the streaming mode for trace recording.

The objective of this work is to introduce you to the streaming mode of operation. This mode must be used if you wish to make significantly longer trace recordings than those gathered by the snapshot operation.

The timing problem produced by the *vDelayUntil* function in exercise 6 is a good example of an issue that calls for further examination. We really need to evaluate this over (relatively) long execution times to assess its full impact on system performance. So, for exercise 7, create a project that implements the requirements specified in Tracealyzer exercise 6.2: then collect the run-time trace data using the streaming mode of Tracealyzer. However, before doing that:

- First, consult the section 'Quick reference guide - setting up streaming mode'.
- Second, ensure that your project contains all necessary include and source files as shown in figure 7.1.

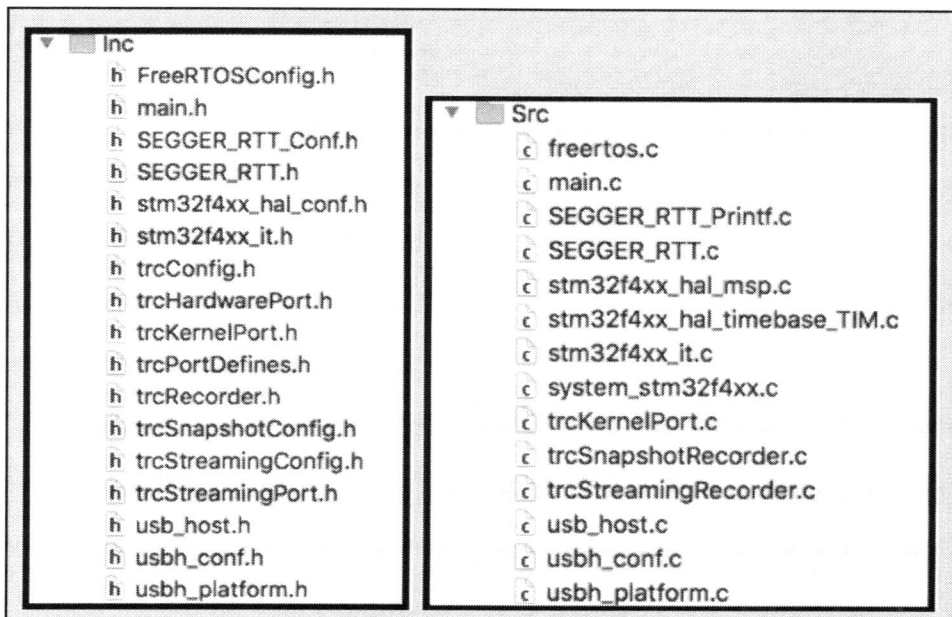

```
▼ 📁 Inc
    h  FreeRTOSConfig.h
    h  main.h
    h  SEGGER_RTT_Conf.h          ▼ 📁 Src
    h  SEGGER_RTT.h                   c  freertos.c
    h  stm32f4xx_hal_conf.h           c  main.c
    h  stm32f4xx_it.h                 c  SEGGER_RTT_Printf.c
    h  trcConfig.h                    c  SEGGER_RTT.c
    h  trcHardwarePort.h              c  stm32f4xx_hal_msp.c
    h  trcKernelPort.h                c  stm32f4xx_hal_timebase_TIM.c
    h  trcPortDefines.h               c  stm32f4xx_it.c
    h  trcRecorder.h                  c  system_stm32f4xx.c
    h  trcSnapshotConfig.h            c  trcKernelPort.c
    h  trcStreamingConfig.h           c  trcSnapshotRecorder.c
    h  trcStreamingPort.h             c  trcStreamingRecorder.c
    h  usb_host.h                     c  usb_host.c
    h  usbh_conf.h                    c  usbh_conf.c
    h  usbh_platform.h                c  usbh_platform.c
```

Figure 7.1 List of project include and source files

- Third, modify the source code to include the Tracealyzer API call, as shown below.

```
///////////////////////////////////////////////////////////////////////////////
Initialize the recorder; start recording later at a designated point.

In main:
/* Configure the system clock */
 SystemClock_Config();

 /* USER CODE BEGIN SysInit */
        vTraceEnable(TRC_START_AWAIT_HOST);
 /* USER CODE END SysInit */
///////////////////////////////////////////////////////////////////////////////
```

Download your machine code to the target, then reset the board (thus starting code execution). You should find that the system enters a pause mode before any tasking operations take place. This corresponds to the point at which the trace recorder API is executed. As a result the system pauses, waiting for a 'start recording' command from Tracealyzer.
   Now start Tracealyzer, then select 'File', figure 7.2.

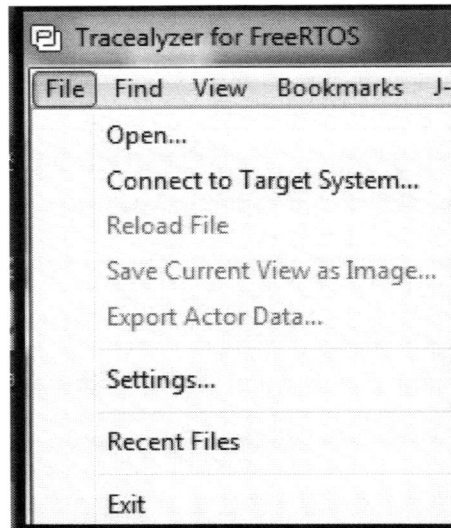

Figure 7.2 Tracealyzer 'File' drop-down menu

From the drop-down menu select 'settings' and check the 'Streaming Trace Settings' correspond to those shown in figure 7.3

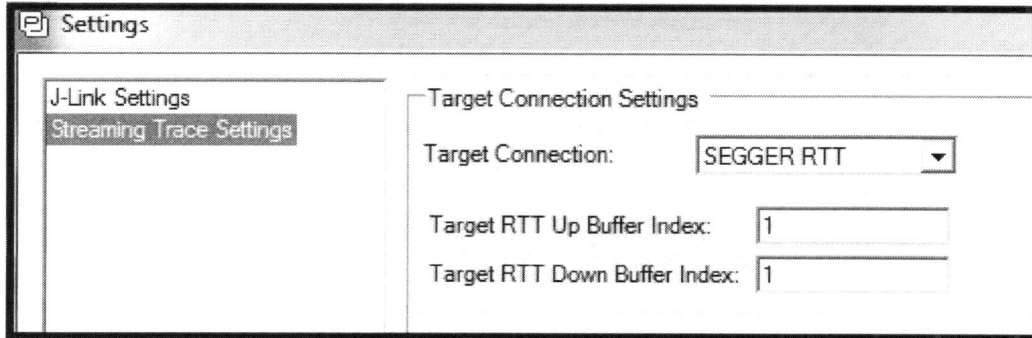

Figure 7.3 Tracealyzer 'Streaming Trace Settings'

Return to the drop-down menu and select 'Connect to target system', figure 7.4.

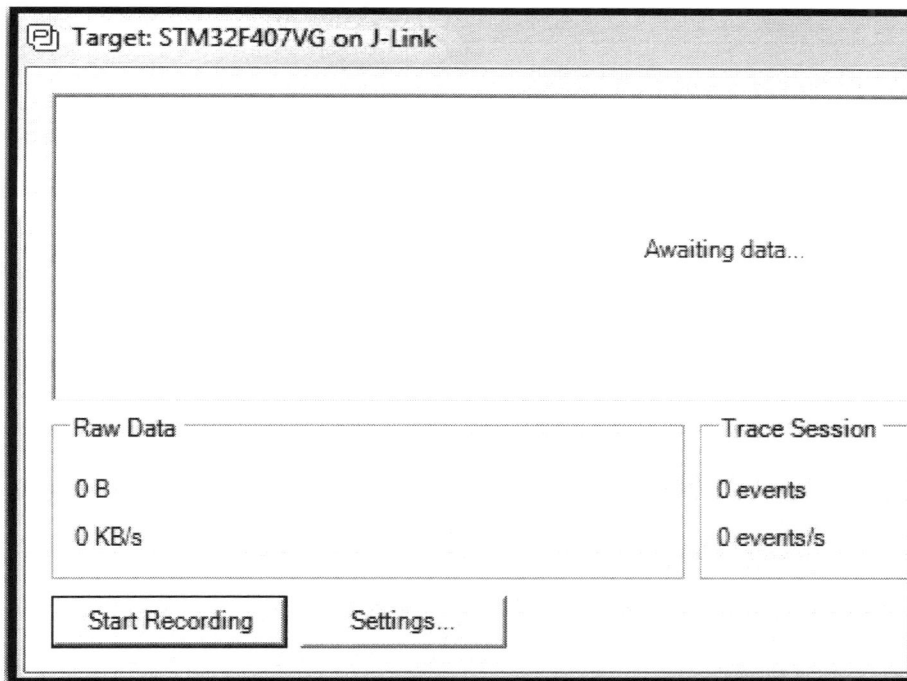

Figure 7.4 Tracealyzer recording window - ready to start recording

Click on 'Start Recording'. You will find that the target system now continues with its normal execution but with trace recordings in action, figure 7.5.

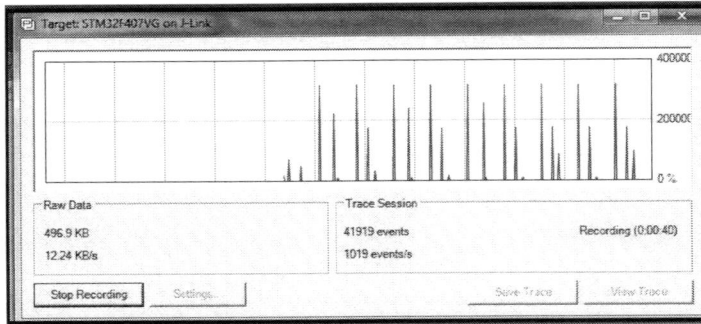

Figure 7.5 Run-time recording in progress

Stop the recording as and when desired, then view or save the results (an example trace is shown in figure 7.6, its duration being approximately 43 seconds.

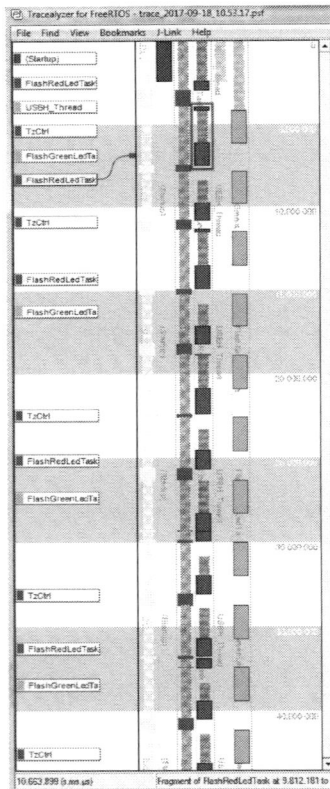

Figure 7.6 Example trace recording

An alternative way to use the tool is to first initialize the recorder: then start recording later at a designated point.

//

```
In main:
 /* Configure the system clock */
  SystemClock_Config();

  /* USER CODE BEGIN SysInit */
      vTraceEnable(TRC_INIT);
  /* USER CODE END SysInit */

In task code:
/* StartFlashRedLedTask function */
void StartFlashRedLedTask(void const * argument)
{
    ............
   /* USER CODE BEGIN 5 */
       vTraceEnable(TRC_START_AWAIT_HOST);
     ............
  /* Infinite loop */
  {
   /* code of task */
  } /* end infinite loop */
}
```
//

Chapter 8

Analyzing resource sharing and task intercommunications.

8.1 Tracealyzer exercise 8 - Mutual exclusion: using protected shared resources.

The purpose of this exercise is to use Tracealyzer to observe task executions that involve accesses to a protected shared resource. The system task diagram for this work is shown in figure 8.1.

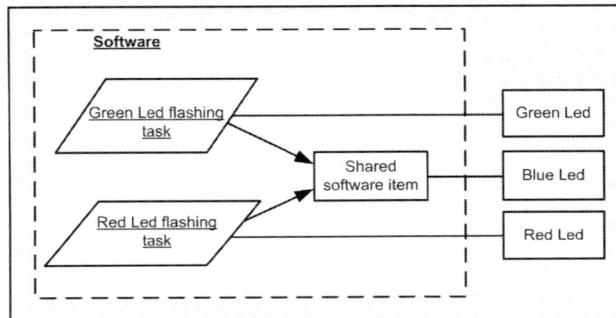

Figure 8.1 System task diagram

The design is to use a priority preemptive scheduling scheme, with the Green task having the higher priority. It is intended to be similar in operation to the original exercise 7 but now having two tasks and modified timings (figure 8.2).

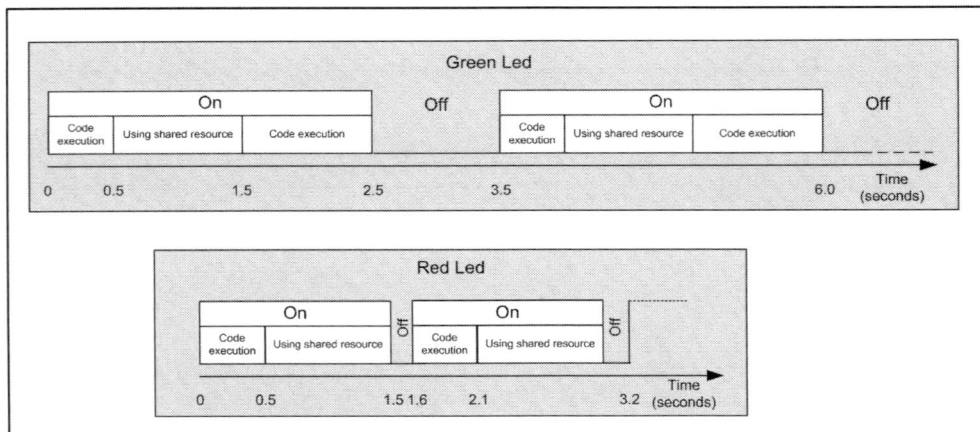

Figure 8.2 Timing diagram of Led flashing operations

(a)Green Led task.

When dispatched it executes non-critical code for 0.5 seconds, then accesses the shared software item. This access lasts for one second. It then resumes executing non-critical code, for a further one second. At this point it enters a one second time-suspended mode; on awakening, the cycle repeats itself.

(a) Red Led task.

When dispatched it executes non-critical code for 0.5 seconds, then accesses the shared software item. This access lasts for one second, followed by a 0.1 second time-suspended mode. On awakening, the cycle repeats itself.

There is only one important feature of these timings; it guarantees that, at some time, the Green task will try to access the shared resource whilst it is held by the Red task (if you wish, use whatever timings appeal to you).

Access to the shared software item is to be protected by a semaphore, as in the original exercise 8:

///

Access shared data function — suggested code:
1. Check if the Start flag is Up.
   If Up then set the Start flag to Down
   else turn the Blue Led on.
2. Simulate read/write operations for one second.
3. Turn the Blue Led off**.
4. Set Start flag to Up.
** Insert this if you wish the Blue Led to turn off after a contention is detected.

///

Configure your code for streaming operations, exercise it in the target system, and capture its operation using Tracealyzer. Inspect it to find where the scenarios described above occurs (i.e. Green task trying to access the shared resource whilst it is held by Red). The trace won't show any semaphore details, but you can deduce the times at which it is accessed (carefully check out all recorded timings shown here and also those of your own design).

In our case the following interactions, figures 8.3 and 8.4 were recorded during a 30 second trace:

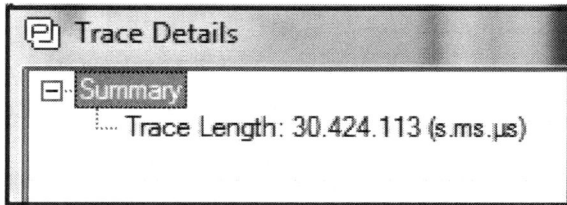

Figure 8.3 Trace streaming length

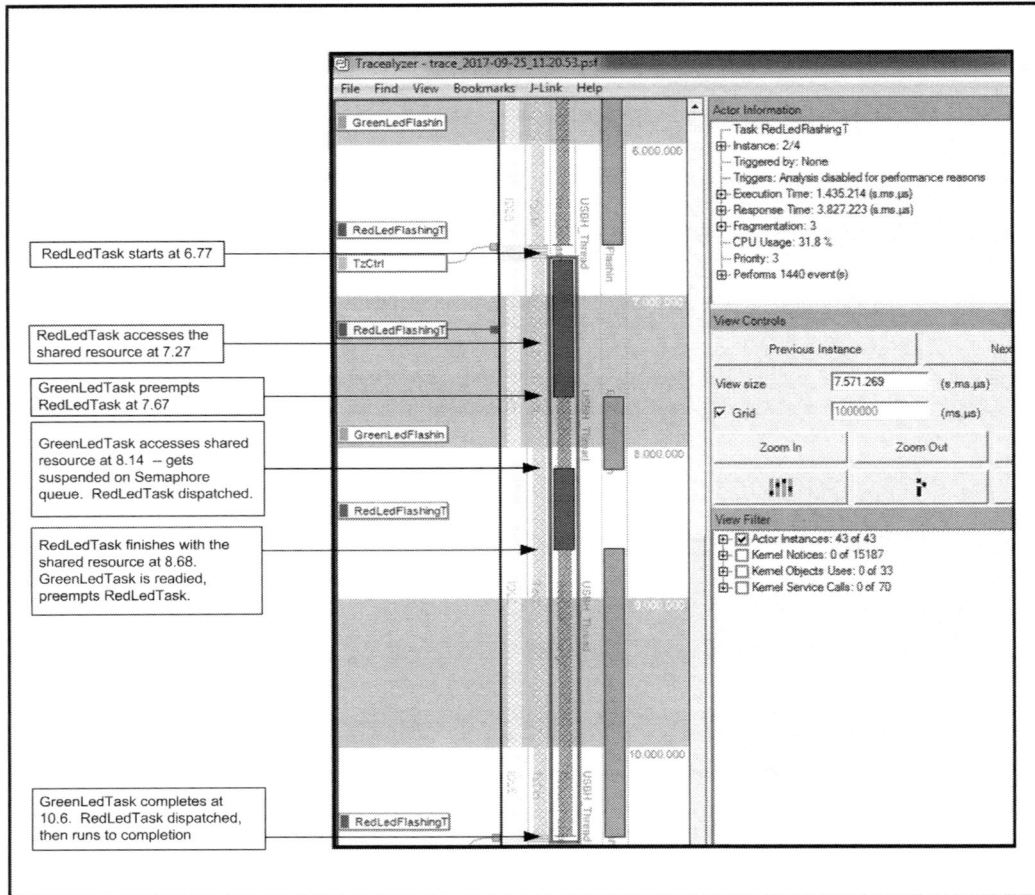

Figure 8.4 Trace recording of Led flashing operations

Note that, in our design, software delay loops were used to simulate code operations. As a result the timings may vary slightly from those defined in figure 8.2.

If you wish to identify precisely when tasks make semaphore calls you need to use the the CPU Load and the Communication Flow graphs (please read about these now in the Tracealyzer documentation). After a trace has been captured, open the CPU Load Graph view and select the time intervals of interest, figure 8.5(a). Position your cursor within this selection, then right click the mouse button. The window shown in 8.5(b) will appear. In this select 'Show Communication Flow', at which point the Communication Flow Graph will open, figure 8.5(c).

In this example the graph shows that it has 'No Data To Display'. This means that there weren't any task-semaphore interactions during the selected time period. However, the selected time interval of figure 8.6 *does* include a call by the Red task to take the semaphore. In informal terms the Red task *acquires* the semaphore.

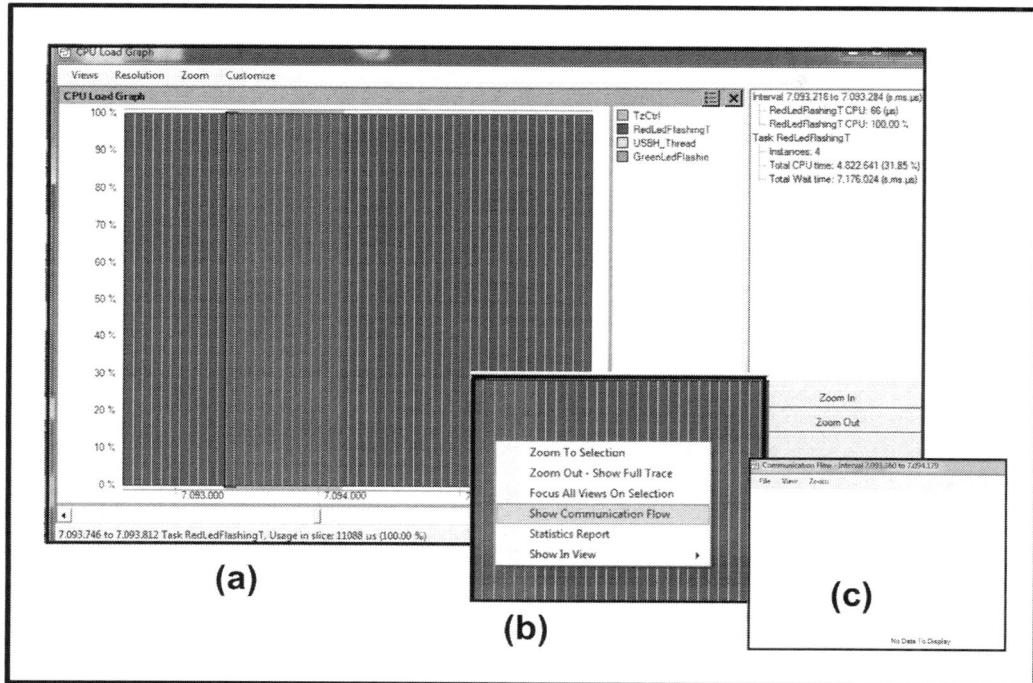

Figure 8.5 Trace recordings 1

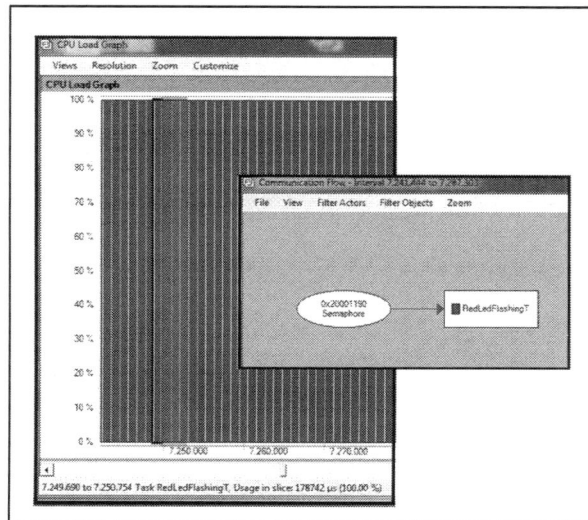

Figure 8.6 Trace recording that includes a *SemaphoreTake* call by Red task

Detailed timing of semaphore operations can be obtained by opening the Kernel Object History view, figure 8.7 (double-click on the semaphore icon).

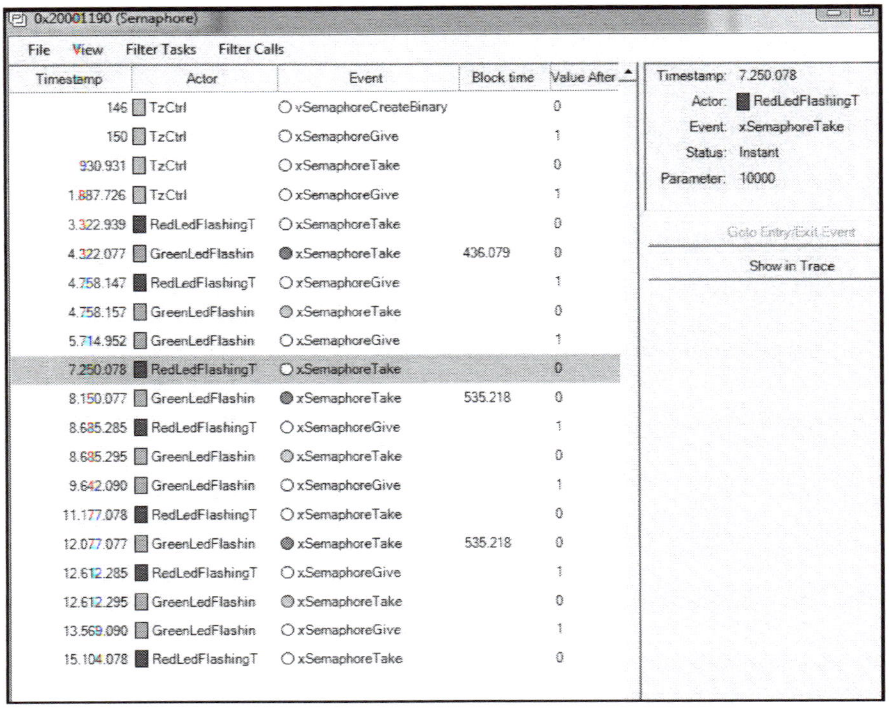

Figure 8.7 Semaphore Object History

In figure 8.5 we'd estimated that the *SemaphoreTake* call was made at 7.27 seconds. But from figure 8.7 we can see that it occurs at precisely 7.250078 seconds (according to the recorder). From the Semaphore Object History graph we can show the corresponding time point in the Vertical Trace View, figure 8.8.

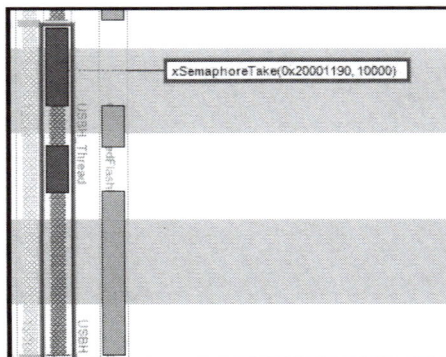

Figure 8.8 Vertical Trace View - *SemaphoreTake* operation by Red task

Moving down one event on the history graph to where the Green task makes a *SemaphoreTake* call: we can show, as before, the corresponding point on the Vertical Trace View, figure 8.9.

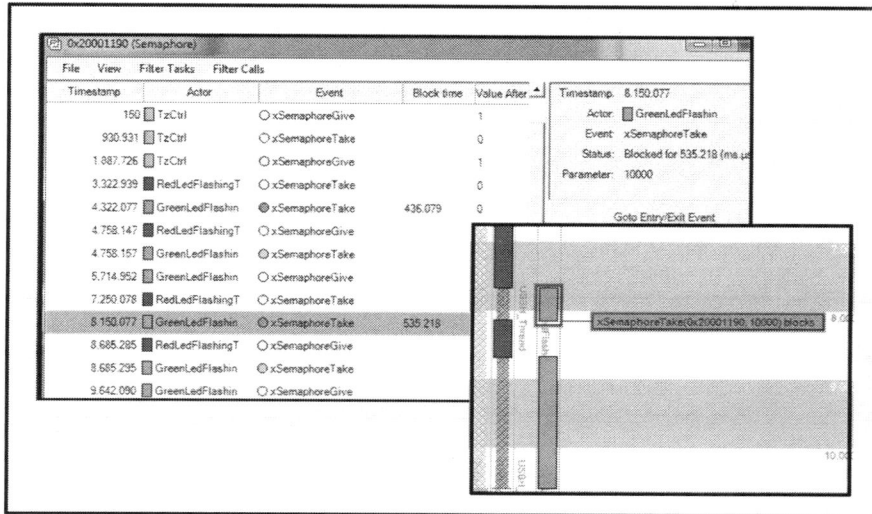

Figure 8.9 Vertical Trace View - blocked *SemaphoreTake* call

It can be seen from the 'Value After' column that the Green task fails to acquire the semaphore (which is precisely as predicted since it is currently held by the Red task). The corresponding CPU Load and Communication Flow graphs are shown in figure 8.10.

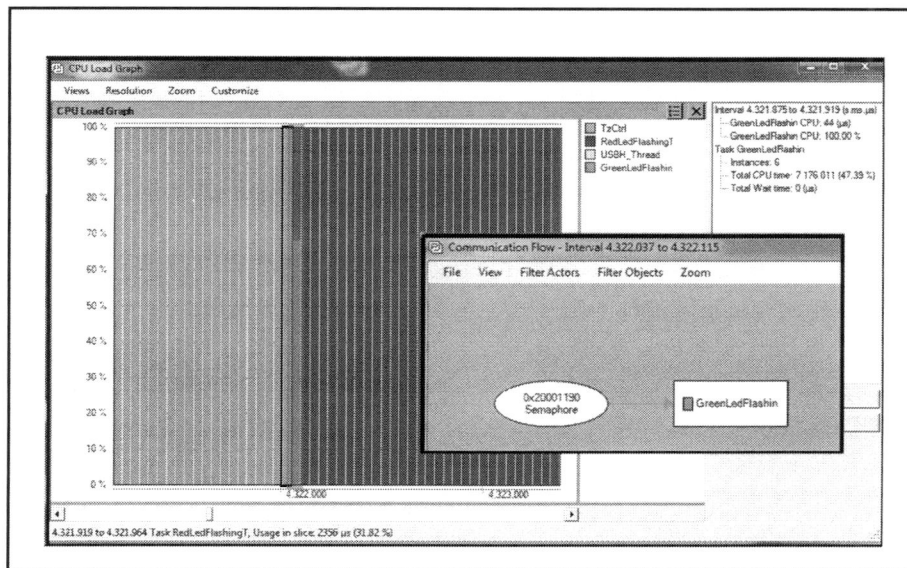

Figure 8.10 Trace recording - blocked *SemaphoreTake* call by the Green task

The next event on the history graph is where the Red task makes a *SemaphoreGive* call; it *releases* the semaphore, figure 8.11.

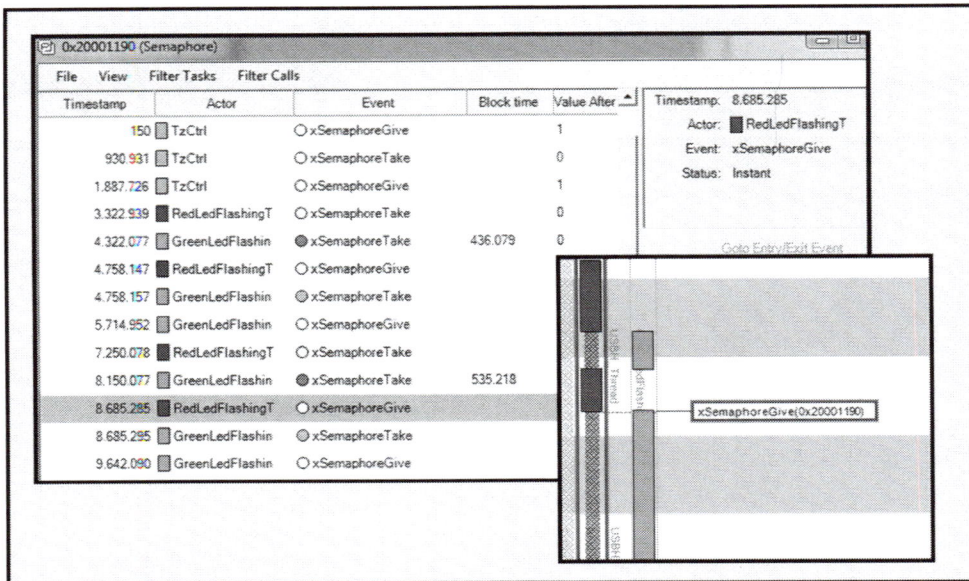

Figure 8.11 Releasing the semaphore - SemaphoreGive event

The corresponding Communication Flow Graph can be seen in figure 8.12.

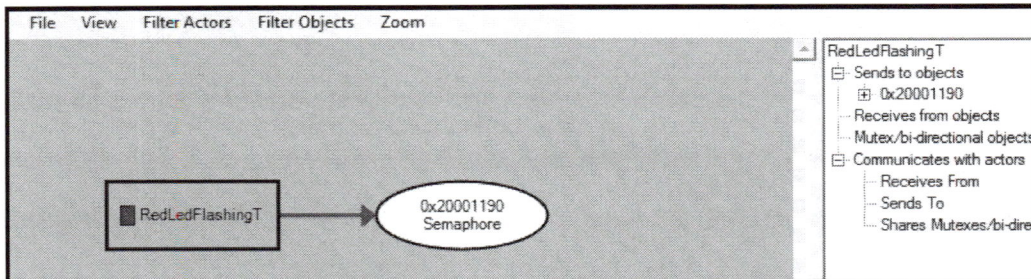

Figure 8.12 Communication Flow Graph - SemaphoreGive event

   This exercise is a fairly straightforward one, one that allows you to quickly understand the tool features.   We strongly recommend that you fully evaluate the tool qualities using such simple designs; it will make it much easier to employ it in real, practical applications (a much more complex task).

8.2 Tracealyzer exercise 9 - Investigating non-synchronized data transfer between tasks.

The purpose of the exercise is to investigate the use of a queue to support data transfer between tasks without any synchronizing actions. Figure 8.13 shows the system task diagram, comprising two tasks and a single queue.

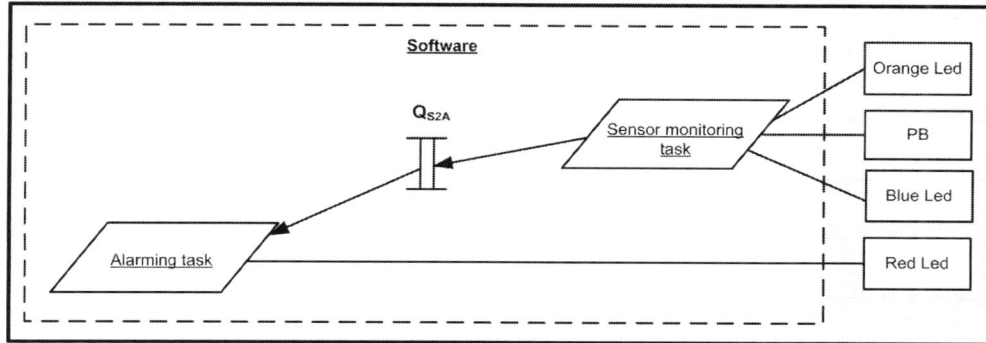

Figure 8.13 System task diagram

Your implementation should be identical to that of the original exercise 19, with one small change (see below).

8.2.1 Behavioural specification - a recap.

Implement the exercise to conform to the specifications detailed below. Both tasks are to run within infinite loops, having equal priorities. Please also consult the original exercise 19 for more detailed information. Here the Leds are used to indicate the current operational state of the system.

Blue Led - is used to display the current state of the push button:
- When off, denotes that the push button is *released*.
- When on, denotes that the push button is *pressed*.

Orange Led - is used to show the system alarm status.
- When off, denotes that the sensor is *Not In Alarm*.
- When on, denotes that the sensor is *In Alarm*.

Red Led - is used to show the status of the Alarming task:
- Initially turned off, denoting that the Alarming task is in a non-alarm state.
- Is turned on when an *In Alarm* signal is received from the Sensor task.
- Is next turned off when a Not *In Alarm* signal is received from the Sensor task.

(a) Sensor monitoring task.
The key points are as follows:

1. The PB mimics the action of an alarm switch.
2. It (the PB) is polled to detect its current state.
3. When the PB is pressed the Blue Led is turned on; when released the Led is turned off.
4. After a PB press is detected and actioned there is a 250 ms delay before checking the button status again.

5. After a PB release is detected and actioned there is a 250 ms delay before checking the button status again.
6. A change in the sensor alarm state is mimicked by depressing the push button (*depress* — press followed by release).
7. The alarm default state is *Not In Alarm.*
8. The first depressing action sets the alarm state to *In Alarm.* This state information is sent as a message to the queue and the Orange Led is turned on.
9. The next depressing action sets the alarm state back to *Not In Alarm.* Again, this information is sent to the queue and the Orange Led is turned off.
10. The next depressing action once again sets the alarm state to I*n Alarm,* which is then sent to the queue, and so on repeatedly.

(b) Alarming task.
1. The queue is polled for messages at a 4 Hz. rate (approximately).
2. If an *In Alarm* message is received:
    • The Red Led is turned on.
    • Alarm processing is simulated (in software) for 500 milliseconds.
3. If a *Not In Alarm* message is received the Red Led is turned off (if it was already on).

8.2.2 Trace recordings - alarm generated by sensor task.

The following recordings relate to events that take place:

   (a) Just prior to the sensor task going into alarm and
   (b) When an alarm occurs in the sensor task.

The Vertical Trace View covering this period is shown in figure 8.14.
   To start with, we'll highlight the run of the Alarming task that takes place just before an alarm occurs, denoted as instance 34/61. At this point the Alarming task is active, polling for a message (where its first action is to check the queue state by making the *xQueueReceive* call). No message is present; thus it continues executing the remainder of the task code. At this point it then suspends for 250 milliseconds.

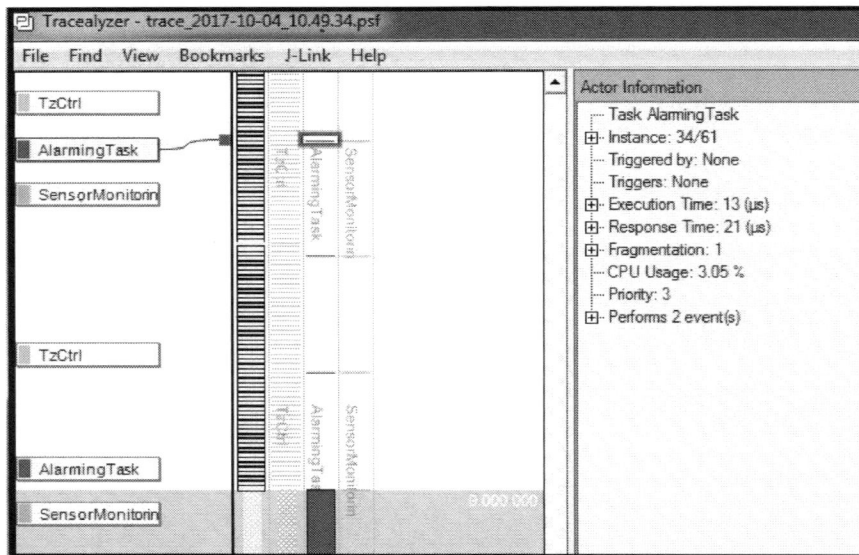

Figure 8.14 Vertical Trace View 1

During the period preceding alarm signalling the queue interacts only with the Alarming task, figure 8.15.

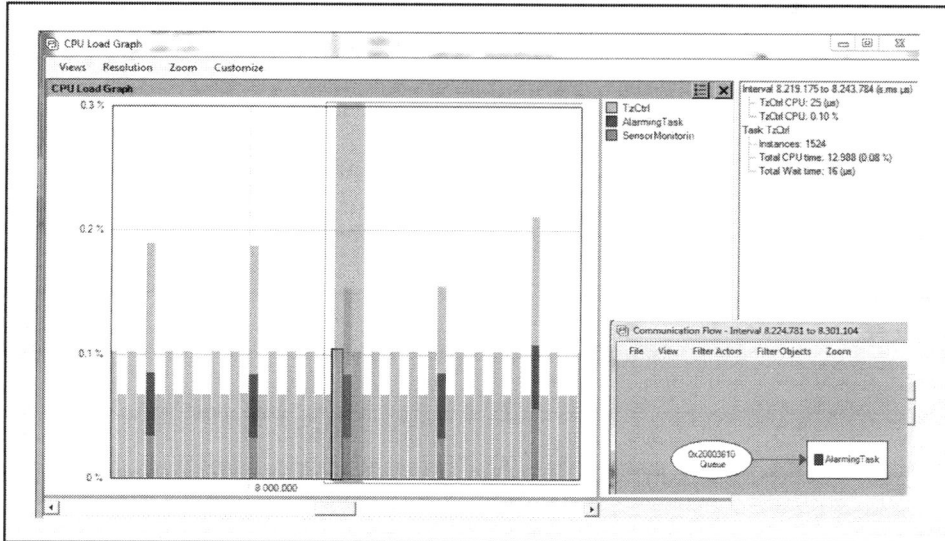

Figure 8.15 Queue-task interactions before a sensor alarm is signalled.

Further communication flow details are shown in figure 8.16.

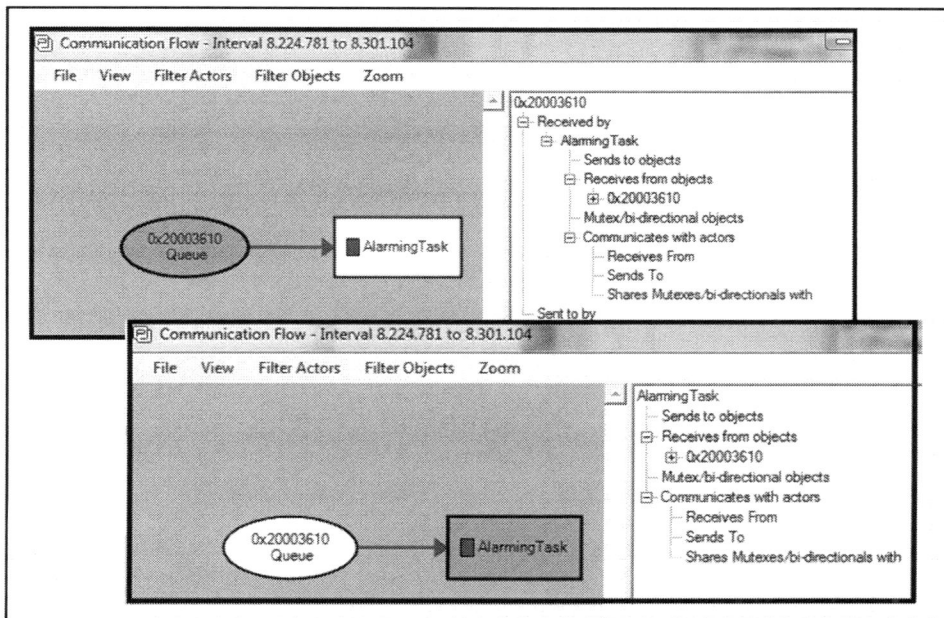

Figure 8.16 Further communication flow details

By double-clicking on the queue and task icons you can obtain further information about their behaviours, figure 8.17.

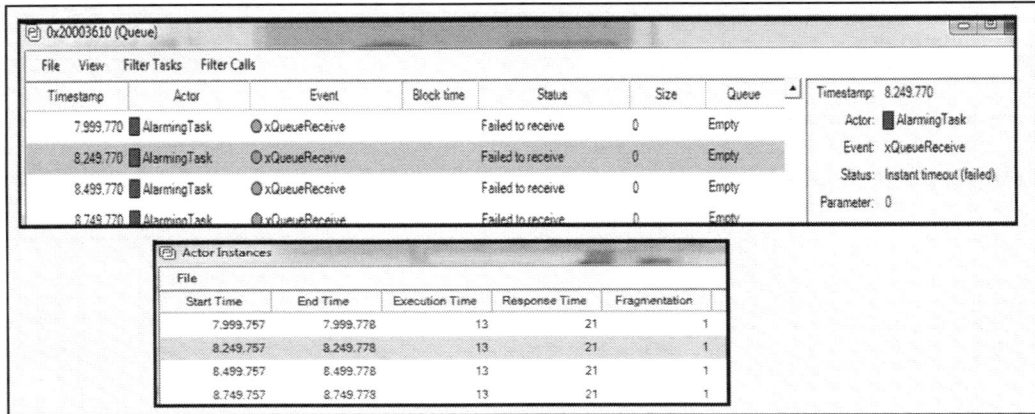

Figure 8.17 Queue and task - detailed information

Shortly after this the Sensor task goes into alarm. As a result it sends a message to the Alarming task (figures 8.18, 8.19), which then performs alarm processing for 0.5 seconds.

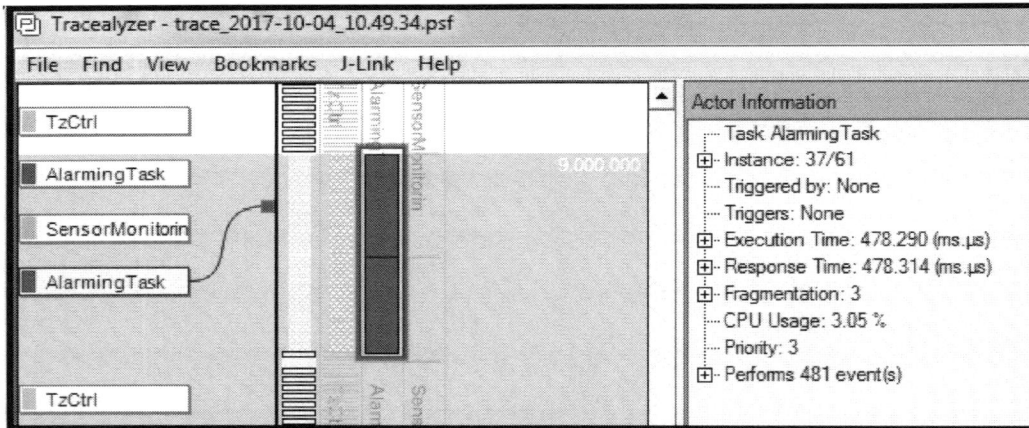

Figure 8.18 Vertical Trace View 2

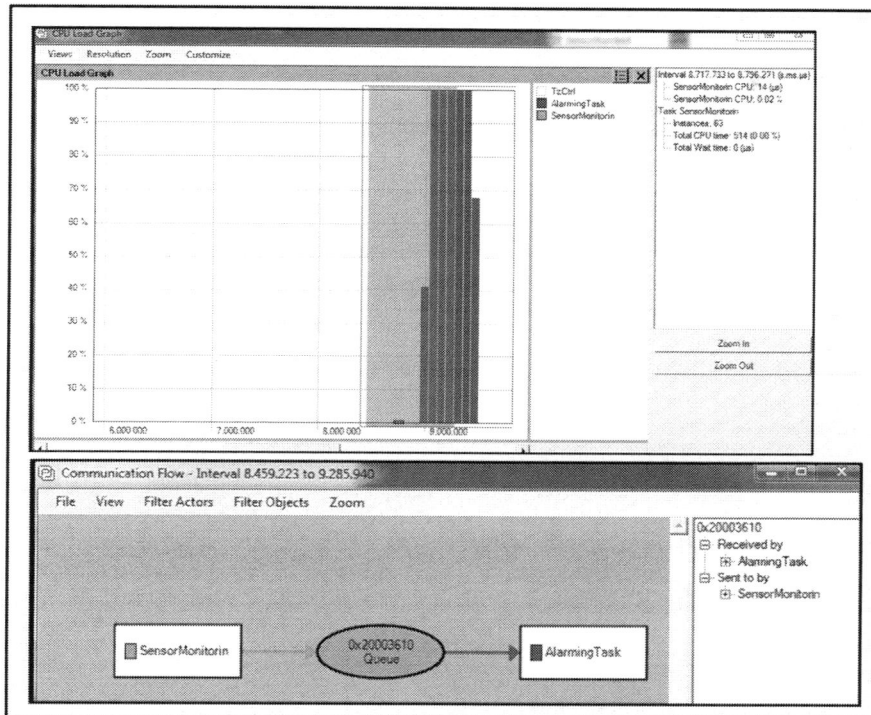

Figure 8.19 Queue-task interactions when a sensor alarm is signalled

Detailed information relating to both tasks and the queue is shown in figure 8.20. The overall sequence of messaging interactions is given in figure 8.21.

1. At time stamp 8.749.770, figure 8.21a, the Alarming Task makes an *xQueueReceive* call to the queue. However, as there isn't a message in the queue, it completes its processing, then suspends for 250 milliseconds.
2. The next event, figure 8.21b, occurs at time stamp 8.749.782, when the SensorMonitoring Task makes an *xQueueSend* call to the queue (that is, sends a message to the queue - see Queue column of figure 8.21b).
3. Lastly, in figure 8.21c, at time stamp 8.999.770, the Alarming Task once again makes an *xQueueReceive* call to the queue. This collects the message, thus emptying the queue (confirmed by the Queue column info at time stamp 8.727.668). After it has acquired the message it processes it for 500 milliseconds.

The recordings given here have covered the most important features relating to the use of queues.
    A last comment: if you really wish to understand FreeRTOS, it is well worth spending time investigating its detailed behaviour using Tracealyzer.

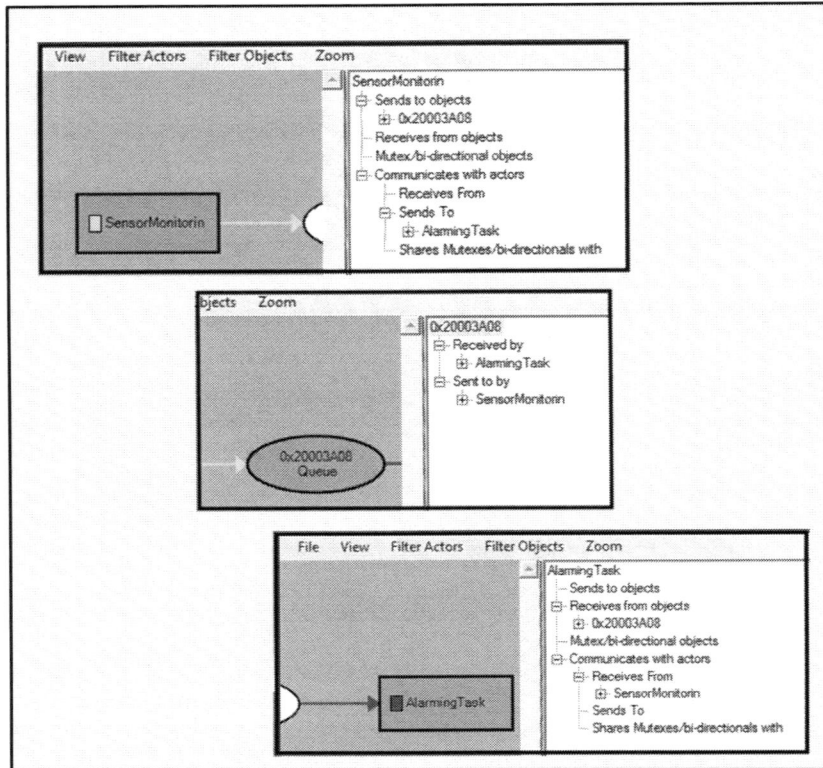

Figure 8.20 Queue and tasks - detailed information

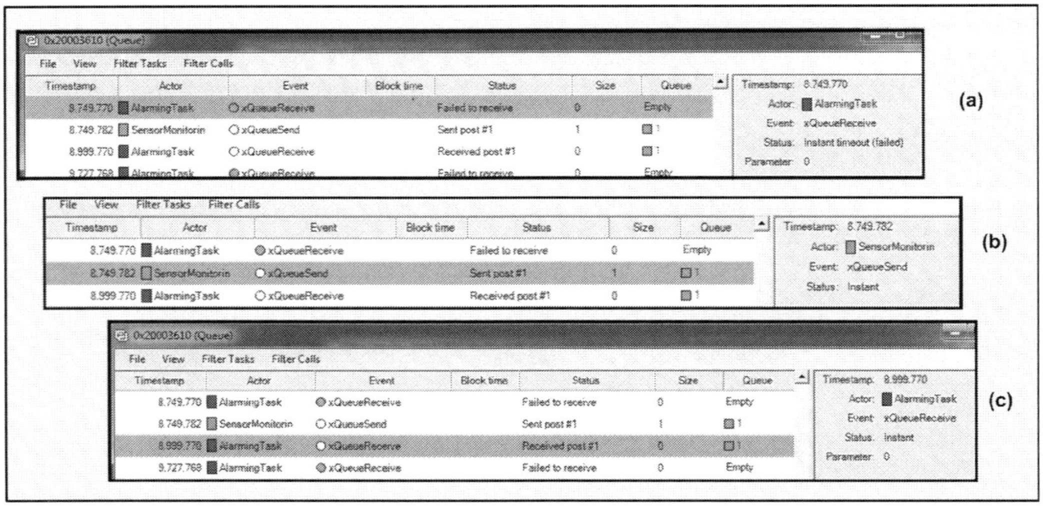

Figure 8.21 Message signalling interactions

8.3 Tracealyzer exercise 10 - Investigating synchronized data transfer between tasks.

The purpose of the exercise is to demonstrate task synchronization with data transfer, applied to the system of figure 8.22. In this case synchronization is unilateral, with the Alarming task acting as a deferred server. A mailbox is used as the signalling/synchronization mechanism, this being based on a single queue.

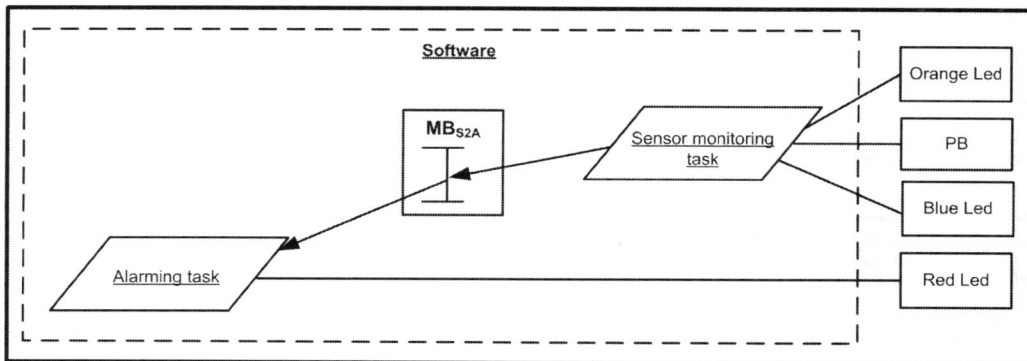

Figure 8.22 System task diagram

Your implementation should be the same as Tracealyzer exercise 9, but with some important changes:

- The Alarm task does not continuously poll for a message arrival; instead it waits indefinitely (suspended on the queue) until one is received.
- When an *InAlarm* message arrives the task is 'released', and performs processing for 500 millisecond (as before). Following this it once again checks the queue state, suspends and then waits until a message arrives.
- When a *NotInAlarm* message arrives the task is 'released', and performs processing for 250 millisecond. After this it once again checks the queue state, waiting indefinitely until a message arrives.

All other actions are to be as defined in exercise 9. Also, these times aren't critical, but the processing must be simulated in software (and *not* using a Delay function).

The following set of figures are Tracealyzer recordings of the more important task interactions. These are a sequence of Vertical Trace View recordings, starting with a run of the Sensor Monitoring task, figure 8.23. In this case the system was normal, i.e. not in alarm.

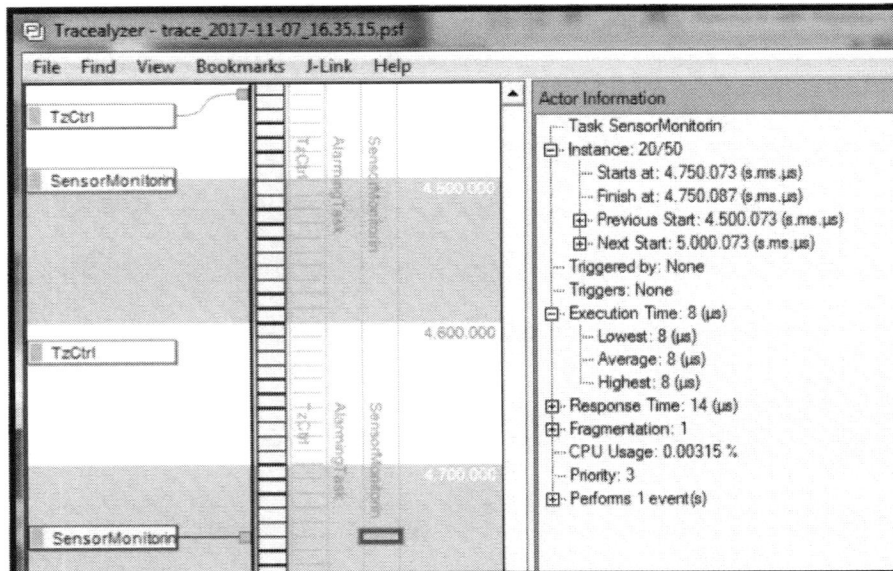

Figure 8.23 Vertical Trace View - Sensor Monitoring Task execution (non-alarm)

Observe that there aren't any executions of the Alarming task, confirming that it is in a suspended mode.

At the next execution of the Monitoring task, instance 21/51 (figure 8.24), an alarm has been generated.

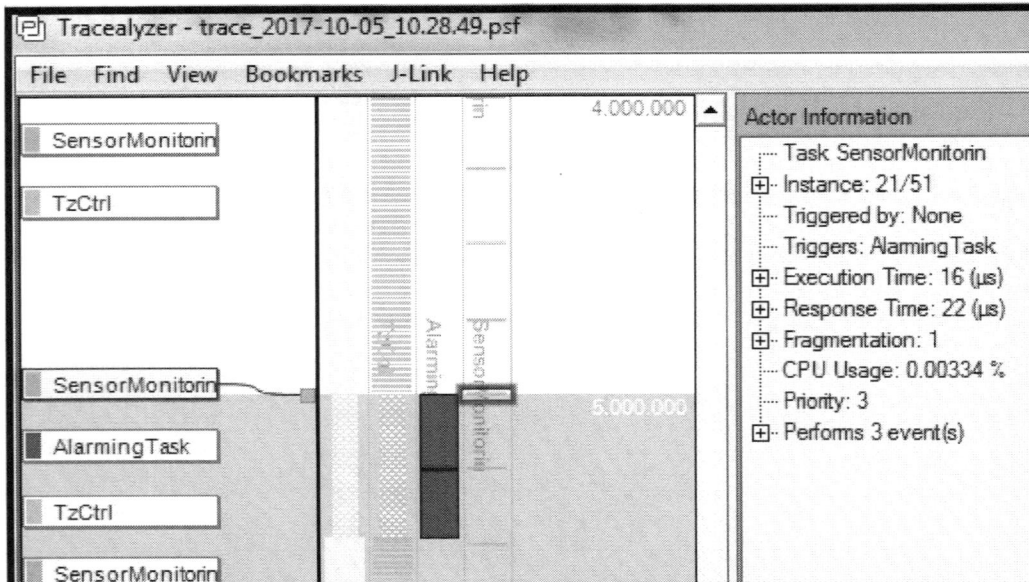

Figure 8.24 Vertical Trace View - Sensor Monitoring Task execution (alarm)

It therefore sends a message to the Alarming task, thus triggering it into action (figure 8.25). The resulting task execution time shown in the Actor information confirms that it was an *InAlarm* message.

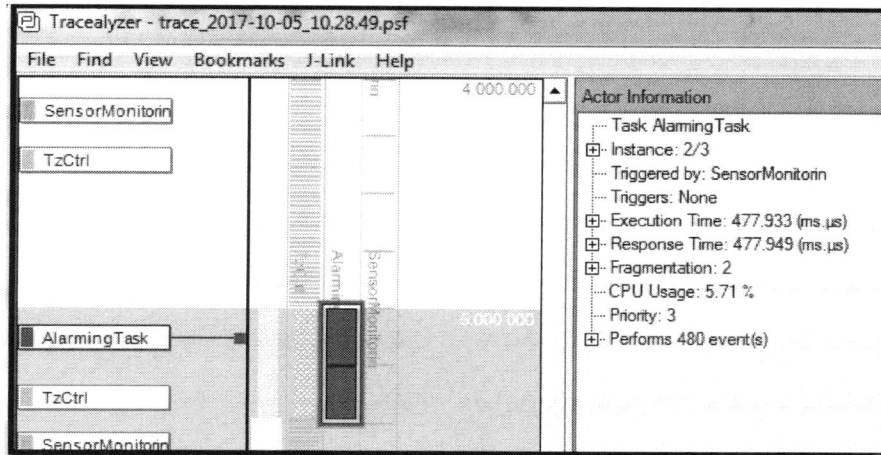

Figure 8.25 Alarming (server) Task triggered by the Sensor Monitoring task

Here, for simplicity of operation, the Monitoring task sends only one *InAlarm* message when an alarm is detected. Hence there is no re-triggering of the Alarming task the next time the Monitoring task runs (instance 22/51, figure 8.26). Note: the Alarming task is fragmented by the run of the Monitoring task.

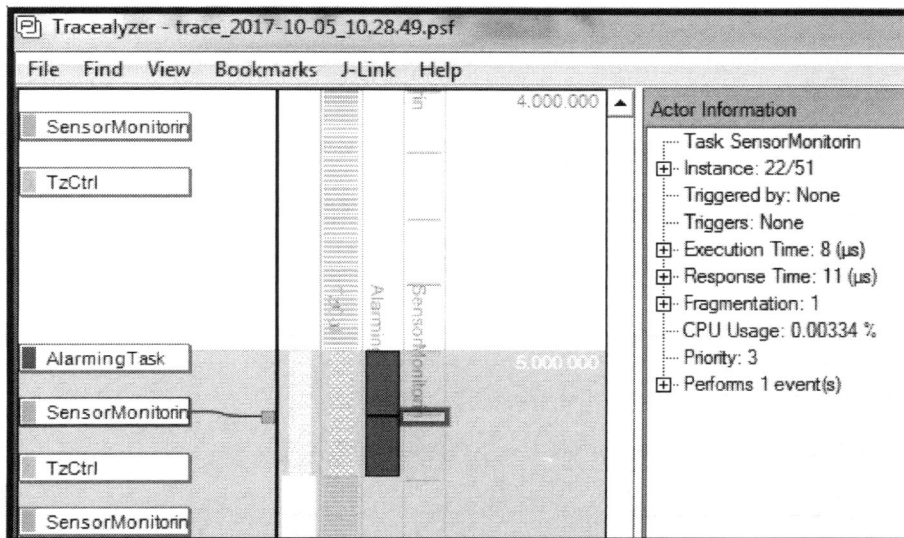

Figure 8.26 Periodic execution of the Sensor Monitoring task (non-alarm)

After the Alarming task has completed its processing it makes a read of the mailbox. As there isn't a message ready for collection the task once again goes into a suspended-on-queue mode.

It is woken up from this when the Monitoring task signals *NotInAlarm*, instance 33/51, figure 8.27.

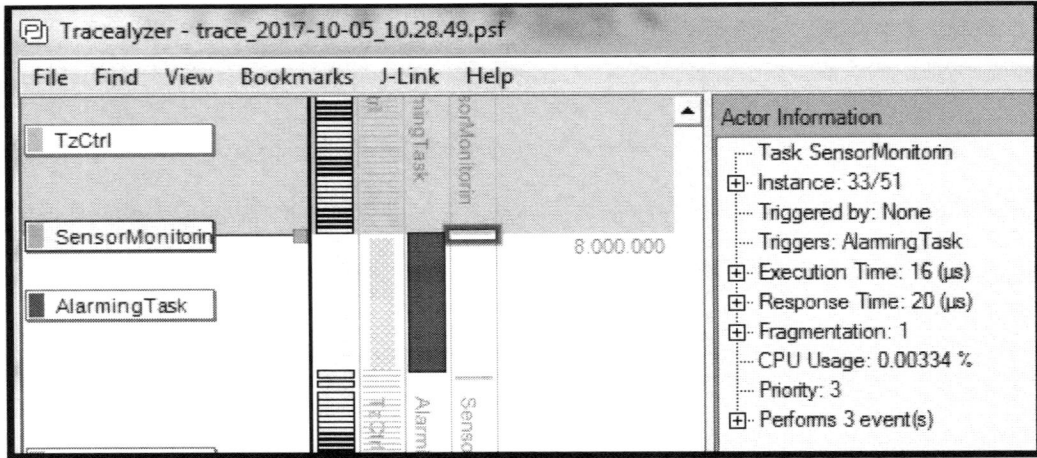

Figure 8.27 Sensor Monitoring Task execution - *NotInAlarm* message generated

This triggers the Alarming task into action (figure 8.28), the processing time of 238 ms confirming that the message was a *NotInAlarm* one.

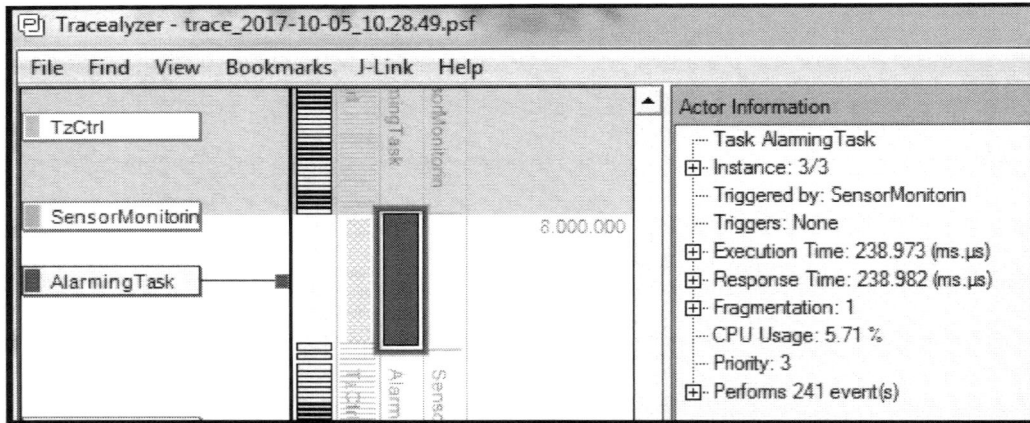

Figure 8.28 Alarming (server) Task triggered by *NotInAlarm* message

There is little point in us here exploring the recordings in more detail, as it'll just retread familiar ground. However, if you carry out this exercise, we recommend that you do analyze it fully; it's a good way to deepen your understanding of RTOS operation.

8.4 Tracealyzer exercise 11 - Evaluating the use of deferred server techniques.

This exercise demonstrates the use of Tracealyzer to observe the activation of a deferred server task using interrupt-driven operations. The overall system is shown in figure 8.29.

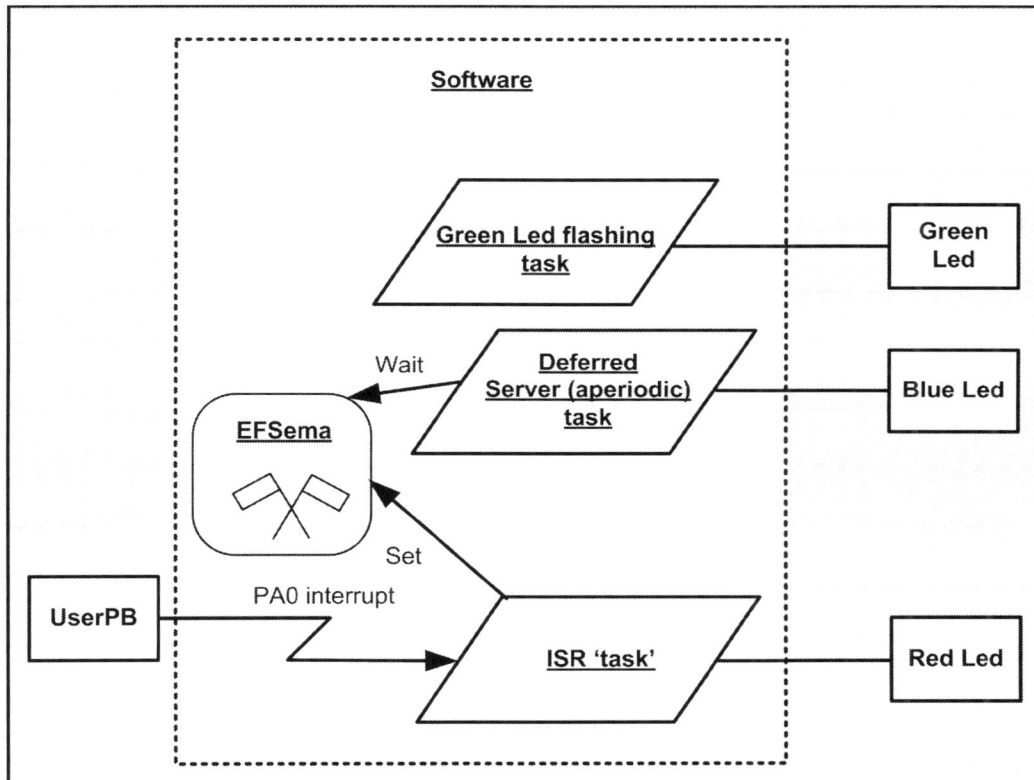

Figure 8.29 System task diagram

8.4.1 Overall description of operation.

With reference to figure 8.29: until an interrupt occurs the only active task is the Green Led one. This is a straightforward periodic one, whose role in the scenario will become clear later in this section.

The aperiodic task is a classical deferred server type, one that spends most of its life in suspension (waiting on a Semaphore queue). The task, when first activated, immediately makes a *Wait* call on the semaphore. Provided the semaphore is correctly initialized it will now suspend, waiting for a wake-up signal. As can be seen, the semaphore is *Set* by the ISR code, which results in the Deferred Server (DS) task being released. The ISR itself is invoked when the user push-button generates a hardware interrupt signal.

Once the Deferred Server task is released it transits from the suspended to the ready state: subsequent execution is controlled by the RTOS scheduler. As the task runs in an infinite loop it eventually returns to the point where it once again makes a *Wait* call.

Very important point: the priority of the Green Led task *must* be greater than that of the Deferred Server one. Remember: we use the deferred server technique to implement designs where:

- The activating signal (in this case a press of the push-button) must be responded to immediately but
- The DS task must have minimal effect on the scheduled (periodic) task set.

This implies that it isn't especially time-critical and thus can be safely run under the control of the scheduler.

8.4.2 Task timing aspects.

Let us deal first with the ISR/DS task aspects. This will involve two scenarios, the first being shown in figure 8.30. Please note, for these exercises, timings are *not* critical.

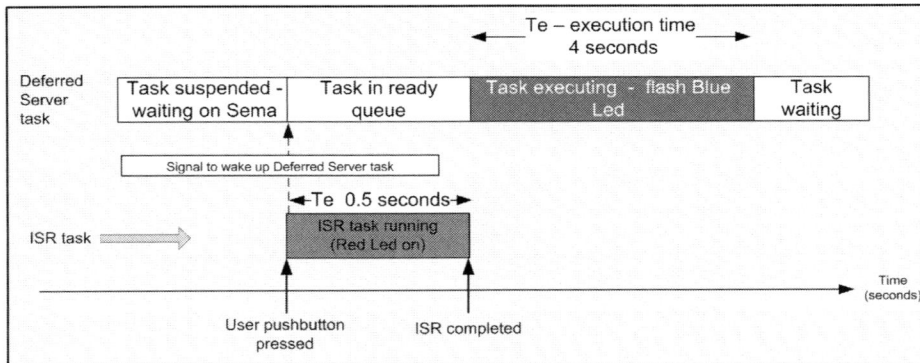

Figure 8.30 ISR/Deferred Server task timing aspects - scenario 1

The DS task is a 'one-shot' type that, when activated, executes for four seconds. During this period it flashes the Blue Led. The ISR task, when invoked:

(i)   Sends a *Set* signal to the semaphore.
(ii) Turns on the Red Led.
(iii) Runs for 0.5 seconds.
(iv) Turns off the Led.
(v)   Completes - returns from interrupt.

The second scenario is shown in figure 8.31. Here the ISR task, when invoked:

(i)   Turns on the Red Led.
(ii) Runs for 0.5 seconds.
(iii) Turns off the Led.
(iv) Sends a *Set* signal to the semaphore.
(v)   Completes - returns from interrupt.

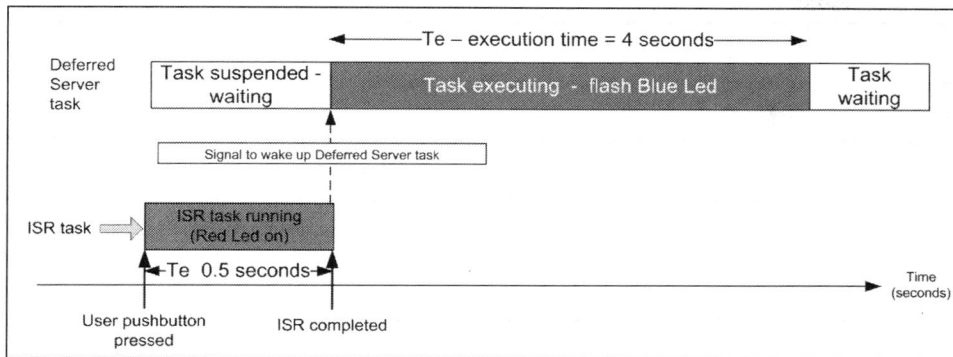

Figure 8.31 ISR/Deferred Server task timing aspects - scenario 2

Moving on: details of the periodic task are given in figure 8.32, which should be self-explanatory.

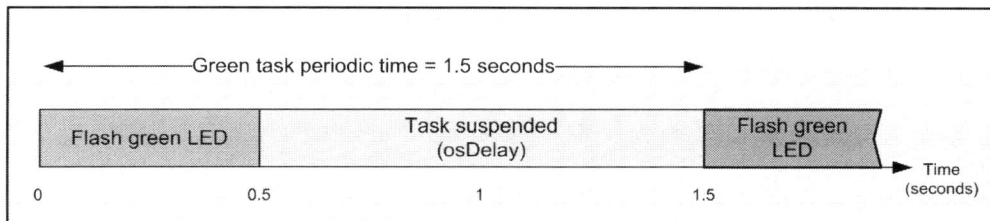

Figure 8.32 Timing diagram of the periodic (Green Led) task.

Now let's describe the reasons for choosing these particular behavioural and timing factors.

(a) ISR task.

In normal circumstances the run-time of an ISR should be as short as possible (to minimize disruption of scheduled tasking operations). Here though it is intended to run for 0.5 seconds (abnormally long in embedded work). This, however, is purely for demonstration purposes. While the ISR is active it *must* execute code - a software delay loop is sufficient for this purpose.
There are two reasons for implementing the design as described in the previous figures. First, the ISR execution time is long enough to give us clear visual feedback of its operation. Second, the interactional and timing behaviours in the two scenarios provide us with interesting and instructive data. This will be described later when viewing the trace results.

(b) Deferred Server and Green Led tasks.

Here the selected timings guarantee to produce multiple interactions between the tasks at run time (needed for demonstration purposes). The exercise will actually be done in three stages as described below.

  (i) Exercise 11a: Scenario 1, with Green Led task disabled.
  (ii) Exercise 11b: Scenario 2, with Green Led task disabled.
  (iii) Exercise 11c: Scenario 2, with Green Led task enabled.

8.4.3 Exercise 11a: Scenario 1, with Green Led task disabled.

Here the semaphore is Set at the start of the ISR. The reason for disabling the Green Led task during this exercise is to focus entirely on the ISR/DS task operations and interactions. Figure 8.33 below is a Vertical Trace View which highlights the behaviour and timings of the ISR.

Figure 8.33 Ex.11a Vertical Trace View 1

It clearly demonstrates where and when the DS task was released, thus implying that the ISR set

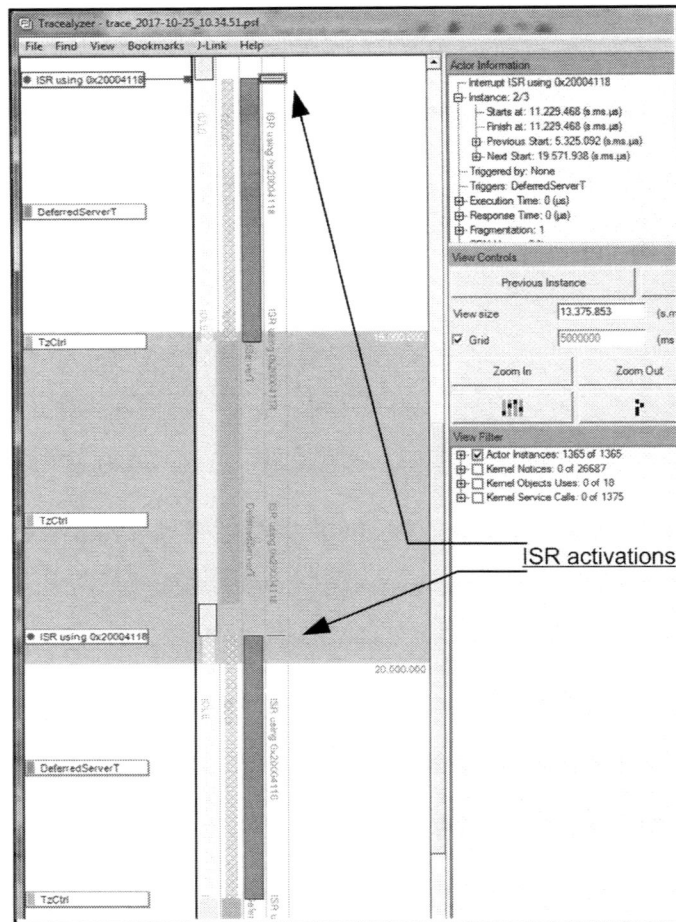

ISR activations

the semaphore. But the Actor Information shows an ISR execution time of zero seconds, clearly not true.
   We have included this result to bring it home to you that extra Tracealyzer calls are need to get interrupt timing data. These are:

(a) xTraceSetISRProperties.
This stores a name and priority level for an ISR and returns a trace handle. This handle is used to identify the ISR.

(b) vTraceStoreISRBegin.
This registers the beginning of an ISR, using the trace handle.

(c) vTraceStoreISREnd
This registers the end of an ISR.

The call to *xTraceSetISRProperties* must be made before tasking begins. Hence it makes sense to include it in main.c. The other two calls (essentially a matching pair) are used to 'bookend' the code of the ISR. The Tracealyzer Recorder Library documentation has full details of these APIs. However, to introduce the topic, a brief outline of their usage is given below.

1. Defining the trace handle.

        traceHandle PBsignalHandle = 0;

Note that you must make the trace handle - here named as PBsignalHandle - visible to all its users (i.e. the client code units).

2. Setting the ISR properties in main.c.

  /* USER CODE BEGIN 2 */

        PBsignalHandle = xTraceSetISRProperties("PBsignal", PriorityofISR);
        vTraceEnable(TRC_START_AWAIT_HOST);

  /* USER CODE END 2 */

The value of *PriorityofISR* can be found in the NVIC Configuration information of the CubeMX project, figure 8.34.

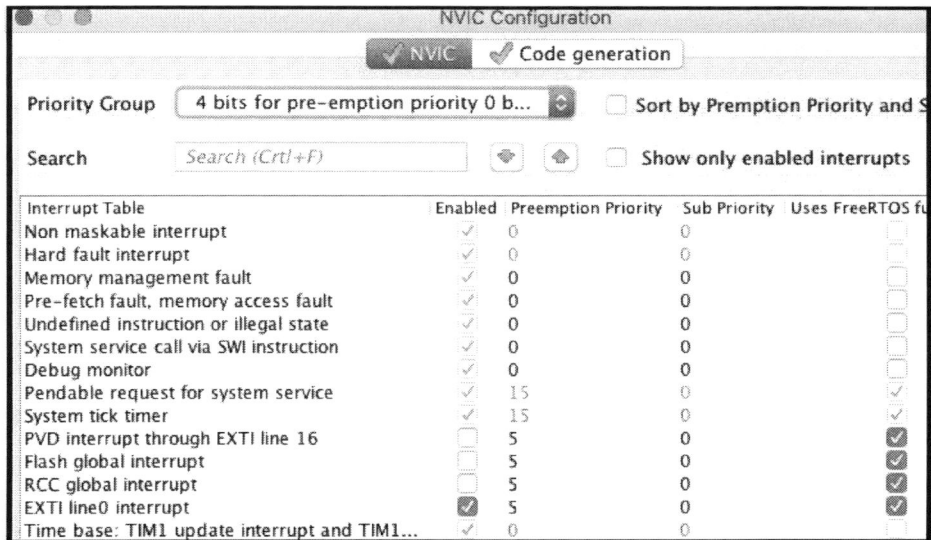

Figure 8.34 Priority of the pushbutton-generated ISR (EXT1 line 0 interrupt)

3. Instrumenting the ISR.

```
void EXTI0_IRQHandler(void)
{
 /* USER CODE BEGIN EXTI0_IRQn 0 */

        vTraceStoreISRBegin(PBsignalHandle);

                BODY OF THE ISR CODE

        vTraceStoreISREnd(0);

 /* USER CODE END EXTI0_IRQn 0 */
```

As a result of modifying the exercise code in this way the tool generates the correct timing data, figure 8.35.

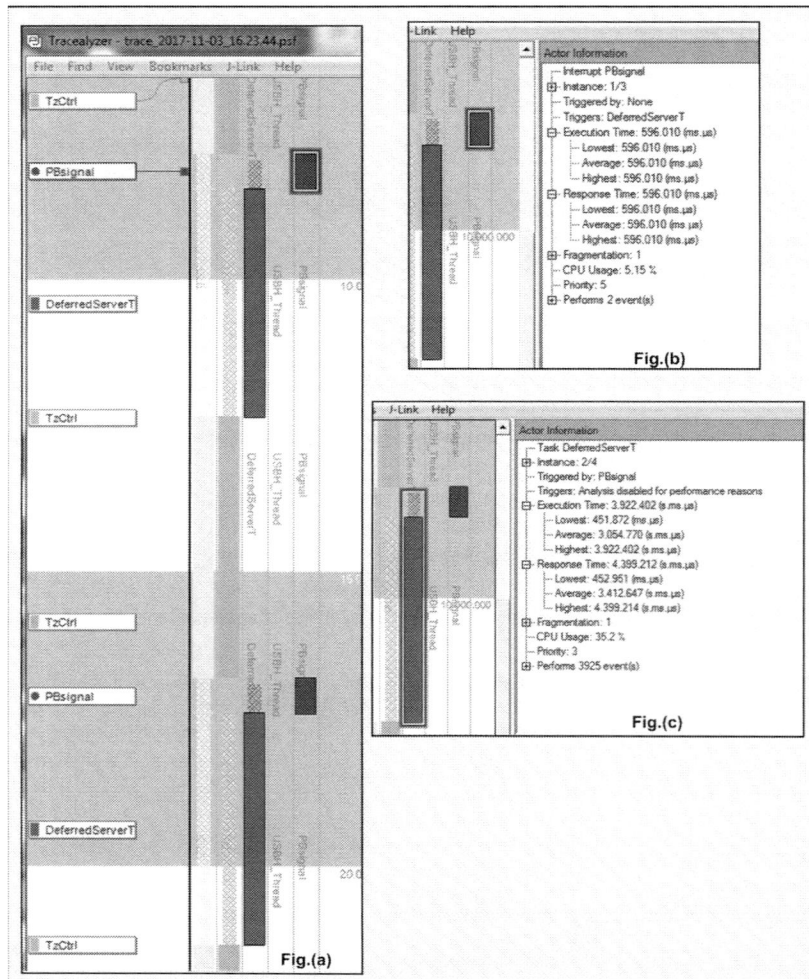

Figure 8.35 Ex.11a Vertical Trace View 2

Figure 8.35a is a trace that has captured two ISR activations. You can see that these are essentially identical in operation, to be expected in this scenario. Figures 8.35b and 8.35c provide Actor Information relating to the ISR and DS tasks. Please study these figures carefully and in depth.

Figure 8.35b shows that the execution time of the ISR is 0.596 seconds, which is identical to its response time. Figure 8.35c shows the DS task execution time as 3.922 seconds but with a response time of 4.399 seconds (a difference of 0.477 seconds). This difference corresponds to the time the DS task is in a suspended state before beginning execution (figure 8.36 highlights these aspects).

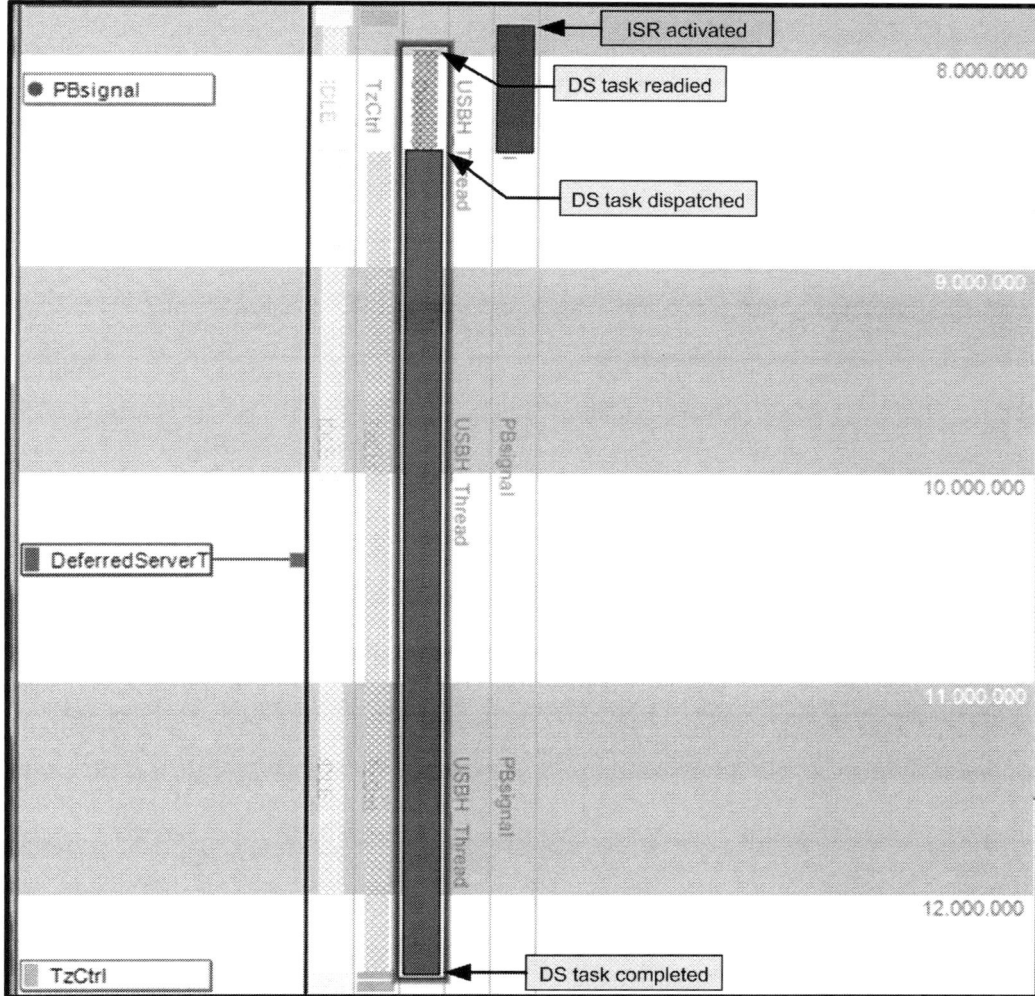

Figure 8.36 Ex.10a Vertical Trace View 3

Further information can be gleaned from the Kernel Blocking Times View, figure 8.37.

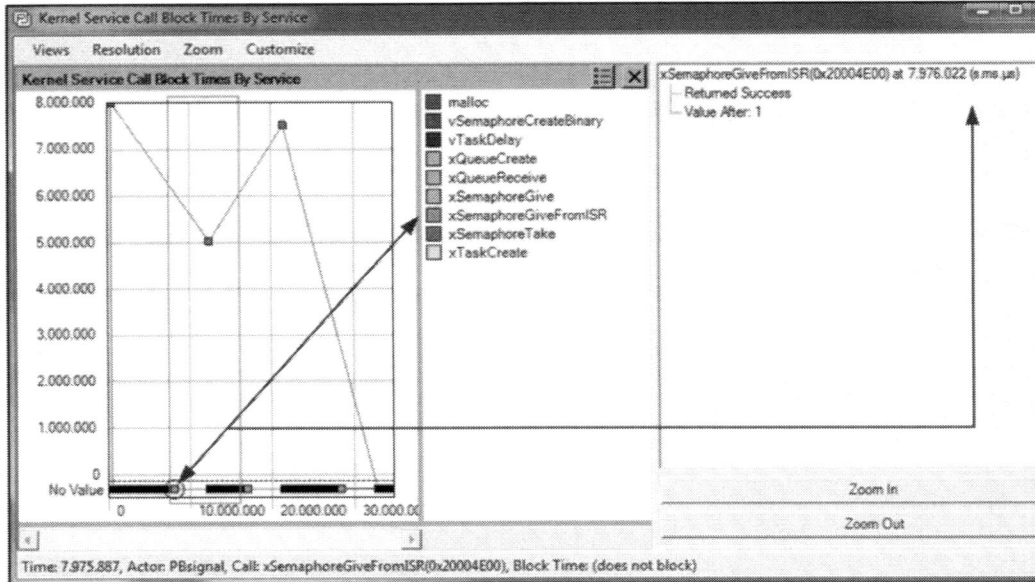

Figure 8.37 Ex.11a Semaphore Kernel Blocking time info 1

From this we can see that the ISR generates, in this case, a *Set* (semaphore give) call at timestamp 7.976 seconds. The next Blocking Times View, figure 8.38, provides data relating to the DS task:

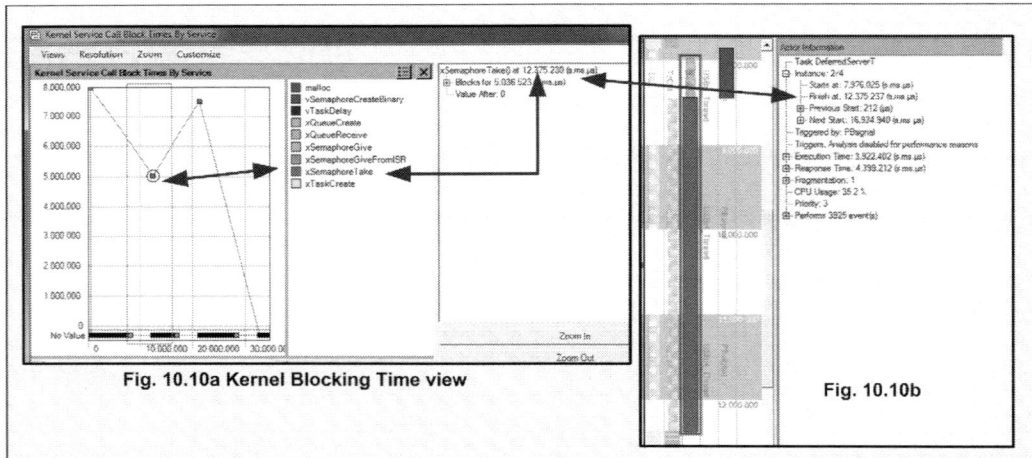

Figure 8.38 Ex.11a Semaphore Kernel Blocking time info 2

Each data point in these figures represents a specific kernel service call made by the DS task. The x position provides the time stamps, while the y position denotes the blocking time. In figure 8.38 for example, the DS task makes a semaphore *Get* (*xSemaphoreTake*) call at 12.375 seconds, followed by a block time of 5.036 seconds. The call time corresponds to the end of the

DS task, where the task once more goes into a suspended mode (waiting on the semaphore queue).

8.4.4 Exercise 11b: Scenario 2, with Green Led task disabled.

Remember, for this scenario the semaphore is *Set* at the <u>end</u> of the ISR. Two trace views relating to this scenario are shown below. The first, figure 8.39, emphasizes the timings of the ISR. The second, figure 8.40, provides information about the execution of the Deferred Server (DS) task.

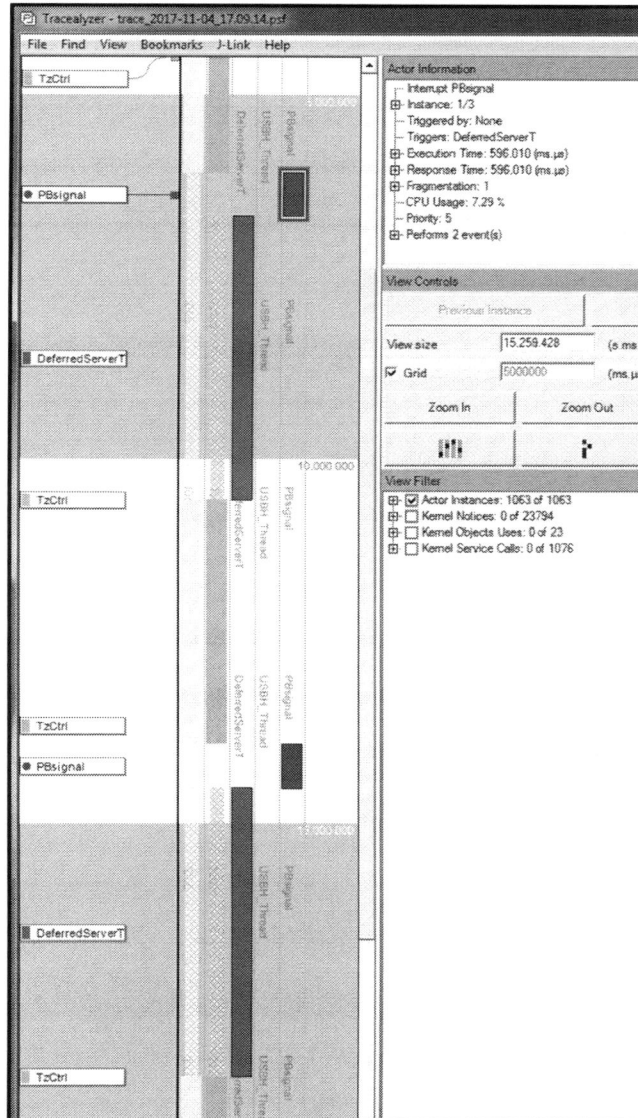

Figure 8.39 Ex.11b Vertical Trace View 1

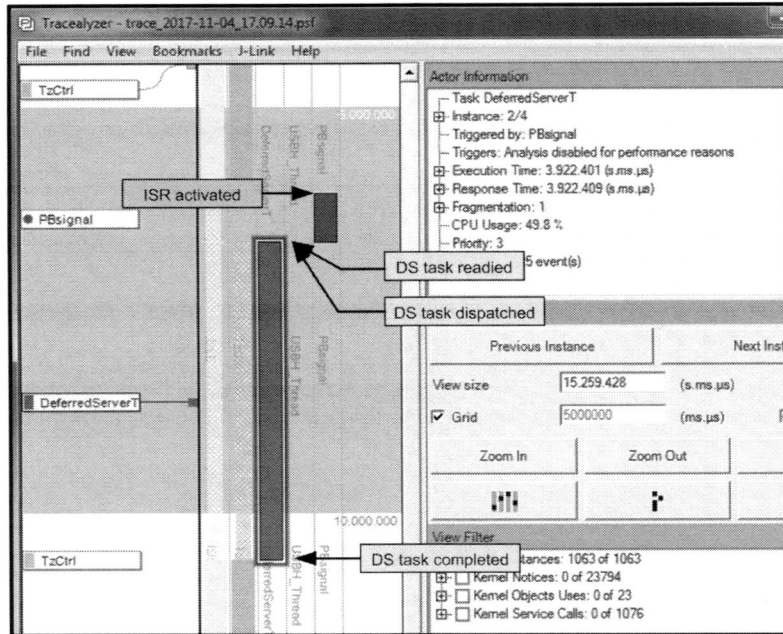

Figure 8.40 Ex.11b Vertical Trace View 2

From these you can see that once the ISR has completed, the DS task begins to execute.

Observe that the response time is now equal to the execution time (unlike that shown in figure 8.36). But note: the latency (the time between the arrival of the interrupt signal and the completion of the DS task) is exactly the same in both scenarios.

The Communication Flow View for this exercise is shown in Figure 8.41 below:

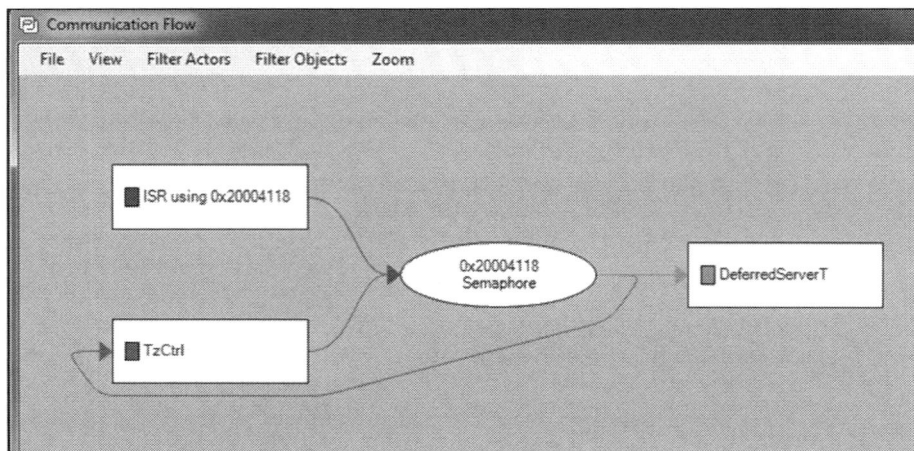

Fig 8.41 Ex.11b Communication Flow View 1

Figures 8.42 to 8.44 provide details of the interactions of the individual communication components.

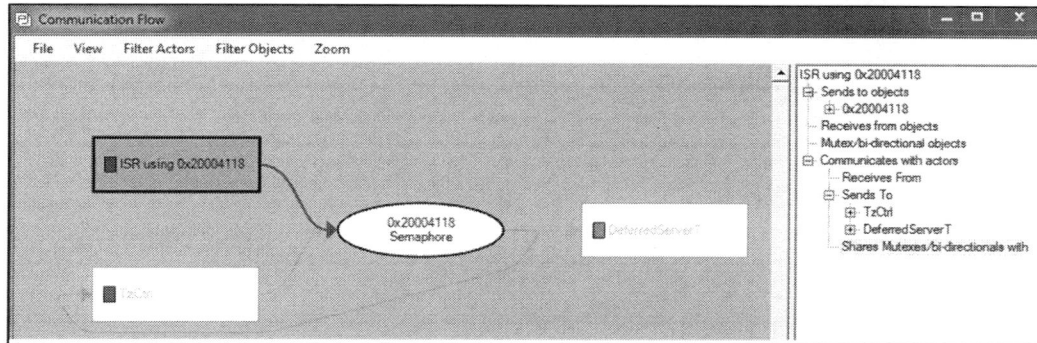

Fig 8.42 Ex.11b Communication Flow View 2

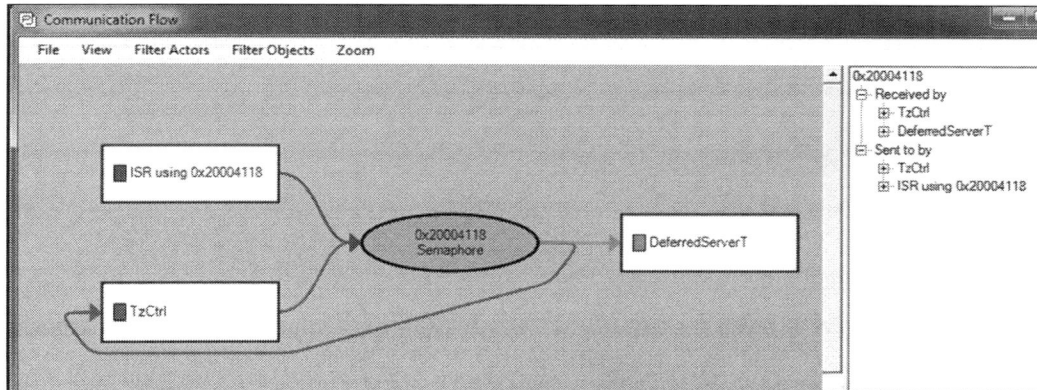

Fig 8.43 Ex.11b Communication Flow View 3

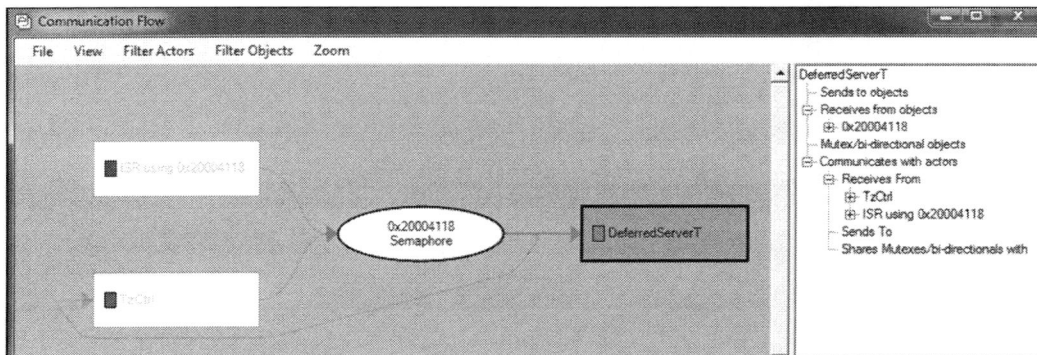

Fig 8.44 Ex.11b Communication flow View 4

8.4.5 Exercise 11c: Scenario 2, with Green Led task enabled.

In this exercise the Green (periodic) task is active, its priority being greater than the DS one. The run-time behaviour of the system for two consecutive interrupts is shown in the Vertical Trace View of Figure 8.45.

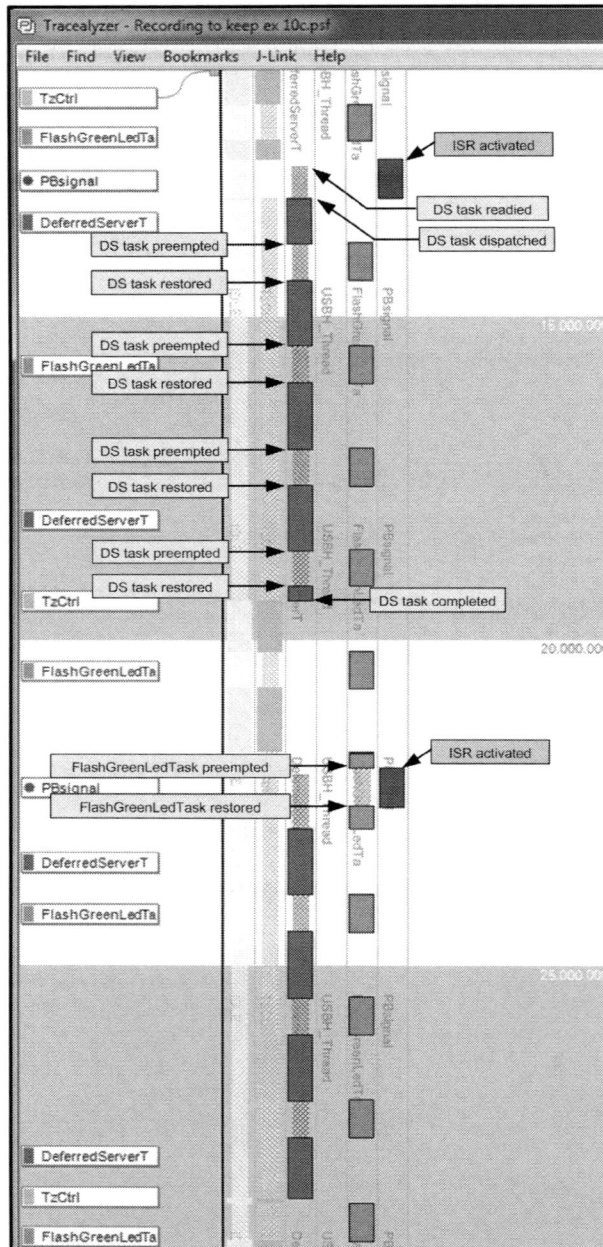

Figure 8.45 Ex.11c Vertical Trace View 1

There is much detail here, so work your way carefully through the diagram.

The first ISR activation occurs while the Green task is in a suspended state.   Hence the response of the system (in terms of readying and dispatching the DS task) is identical to that shown in figure 8.35.   Now for the first difference: once the Green task is re-readied it preempts the DS task (as it has the higher priority).   It (the Green task) runs to completion, goes into a timed-suspension mode and allows the DS task to be restored.   You can see that the DS task is preempted and restored a number of times before it eventually completes.

When the ISR is activated for the second time it, in this case, interrupts execution of the Green task.   The trace clearly shows the preemption of the Green task.   At this point it returns to the ready queue as the ready head.   The DS task is also awoken and placed into the ready queue, behind the Green task.   Hence, when the ISR completes execution, the Green task is restored to continue to completion (where it once again goes into a timed-suspension state).   Subsequent operations should be self-evident from the trace details.

Three important aspects of the DS task are shown in figure 8.46. Observe that:

(i) The first execution is fragmented into five segments while that of the second has four fragments.

(ii) The *execution* times of both activations are virtually the same in spite of the different fragmentation.

(iii) The *response* times are different, the result of the different fragmentations.

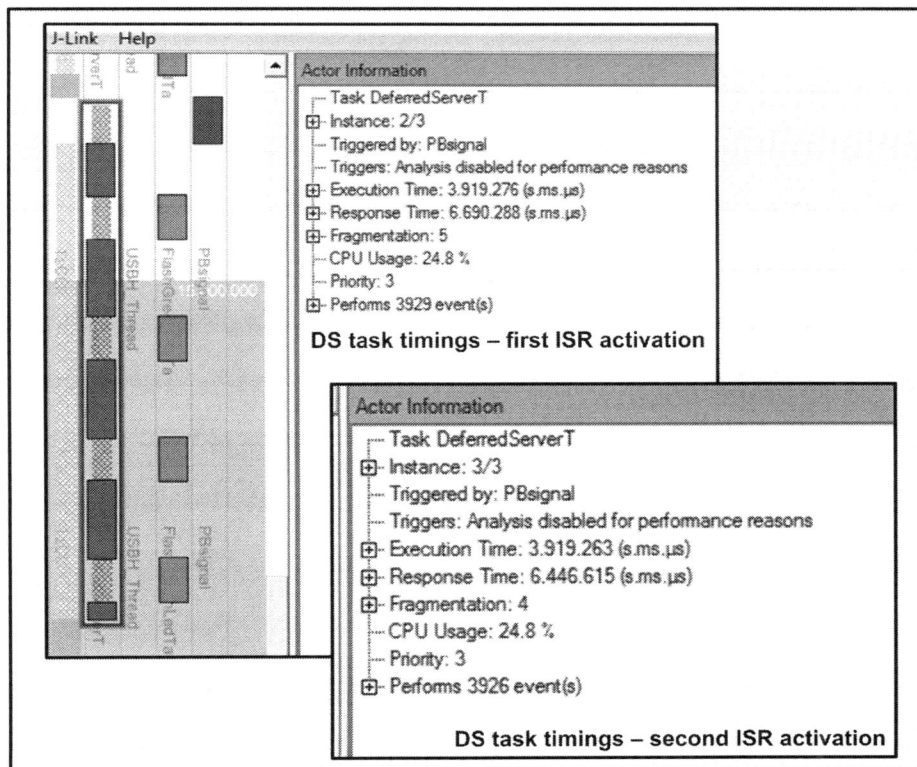

Figure 8.46 Ex.11c DS task key timings

Figure 8.45 also contains one further important feature (which eagle-eyed readers may well have spotted). The Green task periodicity is constant apart from the time section that includes the ISR activation. This is marked up on figure 8.47 below:

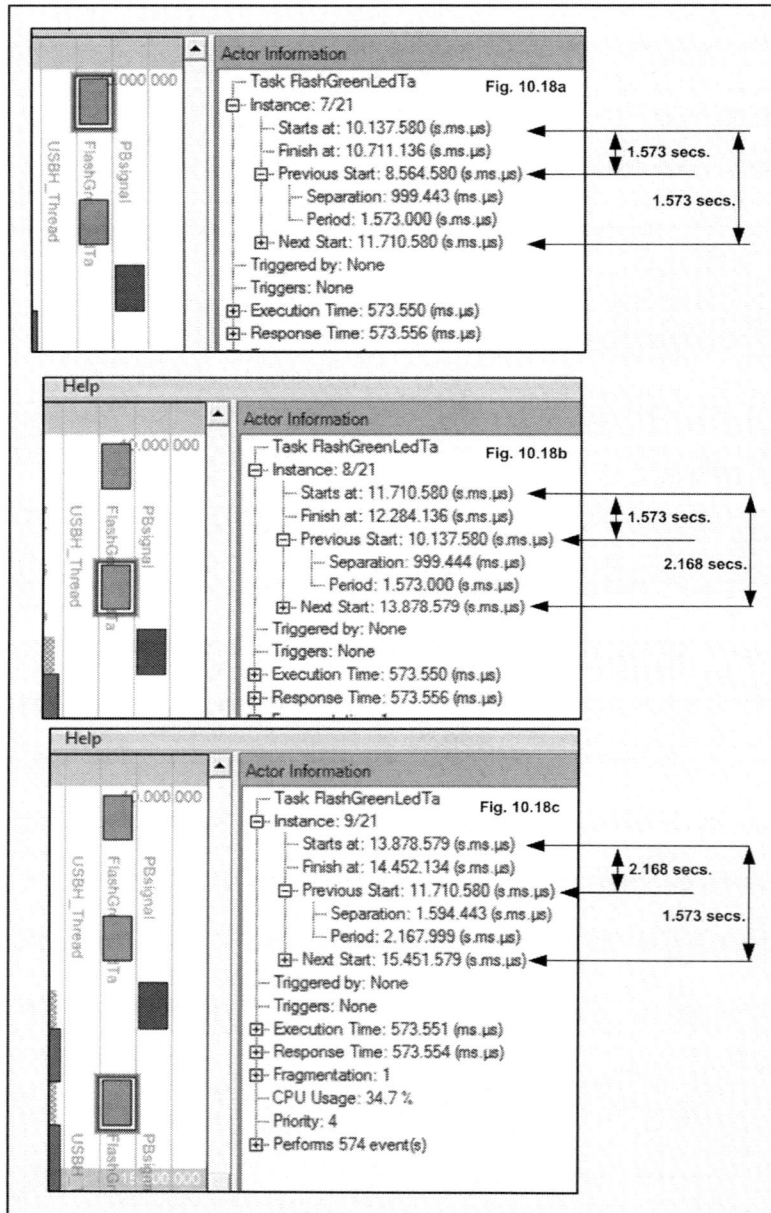

Figure 8.47 Ex.11c Periodic task timing details

It seems that FreeRTOS 'shifts' the schedule of periodic task activations; this shift corresponds to the execution time of the ISR (what is interesting is that, in this case, there is theoretically enough time to maintain the schedule).

The results from this exercise contains many useful pointers for producing high-performance multitasking systems:

- Wherever possible don't use aperiodic tasks. These make it impossible to deliver deterministic behaviour.
- If you *do* need to employ aperiodic tasks use the deferred server technique as a default approach.
- Make sure that these DS tasks have priorities lower than the periodic ones, to allow you to retain some predictability of behaviour.
- In such circumstances the response times of DS tasks are likely to be much longer than their execution times (especially when a number of periodic tasks are present)
- There may well be significant variation in response times from activation to activation (much depends on the current state of the system).
- ISRs, by default, should be very fast, to minimize their effects on system performance.
- Lengthy ISRs should be used only when it is *essential* that full responses must be produced extremely quickly.
- If you want to develop reliable, fast and near-deterministic systems, much effort is needed at the design stage. This requires careful planning, analysis and, ideally, simulation of the task set.
- Any time you modify your current multitasking designs always try to evaluate and predict consequential effects (and if someone suggests that the solution to a problem is to 'merely spawn another thread', avoid the urge to throttle them!).

Part 4

Epilogue - looking to the future

By now you'll have gained a very good understanding of RTOS features, behaviour and the usage of individual constructs.   So, what next?   How can you continue your self-improvement programme in a practical, useful and relevant fashion? Well, what follows are some pointers that might help you in that quest.

Chapter 9

A self-help improvement guide

9.1 The influence of work practices.

Work practices are probably going to have the greatest influence as to how you use the knowledge gained here. At one extreme you may intend to apply this to company projects, ones which use defined processors, tools and RTOSs. At the other end you may be doing it both for self-satisfaction and to increase your professional knowledge (these aren't mutually exclusive, of course). There is a good chance that your future work will follow one or more of the routes shown in figure 9.1.

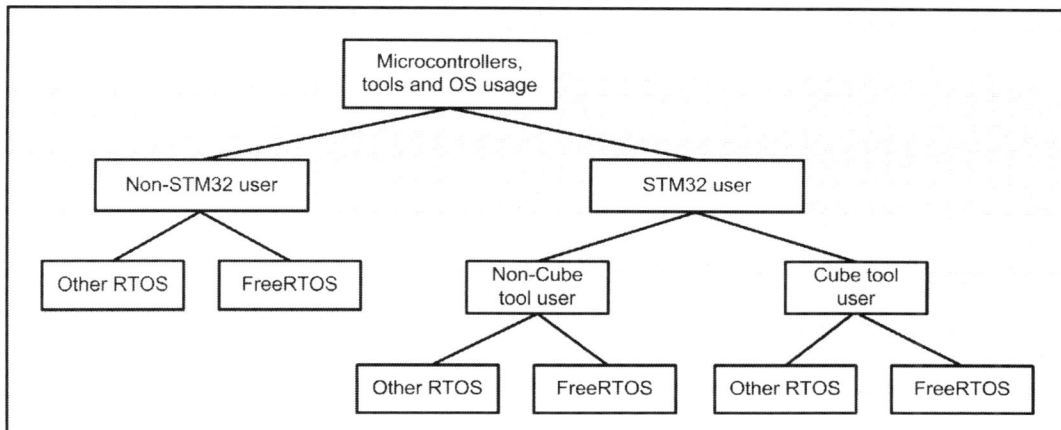

Figure 9.1 Future work routes

What you now need do to advance your knowledge depends to a large extent on your chosen path. It depends on many factors: some being generally applicable, others being very specific. In the following sections we will look at three important aspects: OS issues, portability of applications and good structuring of code units.

9.2 OS and related issues.

It's important to build on the things that you've learned so far, both theoretically and practically. However, as pointed out above, it all depends on where you go to from here. So let's try to give some sensible, useful advice.

From figure 9.1 you can see that there are six possible routes. The big divide is between those who intend to continue using STM32 microcontrollers and those that don't. This is an important distinction as the Cube tool can be used only with STM devices.

(a) Route 1 - Non-STM32 user, Other RTOS.

There is little point in delving into the innards of FreeRTOS if you aren't going to use it in future work. However, you can consolidate your RTOS knowledge by doing a few simple things:

- List all FreeRTOS APIs and get to know precisely what they're used for.
- Collect these into logical functional groupings (e.g. task management, software timers, memory management, etc.).
- List all the APIs of your chosen RTOS; cross compare these with the FreeRTOS ones.
- Develop a set of exercises similar to the ones given here, adapted so that they can be executed on your own hardware using your own RTOS.
- Extend the exercise set to cover all 'new' features of the RTOS (i.e. those you haven't met with or used previously).

At the end of this you should be in a very good position to effectively employ your chosen RTOS in real designs.

(b) Route 2 - Non-STM32 user, FreeRTOS.

Clearly you need to get a deep understanding of all the FreeRTOS APIs, their features and their usage.

- List all 'native' FreeRTOS APIs and get to know precisely what they're used for.
- Collect these into logical functional groupings (e.g. task management, software timers, memory management, etc.).
- Extend the exercise set to cover all 'new' features of FreeRTOS (i.e. those you haven't met with or used previously).

(c) Route 3 - STM32 user, Non-Cube tool user, Other RTOS.

The suggestions listed in (a) above are equally applicable to this route. However, you have the advantage of being able to experiment using a familiar, proven platform: the STM32 Discovery board.

(d) Route 4 - STM32 user, Non-Cube tool user, FreeRTOS.

The suggestions listed in (b) above are directly applicable to this route. However, you also have the advantage of being able to experiment using a known target platform.

(e) Route 5 - STM32 user, Cube tool user, Other RTOS.

You also have the advantage of being able to experiment using a known target platform. Note that the suggestions listed in (a) above are directly applicable to this route, with the addition of the following:

- Work out how to integrate your own RTOS code with that produced by the Cube tool.
- Become familiar with the range of driver software provided by the Cube tool.

(f) Route 6 - STM32 user, Cube tool user, FreeRTOS.

This is the easiest path forward as the tools, platform and RTOS are, by now, well known to you. The items listed in route 2 should be performed, together with an extensive review of the STM driver software features.

9.3 Portability of application code.

Before an embedded system becomes operational all code must be fully tested (for that level of release, of course). It could be a prototype version only, not the final product). Now, the last thing we want to do, especially in deployed systems, is to change any code. The reason is simple: to avoid further testing. Unfortunately, the reality is that software always gets changed during its lifetime. Such changes have their greatest impact when application level code is modified, because this calls for a complete *system* retest. For some of you this, at first sight, might not appear to be a big deal. But what if the software is embedded in, say, a remotely-controlled submersible vehicle, an aircraft flight control system or a production line sequencing controller? Now you should see that it is most definitely NOT a trivial consideration. OK. But what has this to do with RTOSs?

In reality it isn't to do with RTOS features per se; it's the problems introduced if we change our RTOS (and this isn't all that unusual, especially in systems that have long operational lifetimes). This problem can be illustrated using the analogy of a 'jigsaw-type' puzzle, figure 9.2.

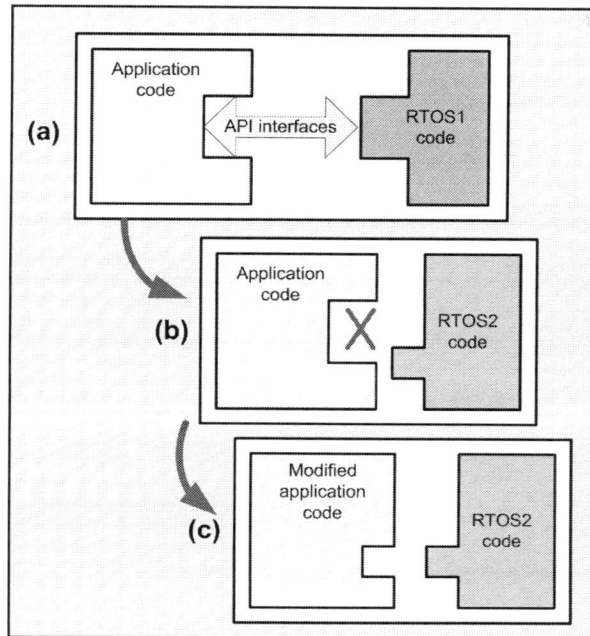

Figure 9.2 RTOS portability issues

The RTOS APIs act as the hooks between the application code and that of the operating system. The call of the API in the application code *must* match its implementation in the RTOS software, figure 9.2(a). If, however, the RTOS is changed (figure 9.2(b)), the application and RTOS code are no longer compatible. The only solution to this is to change *all* API calls in the application code! Also, it is possible that the code definitions and declarations of various program items must be changed. Without a doubt this means that full system testing (including regression testing) *must* be carried out.

Is there a way to avoid this? The answer, fortunately, is 'yes'. The solution is not trivial; it needs careful consideration, planning and coding effort. It can be illustrated (again) by analogy using the jigsaw concept, figure 9.3. Key to solving the problem is to use an additional layer of software: an adaptor (wrapper) code unit as an API translation mechanism, figure 9.3(a). The core aspects of this are as follows:

1. You, the designer, define a full set of 'bespoke' RTOS APIs for use in all application-level software.
2. Adaptor units are built to accept these API calls via custom API interfaces.
3. The adaptor unit is coded to translate the bespoke calls to valid RTOS function calls.
4. The adaptor code make the actual calls on the RTOS functions via RTOS-specific API interfaces.
5. If at any time the RTOS is changed (figure 9.3(b)) then a different adaptor unit is used, one compatible with the new RTOS.
6. The new adaptor unit maintains full compatibility with the bespoke APIs of the application code.

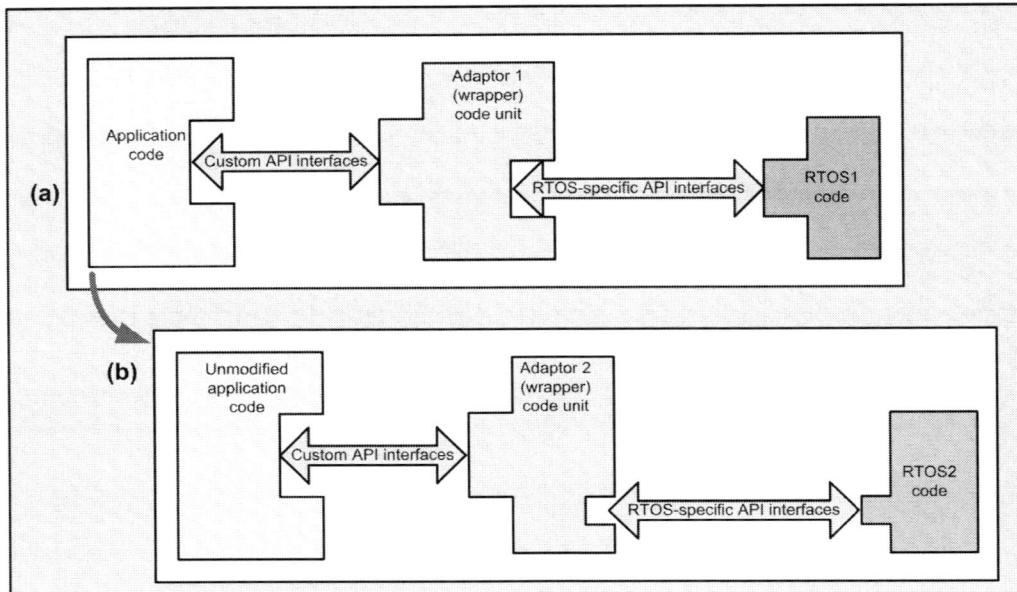

Figure 9.3 The adaption layer

Thus if the RTOS is changed no changes need be made to the application code. This also affects the extent of any software and system retesting that must be done, in two ways:

- First, all RTOS-dependent code modules may be tested extensively in the software (and not system) environment, using proven test harnesses. All test stimuli are injected via the custom API interfaces; resulting responses are collected at the same points. Testing of this type can give us great confidence that our software is correct, robust, reliable, and temporally correct (i.e. meets its performance targets).
- Second, although full system testing is still needed, its extent can be significantly less than in the previous case; after all, the application code hasn't been modified in any way.

   An aside: some developers recommend that your own bespoke APIs should be based on the POSIX standards.

9.4 Code structuring at the application level.

Please understand that what comes next is very much based on my own personal views. Do not take this as being prescriptive — 'you *must* do it like this'. Rather it is descriptive — 'you *can* do it like this'. And it works for me! In the approach used here it is essential that:

- You use the design model to drive the code model; i.e. the code is the implementation of a design specification.
- The design model is defined using a diagram(s), i.e. the task diagram.
- You specify a clear relationship between the task diagram and its implementation (code) model.

The basic set of task diagram elements are shown in figure 9.4.

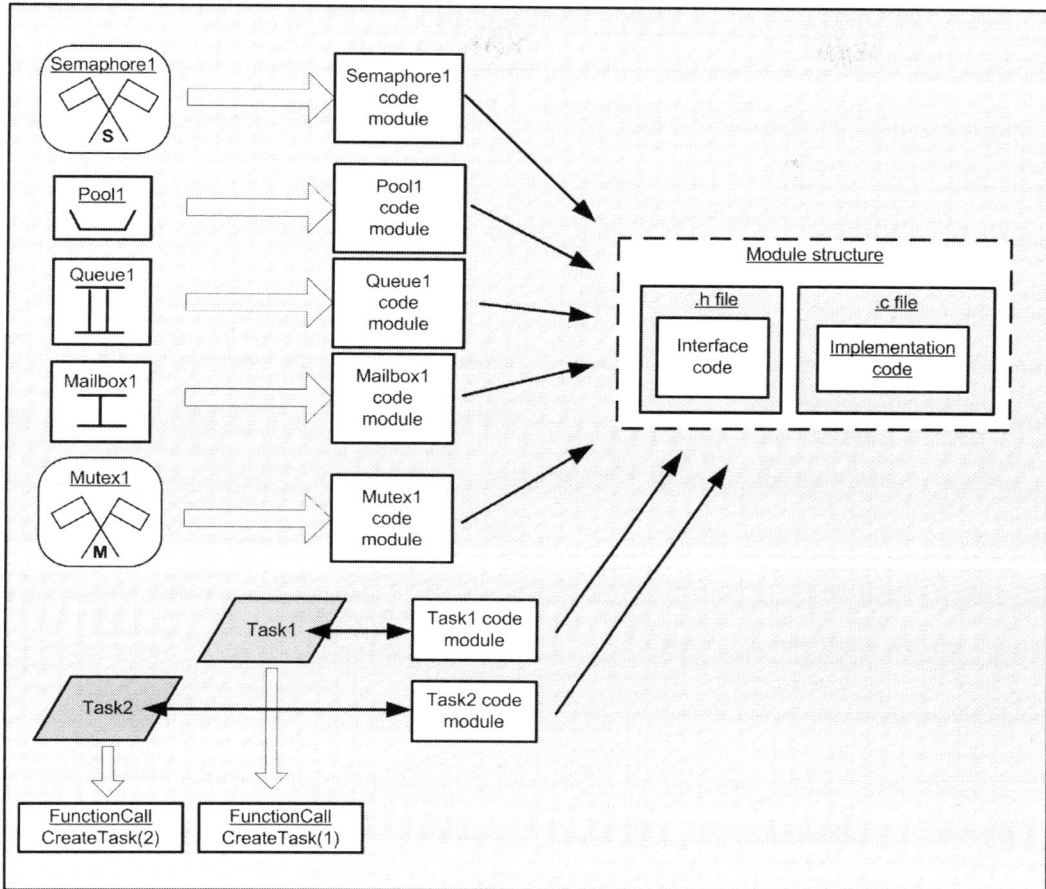

Figure 9.4 Task components and corresponding code structuring aspects

Note this well: each item shown on a task diagram represents a distinct, unique item that is a component part of your design. Make sure that the names you give them are taken from the system domain (e.g. PressureControlTask, TuningCoefficientsPool, etc.). When you produce the code use exactly the same names in the programs. One reason for doing this is to make it easier to confirm the correctness of the code model. Another is that it should also result in clear, understandable and self-documenting code (why use program comments when good naming makes things perfectly obvious?).

I strongly recommend that all communication components are built using a 'modular' structure, as shown above. Also, it is a given that all such components should incorporate access control (mutual exclusion) mechanisms.

The task symbol represents an executable item, constructed by a 'CreateTask' function (perhaps 'executable environment' might be a better description). Precisely what such functions do depends on individual RTOSs, but at the very least they:

- Specify the code to be executed by the task.
- Allocate stack space for the task.
- Define the priority level of the task (if applicable).

The executable code is accessed at task run-time using a pointer (addressing) mechanism. All of this is hidden from you, but you are responsible for writing the task code (as you have seen from the exercises).

The last item worth discussing here is the role of the main.c function. This should do minimal work, as for example:

```
/* ========================================================== */
void main(void)
{
/* code to initialize the system placed here */

/* code to create semaphores, mutexes, pools and channels placed here */

 /* code to create the application tasks placed here*/

 /* Now start the scheduler — FreeRTOS implementation*/
vTaskStartScheduler();

 /* We should never get here as control is now taken by the scheduler. */
 return;

} /* end main */
/* ========================================================== */
```

If you intend to continue using the Cube tool, then you have to live with the way it works. One of the best reasons for using Cube is that is generates all the initialization code, a real boon. It also, as you've seen, generates task, mutex, semaphore and timer creation code if configured for this. Additionally, for each task, it provides a function to house the task code, and populates it with a skeleton program unit, as for example:

```
/* ========================================================== */
/* StartFlashOrangeLedTask function */
void StartFlashOrangeLedTask(void const * argument)
{
  /* USER CODE BEGIN 5 */
  /* Infinite loop */
  for(;;)
  {
    osDelay(1);
  }
  /* USER CODE END StartFlashOrangeLedTask */
}
/* ========================================================== */
```

To keep main.c file as sparse as possible just replace the predefined user code with a function call to your own-design task code module, as for example:

```
/* ========================================================== */

/* StartFlashOrangeLedTask function */
void StartFlashOrangeLedTask(void const * argument)
{
  /* USER CODE BEGIN 5 */
        RunFlashOrangeLedTask();
 /* USER CODE END StartFlashOrangeLedTask */
}
/* ========================================================== */
```

9.5 A closing comment.

To reiterate a point: the material in this chapter is meant to be descriptive, not prescriptive. Its purpose is to get you to start thinking about where you go to and what you do from now on. Moreover, it is very important that you develop your own design philosophy, one based on sound engineering principles. I suggest that a reread of the following sections of book 1 would help guide you in that quest:

Section 1.2 Producing quality software.
Section 1.3 Modelling the software.
Section 1.4 The importance of time and timing.
Section 1.5 Handling multiple jobs.
Section 1.6 Handling complex multiple jobs.

And always remember: there isn't ever a single right solution to a problem - be wary of software fashionistas! Finally, engrave this on your mind: 'think before do'.

Part 5

Useful, helpful and informative online material

This is a brief roundup of freely-available on-line material that can help improve your understanding of the tools used in this book. There is a wealth of material out there on the web; this is just a starting point. I'm sure that as you follow the various links you'll find many more relevant items, especially on YouTube. Any feedback is welcome. Send to cooling@lindentreeuk.co.uk.

Chapter 10

Online material reference guide.

10.1 STM32Cube embedded software.

This consists of the:

- STM32CubeMX graphical configuration tool and the
- STM32Cube embedded software libraries - the firmware package.

These can be downloaded from:
http://www.st.com/web/catalog/tools/FM147/CL1794/SC961/SS1533/PF259242?sc=stm32cube#

For an excellent overview of Cube go to: www.st.com/stm32cube-pr11
Check out the featured videos

10.2 STM32CubeMX features.

Relevant manuals:

- STM UM1718 user manual: *STM32CubeMX for STM32 configuration and initialization C code generation.*

10.3 STM32Cube embedded software libraries and documentation.

Important user manuals:

- STM UM1730 *Firmware package getting started for STM32F4 series.*
- STM UM1725 *Description of STM32F4xx HAL drivers.*

10.4 The hardware - STM32F4 Discovery kit.

Two important documents:

1. ST User Manual UM1467
Getting started with software and firmware environments for the STM32F4DISCOVERY Kit
2. ST User Manual UM1472
Discovery kit with STM32F407VG MCU

Check out the material at:
http://www.st.com/content/

****
****

10.5 Useful and informative videos.

10.5.1 Tutorial CubeMx - 1 - GPIO Out STM32F4Discovery STM32CubeMX.

https://www.youtube.com/watch?v=TcCNdkxXnJY

STM32CubeMX is a very fast way to setup new highly portable projects for STM32 microcontrollers, by using the HAL drivers instead the "old" standard ones. This video shows this process for simple GPIO out functions, using both HAL and mixed register programming. The opinions about HAL drivers are not always favourable, but it is easy to use direct register programming in this environment whenever the needed HAL functions are missing or incomprehensible. The HAL divers are almost mature and they will be improved in the future.

10.5.2 Tutorial CubeMX - 2 - Write HAL Port functions.

https://www.youtube.com/watch?v=Pj-rHjxdq0Y

STM32CubeMX is a very fast way to setup new highly portable projects for STM32 microcontrollers, by using the HAL drivers instead the "old" standard ones. As some standard useful functions are still missing, this video shows how you may write and embed them in HAL. The community should ask STM to include such functions in the future firmware versions.

10.5.3 Tutorial STMCubeMX - 3 - GPIO In Out on STM32F4 Discovery.

https://www.youtube.com/watch?v=p_WyLNI40uU

Using the STM32Cube MX with HAL drivers for GPIO IN and OUT operations seems to be very simple when dealing with pins.

10.5.4 Tutorial CubeMX - 4 - External Interrupts EXTI.

https://www.youtube.com/watch?v=ZA7SUITO35k

Working with external interrupts in a project generated by STM32Cube is shown. Dealing with bouncing contacts by waiting before taking action is demonstrated. Passing variables from the stm32f4xx_it.c module to main.c module is also shown.
Once again Cube let the programmer concentrate more on the C part and less on initializations. However, the understanding of the hardware principles of the interrupts is highly recommendable.

10.5.5 Tutorial Cube MX -5- USART polling STM32F4 Discovery.

https://www.youtube.com/watch?v=A86xjXfyiFk#t=3.866122

Working with USART in polling mode in a project generated by STM32Cube on STM32F4 Discovery is shown. Transmitting is OK, but receiving in polling is in principle not working if the loop contains any other instructions, because the transmission from the external source may finish while dealing with them. That is why using interrupts at receptions is highly recommendable, as shown in the next tutorial

10.5.6 Tutorial CubeMX - 6 - Tx polling Rx interrupts STM32F4 Discovery.

https://www.youtube.com/watch?v=Mbd2ASl78Tc

Using HAL API and Cube Mx code generator, only 5 lines in main.c and 2 lines in ISR are necessary for Tx and interrupts Rx for STM32f4 Discovery. The major issue is understanding the ways of activating and deactivating the interrupts made by HAL instructions and macros. Here we use the blocking instructions (the Tx instruction is blocked by reception, as one may notice at the end). Anyway, we recommend the non-blocking method using the HALxxxIT instructions, as in the next video.

10.5.7 Tutorial CubeMX - 7- USART RxTx Interrupts STM32F4 Discovery.

https://www.youtube.com/watch?v=vv4KB-TSJFU

Using HAL API and Cube Mx code generator, only 5 lines and 2 declarations are necessary in main.c and ISR for Tx and Rx interrupts, working with STM32f4 Discovery in non-blocking mode. Here we use the real HAL...IT instructions, which are very powerful, but a lot of attention must be paid to the activating and deactivating of the corresponding interrupt flags.

10.5.8 Tutorial CubeMX - 8 - ADC_DMA+USART_DMA STM32F4 Discovery.

https://www.youtube.com/watch?v=oidnujpelvI

Using HAL API and Cube Mx we program an ADC in DMA circular mode, and the results are transmitted using USART with DMA. The very high speed of the transmission needs a proper USB-TTL adapter (FTDI and CH340 worked well, other China clones didn't!).

10.5.9 Tutorial Cube MX - 9 - DAC ADC USART on STM32F4Discovery.

https://www.youtube.com/watch?v=TFBLGt7M8Sg

A waveform generator using DAC on STM32F4Discovery is built. Connecting the generator output to an ADC input, the waveform may be visualized via USART on the PC by a LabView virtual instrument using VISA. Both direct conversions and DMA conversions are presented. The USB to TTL adapter used is CH340, which worked well even at 921600 bps.

10.5.10 Tutorial Cube MX - 5 - FreeRTOS STM32F4 CubeMX.

https://www.youtube.com/watch?v=qyFHsrlLfA4

FreeRTOS với STM32F4 CubeMX

10.5.11 #1 STM32CubeMX Tutorial.

STM32CubeMX full Introduction Video.

How to start using the program, all its features and settings.

https://www.youtube.com/watch?v=imXauCiwEfs

You can download the STM23CubeMX software from the ST Product page:

http://www.st.com/content/st_com/en/products/development-tools/software-development-tools/stm32-software-development-tools/stm32-configurators-and-code-generators/stm32cubemx.html?sc=microxplorer

Or Directly from:

http://www.st.com/content/st_com/en/products/development-tools/software-development-tools/stm32-software-development-tools/stm32-configurators-and-code-generators/stm32cubemx.html?sc=microxplorer

Please subscribe so you will get notifications when more training videos on the STM32 are loaded.

10.5.12 #2 How the cube generates the code .

https://www.youtube.com/watch?v=SZub9bFGXak

In this video, you will learn how to:
* Start a new project using the STM32CubeMX
* How the cube generates the code structure for the IDE
* How to use the project correctly

10.5.13 #3 STM32CubeExamples.

https://www.youtube.com/watch?v=p3q3kaftvDQ

In this video, you will learn how to:
* To find the STM32CubeMX Examples
* How they are built

10.5.14 #5 STM32CubeMX Power Consumption Calculator.

https://www.youtube.com/watch?v=GZEX3HmzCfI

In this video, you will learn how to start a new project in the STM32CubeMX

10.6 FreeRTOS documentation.

http://www.freertos.org/Documentation/RTOS_book.html

10.7 Percepio Tracealyzer RTOS trace analysis tool.

Tracealyzer for FreeRTOS version 3.1:
https://percepio.com/2016/12/07/tracealyzer-freertos-3-1/

Video: Tracealyzer for FreeRTOS Tutorial 1 - CubeMX Projet creation
https://www.youtube.com/watch?v=0CpJocMjvMA;charstyle:URL

The following explains how to get started with Tracealyzer for FreeRTOS on STM32 devices:
https://percepio.com/st/;charstyle:URL

Using ST-Link for RTOS trace streaming:
https://percepio.com/2016/06/16/st-link-rtos-trace-streaming/